A Radical Stage

Theatre in Germany in the 1970s and 1980s

A Radical Stage

Theatre in Germany in the 1970s and 1980s

Edited by
W. G. Sebald

BERG
Oxford / New York / Hamburg
Distributed exclusively in the US and Canada by
St. Martin's Press New York

First published in 1988 by
Berg Publishers Limited
77 Morrell Avenue Oxford OX4 1NQ UK
175 Fifth Avenue/Room 400 New York NY 10010, USA
Nordalbingerweg 14 2000 Hamburg 61, FRG

© Berg Publishers Limited 1988

British Library Cataloguing in Publication Data

A Radical stage: theatre in Germany in
the 1970s and 1980s
1. Germany. Theatre 1970–1987
I. Title   II. Sebald, W. G.
792'.0943

ISBN 0-85496-038-4

Library of Congress Cataloging-in-Publication Data

A Radical stage : theatre in Germany in the 1970s and 1980s / edited
by W. G. Sebald.
Papers from a colloquium held at the University of East Anglia in
spring 1987.
Includes index.
ISBN 0-85496-038-4 : $40.00 (U.S. : est.)
1. German drama—20th century—History and criticism—Congresses.
2. Theatre—Germany—History—20th century—Congresses.   I. Sebald,
Winfried Georg, 1944–
PT667.R34 1988
832'.914'09—dc19   88-14793

Printed in Great Britain by Billings of Worcester

Contents

Preface   vii

Surveying the Scene—Some Introductory Remarks
W. G. Sebald   1

1. The State of the Stage—The Decline of Commitment in
the Contemporary German Theatre
Sybille Wirsing   9

2. Blacking Up—Three Productions by Peter Stein
David Bradby   18

3. Myth and Mythology in the Drama of Botho Strauss
Irmela Schneider   31

4. 'Dramatisches Talent hat sie nicht, doch viele schöne
Worte'—Friederike Roth as a Playwright
Lucinda Rennison   52

5. The Anxiety of Influence Tankred Dorst's *Deutsche Stücke*
Steve Giles   64

6. Subject, Politics, Theatre—Reflections on Franz Xaver
Kroetz
Moray McGowan   77

7. The Child Grows Up—Towards a History of the Grips
Theater
Horst Claus   93

8. A New Definition of 'Eingreifendes Theater'—Some Recent Productions in the Theatre of the GDR
   Anthony Meech   110

9. Back to the Future—Volker Braun and the German Theatrical Tradition
   Julian Hilton   124

10. Homburg-Machine—Heiner Müller in the Shadow of Nuclear War
    J. H. Reid   145

11. The Excitement of Boredom—Thomas Bernhard
    Rüdiger Görner   161

12. The Art of Transformation—Herbert Achternbusch's Theatrical Mission
    W. G. Sebald   174

Notes on Playwrights and Directors   185

Notes on Contributors   192

Select Bibliography   195

Index   196

Preface

THE papers collected in this volume were given at a Colloquium held at the University of East Anglia, Norwich, in the Spring of 1987. Among the participants were members of German and Drama Departments as well as theatre practitioners and critics from the UK and from Germany.

Many of the plays which have come out of Germany during the last fifteen or so years pose severe problems of understanding. The style of production evolved by leading German directors such as Peter Stein or Klaus Michael Grüber over the same period of time is no less perplexing. Critical reception has therefore been rather delayed. This, however, has not prevented the quite marked success which German playwrights and producers have begun to enjoy abroad in recent years. Grüber and Stein have been repeatedly produced in Italy, France and in England, and to a much greater extent than at any time since the late Weimar years, German plays are being performed in Romance countries and in the English-speaking world. Such names as Kroetz, Strauss, Braun, Bernhard, Achternbusch and Müller, whose collaboration with Wilson epitomises the growing trend, are familiar to theatre practitioners not only in Paris and London but also in Strasbourg, Lyons, Glasgow and Cardiff. They appear to represent, yet again, something that can be construed as prototypically German, something horrendous and fascinating at the same time, and, in its impact, not unlike the radical experiments which characterised the stage works of the Weimar era. Though some of the playwrights mentioned, notably Franz Xaver Kroetz, have by now received a good deal of critical attention, the wider scene has remained largely unexplored and the real questions thrown up by the new German theatre have scarcely been identified.

It was the intention of the Norwich colloquium to map out some of the territory, to provide profiles both of the more important and of some of the lesser playwrights currently writing for the German stage and to explain some of the issues raised in their difficult works and by the contemporary style of production. The contributors' brief was to offer an overview and a general assessment but to avoid the humdrum patterns of introductory papers. As a result the contributors vary in their approaches and tend to focus on quite particular angles. We hope that we have struck a sensible balance between information and exploration and that the volume will prove useful not only to students generally but also to students of drama and to practitioners of the theatre.

As the present volume is, not least, designed to interest readers whose command of German may be limited, we thought it best to give all quotations within the texts in English. (The German originals can be found in the notes.) These translations are by the authors of the papers in question except in the case of the contributions by Sibylle Wirsing, Irmela Schneider and my own essay, which were translated by Anthony Mathews to whom I am very grateful for his patient and painstaking work.

The Colloquium was supported by the Goethe Institute, the German Academic Exchange Service, the British Academy, the British Council and the host institution, the University of East Anglia. I owe particular debts of gratitude to Frau Marga Schmitz of the German Academic Exchange Service's London Office and to Herr Günther Coenen, Director of the Goethe Institute (London). Without their unbureaucratic assistance and generous support this Colloquium would not have been possible.

Last, but not least, I feel much indebted to Janet Godden of Berg Publishers who read the typescript with exemplary care. The book benefited a great deal from her suggestions.

W. G. SEBALD
Norwich, June 1988

Surveying the Scene—Some Introductory Remarks

W. G. Sebald

THE reconstitution of cultural life in West Germany during the post-war era was, in a number of its aspects, a rather disheartening affair. Hopes for a truly new beginning had soon been dashed as it became apparent that the cultural climate of the 1950s, determined by the atmospheric conditions of the Cold War, did not encourage new departures in the arts but tended to promote a programme of restoration. Under the implicit terms of this programme it was the function of the arts to affirm the status quo rather than to ask awkward questions about it.

The theatre, more dependent upon the state than any other form of art, was severely affected by the unpronounced dictates of public propriety. The theatrical landscape of the 1950s and early '60s can only be described as a desert strewn with the incongruous remnants of a misunderstood and maltreated tradition. To be sure, the infra-structures had been rebuilt with amazing efficiency. Like the Phoenix from the ashes the new playhouses rose from the rubble and there was, on the part of the audiences, a veritable craving for culture which was fed with productions of the classics and a staple of imported plays—O'Neill, Wilder, Williams, Sartre, Camus, Anouilh—all of which were 'adapted' to the needs of the system in a manner certain not to undermine the collective amnesia which was the blind spot in the public consciousness of the first fifteen years of the Federal Republic. In other words the inner state of the nation was not, at that time, considered a topic suitable for the stage. In the years from 1948 to 1963 West Germany's contribution to dramatic literature is insignificant, if not non-existent. This in turn meant that the theatre too remained uninspired and uninspiring. The difference it would have made in this general malaise, if at least some of the

1

exiles had been won back can be judged by the example of Brecht who created what was perhaps the most influential ensemble in post-war Europe at the Theater am Schiffbauerdamm in East Berlin and whose brief séjour, after his return from the United States, at the Zurich Schauspielhaus also prompted into action the two Swiss playwrights Frisch and Dürrenmatt.

The breakthrough in West Germany came with an increasing willingness to face the repressed past. The war-crime trials which got under way in West German courts from the late 1950s onwards made it plain to all who wanted to know that there was a vast unresolved chapter in recent German history, and in the wake of Hochhuth's notorious *Der Stellvertreter* (1963) a number of writers—notably Martin Walser, Heinar Kipphardt and Peter Weiss—began the dramatic process of re-examining the past and presenting the results on a public stage to an audience which, used as it was to cultural sedatives, reacted to this confrontation with considerable bewilderment.

In spite of its aesthetic austerity documentary drama, the first indigenous form of writing for the stage to come out of West Germany, did have very positive implications for theatre as an art form, at least inasmuch as it went against all preconceived notions of what a play ought to look like. Once the ice had been broken, theatre in West Germany began to make up for the moral and aesthetic deficit which it had incurred since the desertification of the minds had been systematised in 1933; the gap which had to be bridged was that of one entire generation. Significantly, the second important dimension in the regeneration of playwriting—the neo-verist approach propagated by such dramatists as Martin Sperr, Rainer Werner Fassbinder and Franz Xaver Kroetz—had as its point of reference the plays of Ödön von Horváth and Marie-Luise Fleisser that had been written during the late years of the Weimar Republic and were now, in the late '60s, at last rescued from obscurity.

From the mid-sixties onwards the context changed rapidly. The atrophied body of the *Stadt-* and *Staatstheaterkultur* was rocked by the shock waves of the events of 1968, and it was out of these events and out of the changing consciousness of which they were manifestations that the most important new school of post-war German theatre was born. This school had as its energetic centre a group of young producers and actors—Peter Stein, Klaus Michael Grüber, Bruno Ganz, Edith Clever, Jutta Lampe and

Werner Rehm—who had come together under the aegis of the Bremer Bühne. Kurt Hübner's courageous management had turned this stage into the most important training ground for new talent in the 1960s and it was here that were sown the seeds from which grew the now famous Berliner Schaubühne.

There can be no doubt that the dozen or so years from 1968 to the early 1980s were among the most inspiring in the history of twentieth-century German theatre. The political and moral impulses generated in the late 1960s, combined with new aesthetic ambitions, encouraged playwrights and producers to undertake a reconstructive review of their dramatic and theatrical inheritance. From Peter Stein's revolutionary production of Goethe's *Tasso* and Franz Xaver Kroetz's reworking of Hebbel's *Agnes Bernauer* to Heiner Müller's treatments of Kleist and Klaus Michael Grüber's radical adaptation of Goethe's *Faust* for the Freie Volksbühne in Berlin (1981–82), much of the canon of German dramatic literature was virtually rewritten. In the sense in which Brecht had instigated it through his *Bearbeitungen* in the 1950s, theatrical practice redefined itself as a critical encounter with received precepts and materials. Grüber's adaptation of *Faust*, to give just one example, resulted in an entirely new understanding of a play which had been preserved forever, or so it seemed, in the neo-neo-classicist form that Gustav Gründgens had contrived for it in 1960. Grüber's productions made deep cuts into Goethe's sacrosanct text, reduced the score, actors and stage business to an absolute minimum, and through this reductive approach revealed layers of meaning which had escaped generations of producers. What had always been a rather trite element in the *Faust* plot, the seduction of poor Gretchen by the scholar turned gentleman, was translated in Grüber's version into a deeply moving tale of love between an old man (played by Bernhard Minetti, then in his late seventies) and a very young girl (played by Nina Dittbrenner, an amateur actress). Pitch and balance of visual and verbal intensity in this production were such that all discussions concerning the legitimacy of theatre in our time were rendered superfluous.

The reconsideration of the theatrical heritage went hand in hand with the continuing re-examination of Germany's notorious past, a process which has still not been completed as Bernhard's *Vor dem Ruhestand* (1979), Kipphardt's *Bruder Eichmann* (1983) and Achternbusch's (unfortunately rather misbegotten) play *Linz* (1987) demonstrate. It was the re-opening of the crucial chapters in Ger-

3

man history, so prematurely foreclosed by collective amnesia during the era of restoration, the rediscovery of the idealist programme with its ultimate ignominious betrayal, the gradually developing insight into the dialectics of humanism and terror, which created the conditions for a veritable renaissance of dramatic literature in Germany. The present volume is an attempt to provide some insights into a radically transformed scene.

Sybille Wirsing, one of the most informed observers of the German stage, suggests in Chapter 1 that the astonishing revival was a rather short-lived affair. In Sybille Wirsing's view the heroic years during which a deeply felt moral and aesthetic commitment on the part of producers and performers restructured German theatre from the inside were submerged by the well worn routine of the *Staats-* and *Stadttheaterkultur*. The new theatre also had a way of upstaging itself in ever more spectacular extravaganzas. In her regretful statement Sibylle Wirsing argues that the circle of influential producers has remained suspiciously small, that the erstwhile rebels, the clan of '68, knew well how best to keep a closed shop. And this is indeed the overriding impression conveyed by the game of musical chairs which producers such as Palitzsch and Peymann, Hübner and Zadek seem to conduct among themselves, succeeding each other in the key positions of the major German playhouses. The sense of purpose which inspired the years around 1970 has given way to circular patterns in which the same names and notions dominate the scene. That there is a feeling of disenchantment among leading producers can hardly be denied. The turn Peter Stein's career has taken after an unprecedented series of great productions bears this out. Ironically, it was the very success of productions such as the ones referred to by David Bradby in Chapter 2 which may have precluded further developments of the art of staging a play. The more successful a production is in artistic terms, the more likely it is to conceal the conflicts which generated the new theatrical vision. Perhaps this is one of the laws governing the relation between ethics and aesthetics. At any rate, the trend towards increasingly ambitious stage designs was facilitated by the subsidies which the two German states lavish upon their theatres. The Schaubühne's total budget in 1985 was near enough 19 million Marks of which over 14 million were subsidies. Even a provincial stage like the Landestheater Coburg with a total budget of 13 million Marks is subsidised to the extent of 11 million Marks. Support on this scale does amount to a kind of double bind which ensures that more often than not the intended radicality of the message is submerged by the staggering display of theatrical means. The stylistic correlative of all this is a grandiose *Theater der Bilder* which at times approaches the point of stasis, when an audience can do no more than sit and watch in amazement. Hence the touch of the operatic noticeable in so many of the great productions of recent years. Stein's *Otello* arrangement for the Welsh Opera, described by David Bradby, a strange project as it may have seemed to some, was perfectly in keeping with the developments of theatrical practice in Germany over the last fifteen years.

The Schaubühne promoted playwrights like Botho Strauss whose eclectic approach—very much that of a connoisseur of traditions—is the subject of Chapter 3. Strauss may not have remained sufficiently resistent to the temptations of beautifully organised displays of despair which can be as insincere as they are ostentatious. On the other hand it is true to say that Strauss does attempt to reflect the process which gave rise to the discontinuity in his dramatic inventions. His plays mark a phase of societal evolution where the dynamics of social intercourse have become almost entirely opaque and where conflict—the stuff of drama—can only be represented, figuratively, in terms of battles fought and lost many times before. This is why Strauss uses myths and mythology as structuring devices in his plays.

Kroetz, by contrast, seeks to show, as Moray McGowan points out in Chapter 6, that the subject is far from unreal, that it can be defined in its social and political environment and that the theatre is the proper place for such a definition to be made. Like all writers with a penchant for verism, Kroetz is in danger of being accused of sentimentality or cynicism, but there can be no doubt that his best work is a serious challenge not only to society in its present form of organisation but also to a theatre intoxicated by its own miraculous achievements.

How easily both producers and playwrights can get carried away is instanced by Tankred Dorst's latest dramatic work, *Merlin*.[1] Unlike *Deutsche Stücke* where Dorst, as Steve Giles shows, restricts himself to an investigation of the legacy of the fascist era, *Merlin* is a stage work in every sense without bounds. Times past and future, episodic and panoramic devices, exemplary passages and pathetic stylistic lapses, utter fatalism and a belief in some sort of latter-day

1. *Merlin oder das wüste Land*, Frankfurt 1981.

magic come together here in a collage the complete scenic realisation of which would demand one entire day. The slightly megalomaniac tendencies manifest in *Merlin* are not unique. From Peter Stein's and Klaus Michael Grüber's early productions large-scale arrangements began to dominate the scene. Audiences had to get used to performances ranging over four to six hours and sometimes over several days. The Schaubühne's *Antikenprojekt* of 1974 can be considered as the model for this kind of theatrical monumentalism.

I would venture the hypothesis that the tendency to exploit the means of production to the full is to do with the fact that theatres in Germany have remained almost entirely male-dominated institutions. Only in recent years have a very few women managed to join the ranks of producers and no German theatre of any standing has, to the best of my knowledge, admitted a woman to the post of general and artistic director. The professional designation *Intendantin* still sounds like a contradiction in itself. However, a number of female playwrights have emerged since the mid-seventies and it is the nature of their work which prompts my conjecture that large-scale stage fantasies may be the hallmark of male producers and of male playwrights who have succumbed to the lure of the grandiose vision. In Chapter 4 Lucinda Rennison examines the plays of Friederike Roth which are reductive rather than expansive in their approach and which, for their proper realisation, rely on a sense of tact and balance, qualities with which, as Lucinda Rennison points out, most of the male producers who have tried their luck with Friederike Roth's plays, do not seem to have been blessed. Friederike Roth's approach to play-writing is shared by other female dramatists currently writing in Germany, notably by Gerlinde Reinshagen and Elfriede Jelinek[2] whose work was not discussed at the Norwich colloquium. There is every hope that the emergence of female playwrights and producers will prove an important corrective factor in the further development of theatre and drama in Germany.

In Chapter 7 Horst Claus deals with a form of theatre which is far removed from any aesthetic pretence. The Grips Theater's principal concern is to provide a new form of entertainment and instruction for the young. Horst Claus reminds us that Grips too had its roots

---

2. See, for instance, G. Reinshagen, *Sonntagskinder*, Frankfurt 1981; *Eisenherz* in: *Theater Heute* 1983, 1, pp. 43–51; *Die Clownin* in: *Theater Heute* 1987, 1, pp. 31–40. Elfriede Jelinek, *Theaterstücke: Clara S. Wass geschah, nachdem Nora ihren Mann verlassen hatte*. Burgtheater, Cologne 1984.

in the late 1960s. Since then Volker Ludwig and the theatre practitioners associated with him have written a large number of scripts
and their productions have met with much acclaim not only in
Germany but also in this country. In Grips productions the message
is more important than the medium, but this does not mean that
they are aesthetically unsophisticated. Their revue character has
much in common with the productions of the Piscator-Bühne in the
late 1920s and they do in fact constitute something like applied
theatre, theatre with a specific purpose or *eingreifendes Theater*.
Though this Brechtian model is clearly highly successful in the case
of Grips which has its home in West Berlin, it seems, from Anthony
Meech's observations in East German theatres, that producers there
have some difficulty in translating this concept into a meaningful
practice. The idea has been reduced to an almost redundant precept
which is no longer operative in the way in which Brecht envisaged
it.

The provincialism of East German theatres which Anthony
Meech's account speaks of is however only one part of the story for
East Germany has produced a number of quite outstanding playwrights in the last fifteen years. The work of two of these, Heiner
Müller and Volker Braun, is discussed in the contributions by James
Reid and Julian Hilton respectively. Müller and Braun both connect
back to Brecht and both took some time to come out from under his
shadow. Only in the 1970s did they manage to shed the epigonal
image and to establish themselves as major dramatists in their own
right. As Julian Hilton explains, their work is quite consciously
linked to the German dramatic tradition. Such names as Lessing,
Schiller, Kleist and Büchner are reference points in many of their
plays. It very much seems, therefore, as though it will be the East
German authors who will, in time, be seen as representing the true
line of descent. Paradoxically though their process of emancipation
from the provincialism of the GDR would have been unthinkable
had they not had access to the West German stage and to West
German publishers. The transfer of East German talent—
playwrights, producers, actors—onto the West German cultural
market has proved a great challenge to all those who work for the
stage. Müller's work particularly is of a radicality which calls into
question all our assumptions. Not only has he brought such issues
as the threat of nuclear war, the prospect of a post-nuclear age, and,
while we are transfixed by such vast and intractable scenarios, the
ongoing and systematic destruction of nature in and around us into

the precinct of dramatic writing; he has also found quite revolutionary dramaturgic devices capable of translating his apocalyptic visions into scenic structures.

Müller is a writer of endgames as are Bernhard and Achternbusch, the playwrights whose pieces for the theatre are examined in the essays by Rüdiger Görner and by myself with which this volume concludes. The difference between Müller on the one hand and the southerners Bernhard and Achternbusch on the other is that Müller is a professional who wants to make the fullest possible use of the theatre machine whereas Bernhard and Achternbusch are both in a sense amateurs whose work shows little awareness of the complexity of the means of production. Bernhard's plays are essentially *Kammerspiele* but no less radical for that. His message is that we need not be concerned about the future as we are all dead souls already, simply feigning or simulating a kind of life. Achternbusch's plays—if plays are what they are—could perhaps best be described as *théâtre brut*. Unlike the theatre engineer Müller who carefully selects the materials for his machines, Achternbusch uses what happens to be to hand, and as in all *art brut* creations in Achternbusch's plays too the author plays a central role as representative of a species which may well become extinct in the not too distant future since it still belongs, after a fashion, to the natural realm which it relentlessly destroys. This prospect in which the subject and the object of destruction are one is a central theme of playwriting in Germany today. It changes all received ideas about nature and humanity showing us adrift somewhere between the devil and the deep blue sea. Heiner Müller's *Verkommenes Ufer Medeamaterial Landschaft mit Argonauten* treats, among other things, of shipwreck. That there is an audience watching the calamitous scene of destruction brings the whole arrangement in line with one of the most pervasive *topoi* of Western literature and art identified by Hans Blumenberg as *Schiffbruch mit Zuschauer*,[3] a topos summed up by Lucretius's famous lines 'Pleasant it is, when over a great sea the winds trouble the waters, to gaze from the shore upon another's great tribulation'.[4]

---

3. See Hans Blumenberg, *Schiffbruch mit Zuschauer*, Frankfurt 1979.
4. *De Natura Rerum*, Cambridge, Mass. and London 1975, p. 95.

1

The State of the Stage—the Decline of Commitment in the Contemporary German Theatre
Sybille Wirsing

THE Germans are living at peace with their theatre. A year and a half ago the Frankfurt Schauspielhaus attempted to put Fassbinder's play *Der Müll, die Stadt und der Tod* posthumously on the stage. It is about a rich Jew in West Germany who takes democracy at its word, a democracy based on economics and at the service of wolves in sheep's clothing. What does the questionable morality post-1945 matter to the survivor of a concentration camp? He takes up residence on a derelict site and does very nicely thanks to his privileges known as *Wiedergutmachung*. Among the old nazis and the new cynics he remains an alien presence, a provocation. Yet, despite all his faults and defects, this survivor of the holocaust may be the only fit subject left for serious drama, a subject moreover which up until now has been assiduously avoided. The play could not be shown to the public. After protests the attempt to put it on was stifled. I cannot think of any other example of conflict between the theatre and the public in recent times. Presumably this has been the only incident of its kind.

The reign of peace in the West German theatre is a hangover from the Third Reich. For a time in the 1960s and 1970s it appeared to waver, when there was considerable ferment within the new theatres, those bastions of culture that had been established in the period of the rebuilding of Germany, counterparts to the department stores and banks. The unplanned excitement spilled over from the stage to the audience, and for a short time the political administrators of culture lost control of the medium of the theatre. It all started with Hochhuth's *Der Stellvertreter*, the documentary play

9

that questions Pope Pius XII's detachment when the Germans dragged the Jews of Europe into concentration camps to be murdered. In 1963 the first production, directed by Erwin Piscator at the Berlin Freie Volksbühne, with its première that had to be put under police protection, was too much for the Catholic Church. Since the Weimar Republic gave way to the Third Reich there had been no political theatre prepared to speak the truth, so for thirty years people had been unaccustomed to the stage taking a political role. The reintroduction of critical theatre in the sixties went hand in hand with the decline of Christian Democrat domination in West Germany. A younger generation of directors, performers and playwrights made themselves heard. Characteristic of the new tone which was now sounded were statements such as: 'We provide the powerful with the artistic spectacle of dislocation and convulsion. In common with the public we are helpless, unable to articulate our own anger and pain.' These are two sentences from the programme notes that the director Peter Stein and his dramatic adviser Yaak Karsunke provided for the Bremen production of Goethe's *Torquato Tasso*. In 1969 on the Bremen stage the poet Tasso was the embodiment of the artist who had sold himself and his talent to the ruling class that provides the money, sets the fashion and controls politics. He is a buffoon, a eunuch in the service of the powerful who keep art like an exotic pet in a cage. Tasso suffers and throws himself about like a mad thing on the stage but he is as good as gold when the official takes him off at the end—a child who has let off so much steam that his eyes are closing with tiredness, his resistance simply dissolves into nothing; the little man is put to bed. The theatres in fact suffered the same fate. But until the *enfants terribles* were given a piggy-back out of the arena by the cultural officials, there were a few years of fun. Today the initiators—those of them who are still alive—have either retired, or survive as highly paid grand old men of the theatre, or are on the slippery slope to provincial obscurity. There remains scarcely a whiff of the barricades of theatrical history about them. Peter Stein, who was apprenticed to Fritz Kortner (a Jew who had emigrated and later returned), Hansgünther Heyme, the pupil of Piscator, Fassbinder, whose scant respect for German hypocrisy soon earned him notoriety, Peter Zadek, who brought a bold and salacious spirit of enterprise to West Germany from his English exile, Peter Palitzsch, one of Brecht's collaborators and a refugee from the GDR, or Kurt Hübner, theatre manager first in Ulm and then at Bremen, a runner of risks, a collector of talent and ever since the Hitler period a sceptical German—these are a few of the names from the hit-parade of those who made the running in the theatre of the '60s. Then there were the writers: Peter Weiss, the German-speaking Jewish dramatist living in Stockholm, Rolf Hochhuth, the provoker of the Pope, Franz Xaver Kroetz and Martin Sperr, young playwrights from Bavaria, receptive to the murky lower depths of the Catholic, conservative 'free state', or Edward Bond, borrowed from England, the author of *Saved* and *Early Morning*.

A decade and a half even before the arrival on the scene of the younger generation, Jürgen Fehling, an old hand in the theatre, noted what was going to be the point at issue in the controversy between the theatre and the culture industry. Fehling was very German and somewhat influenced by the propaganda style of Goebbels' ministry of 'information' to which he was exposed for twelve years of his life. He wrote:

It is extremely interesting that the recent outcry at the end of Tieck's *Blaubart* at the Munich Residenztheater was seen as unique, without parallel, revolutionary and refreshing. It is time to show the colour of our creative ideas—not the old rag of two-handed argument but a banner, a jolly roger, a gaudy pennant flapping in the wind, like a bold warrior battered and torn in the clash of opinions, rather than diplomatically lowering it at the sight of the unapproachable powers-that-be, whose powers are not, however, beyond reproach. We will not trim our sails full of hope to suit the promoters of the abomination that has replaced humanistic culture since the end of the abominable war and that threatens to be almost as destructive in peace time as the war damage itself was. We are not going to take it any more from these faceless men, all we have to do against them is to make so much fuss around the place that people begin to wake up a little. We are expected to applaud everything, particularly when there is nothing to applaud, when we should be rising up against all the charlatans at the gates, against the philistine conspiracy that would turn the theatre into a place where the self-conscious theatre-going public can show off and where seated in their expensive seats they are unashamedly indoctrinated with the sort of poetic and heroic clichés revived from the Nazi period—a malleable mass the object of party political manipulation that is all the more unrestrained in its cheap sophistry.[1]

1. 'Daß der Theaterskandal jüngst im Residenztheater am Schluß des Tieckschen *Blaubart* als einmalig, ohne Beispiel, umwerfend und beglückend empfunden wurde, ist außerordentlich und muß hier interessieren. Damit sind wir an den Punkt gelangt, der geeignet ist, unsere konstruktiven Gedanken daran zu befestigen—nicht wie einen einerseits andererseits nassen alten Lappen, sondern wie eine Standarte, eine schwarze Seeräuberfahne, wie einen lustigen Wimpel, der im Winde knattern soll,

11

Reading such statements makes the hair stand on end. Fehling, who is here speaking in the name of the so-called higher values of our philosophy, music and literature, had grasped everything but understood nothing. He predicted that the authorities would want to get control of the theatre and banish independence of mind from this prestigious institution but he still considered recourse to intellect and fine words to be an adequate form of resistance. It is as though he had not learnt from the experience of the Third Reich that the cultural policy of the Nazi regime was equally based on writing, music and philosophy. The legendary year 1968 provides an example that pinpoints the predicament exactly. On the studio stage of the Munich Kammerspiele Peter Weiss's *Vietnam Diskurs* was to have been performed with Peter Stein as director, and his conception of the performance included a collection in aid of the Vietcong. The general and administrative director of the Kammerspiele, Herr August Everding, who has since become the leading Munich theatre supremo, banned the collection in the auditorium, arguing that this part of the performance could be carried out in the street outside. The cast insisted that the collection was an essential part of the whole thing. The upshot was that the play was dropped. Peter Stein wrote a post-mortem account of the affair in which he compares the episode to the authoritarian practices of the theatre's administrative directors who are prepared to permit 'artistic freedom' only so long as it does not lead to political consequences. Stein claims in his statement that these functionaries of culture are determined to prevent even the most modest political initiatives on the part of the producers and actors who work in the playhouses they run.[2] Whether or not collections, or any other direct involvement of

---

und der eher wie ein Soldat und brav im Streit der Meinungen zerfransen und zerreißen wird, als daß wir ihn kniggebeflissen vor Behörden und ungreifbaren (aber nicht unangreifbaren!) Gewalten herunterholen. Wir werden unsere Segel voller Hoffnung nicht streichen vor den Managern dessen, was anstelle humanistischer Kultur seit dem schrecklichen Kriegsende schrecklich ausgesät wird und was Friedensschäden zu bringen droht, die den Kriegsschäden an zerstörendem Ausmaß nicht nachstehen werden. Sie haben bei uns nichts zu bestellen, die Dunkelmänner, man muß in den falschen Gärtnern nur laut genug übern Zaun zurufen, daß die Schlafenden ringsum aufwachen. Sie hoffen auf unseren Applaus und sie rechnen mit ihm in einem Moment, wo es nicht zu applaudieren, wo es zu revoltieren gilt gegen alle Scharlatane ante portas, gegen alle Verbündeten im Ungeist, die aus den Schaubühnen eine Repräsentationsangelegenheit einer unsicher gewordenen Abonnentenmasse machen möchten, die in chicer Holzklasse lyrisch hymnisch mit wiedererstandenen KdF-Phrasen dreist bepredigt und belehrt werden soll—eine Masse, deren Labilität man mit um so keckerer Halbbildung versteckt parteipolitisch beschießt.' *Theater Heute* 1968, 8, p. 8.
2. 'Die autoritären Praktiken der Theaterverwaltung machen nicht nur die

the audience for that matter, are liable to lead to an increase in political awareness is less interesting in this context than the conclusion that the young people involved with the theatre in 1968 wanted to take possession of their theatre not in the name of Goethe and Schiller or some other big name but simply in their own right. They were arguing in the spirit of Brecht's *Kreidekreis*: the children to the maternal, the fields to those who work them and, by the same token, the theatres not to the officials but to those who have their place of entertainment and their place of work there.

To cut a long story short, the golden words of Brecht's tale initiate a period of struggle. In the days we are talking about, the German fairy-tale of the theatre in the hands of those who *are* the theatre moved on a little in its collective search for independence, a search which has since been abandoned and is now irretrievably turned into various and separate biographies. It was not very long before the bureaucrats could breathe a sigh of relief at the way things were going. The political will was quickly subordinated to an artistic self-expression that did not care what was being lost and ended up as an ego-trip. The directors who had become proverbial captains in the culture industry, stepped up their shock effects and the extravagance of their sets knew no bounds. They became increasingly obsessed with the notion of self-realisation and their vanity reached such a point that in the end the aim of the exercise was largely the deployment of the means of theatrical production. The director Hans Neuenfels, one of the most outspoken supporters of artistic freedom, noted as early as 1980: 'If we continually think we are threatened by a sell-out of artistic means, that surely has something to do with the fact that our theatre has not been produced by the pressure of circumstances. The unholy alliance between life and art is more than ever relevant for an actor or a director. Liberalism seems to make everything possible but we increasingly get the impression that it is in fact running amok.'[3]

Fragwürdigkeit einer "künstlerischen Freiheit" deutlich, die in dem Augenblick, wo sie ein Minimum an politischer Konsequenz anstrebt, administrativ beschnitten wird, sondern zeigen zugleich, daß Kulturverwalter und Ordnungshüter in unseren Theatern die bescheidensten Ansätze zu politischer Willensbildung und Praxis der eigentlichen Produzenten, nämlich der Schauspieler und Regisseure, am Arbeitsplatz zu unterbinden versuchen.' *Theater Heute* 1968, 8, p. 32.
3. 'Wenn wir uns ständig von dem Ausverkauf der Mittel bedroht sehen, so hängt das sicherlich damit zusammen, daß die Theaterabende nicht aus dem Druck der jeweiligen Spezifik entwickelt werden. Die verteufelte Verschwisterung von Leben und Kunst ist für einen Schauspieler oder einen Regisseur mehr denn je aktuell. Der Liberalismus macht scheinbar alles möglich, aber wir merken immer stärker, wie er

Actually it is less a question of a dangerous form of madness than a creeping paralysis. The theatre that has been so quickly deflected away from the hard road to political responsibility into a playground, now has to put up with the political officials speaking on its behalf. If artistic freedom is used principally to work off personal artistic passions, it becomes nothing more than a gimmick to draw the crowds. It has to be accepted that a theatre conscious of its own political role, the stage as a political institution, a form of political education or even activity, would not suit those in local and regional government who would prefer to keep politics in their own hands. Only an institution prepared to perceive its artistic freedom in terms of a direct political struggle and commitment could take on the management. In fact the political will within the theatre is so lacking that the minister with responsibility for culture can go over the heads of the people within a theatre and appoint its artistic, administrative and general directors. As in the days of Absolutism this remains the business of the government. The consequence is obvious: for those few people active in the theatre who still represent a clearly political view it is getting more and more difficult to find a suitable playhouse. However, the official but unspoken staffing policy is only one small aspect of the whole desperate situation. The certain and ominous decision to silence the voice of emancipation in the West German theatre can be judged by the extent to which the younger generation is given opportunities. In sharp contrast to the lavish funding of the municipal, regional and state theatres with their extremely wide range of productions, there is a fundamental lack of training facilities. Moreover there is no sign of a specific policy. The few officially supported drama schools see themselves largely as feeder institutions. The criteria for selection and training are directed neither towards performing talent nor towards the art of the theatre as such but are based on supply and demand. In other words, the aim right from the start is to fit in. Anyone who does not is weeded out straightaway. Conformity and compliance are what is looked for rather than independence and determination. And that is not all. The apprentice is trained strictly within a very narrow area. The aim is to prepare him for the theatre: he is only required to show competence in his professional role. He is not supposed to have ideas about the meaning and potential of the theatre as it is here

Amok läuft.' *War da was?—Theaterarbeit und Mitbestimmung am Schauspiel Frankfurt 1972–1980*, Frankfurt 1980, p. 307.

and now. Actors should be ignorant, the more ignorant the better. The ideal is still the virtuoso, the professional expert who gets on with the job without asking too many questions about what is going on. And that is not the worst of it. For the director, who is becoming more and more the focal point of the theatre, there is no sort of training at all. Anyone who wants to learn how to put a play on the stage soon learns that this is not provided for in the educational system. There are no apprenticeships; the job of directing a play is not taught. As a result, it has no chance of being developed. The new generation of directors just have to manage as best they can as probationers or assistants, trying their hand at everything, rambling all over the place, experimenting outside of their legitimate fields, imitating, plagiarising, getting stuck up blind alleys. Liable to frustration, underprivileged, they are good-for-nothings, still beginners at thirty and at forty—if they are lucky—self-made men who use the proud claim that they have learnt their trade from the shop-floor up to conceal the humiliating fact that their training has been barely adequate. Of course this may be sufficient for the day-to-day running of the theatre but no great strides can be made with such meagre equipment.

The cultural policy could not be more explicit. On the one hand it plays a decisive part in the running of the theatres, on the other hand it refuses to provide the next generation with training. From these two things we can conclude that an independent theatre is not welcome, indeed it finds severe obstacles set in its way. The less education and training, the more docile the theatre will be—that is the idea behind it. The theatre as the institution of prestige predicted by Fehling upsets no one. The theatrical peace that has already led to a lethargic coexistence of stage and audience will end up as a theatrical silence that nothing can disturb.

The sounds coming from the theatres bear a nasty resemblance to such a declaration of bankruptcy. Ivan Nagel, an outstanding man of the theatre who came back to West Germany and its stage after a long absence, found that first-rate actors gave the impression of having been crushed, that they did not identify with the company and lacked the will to communicate anything to an audience. After productions that were still often conscientious, sincere and even, as if by accident, lively and impressive, the performers sat at the first night party as if at some sort of wake: they stared into their beer in the dimly lit canteen and muttered that there was no point any more. 'I find such a state of affairs criminal', Nagel sums up,

15

'because it is anti-life and anti-theatre.'[4] Nagel's decision to help put the theatre back on its feet did not last very long. His most recent experience as the head of one of the more famous West German theatres must have been truly catastrophic for him to have announced his departure from theatre management and resigned. Yet another one gone. I do not want to make any prognosis—the death of the theatre or some such foreboding. I see only what I see—depression all round—and I ask myself what could bring about a change. Those involved with the theatre would have to admit to their desperate plight instead of repressing it, they would have to ask themselves what they themselves have failed to do instead of pushing the responsibility onto management. The theatre that is put on the West German stage wavers between two extremes that, from the point of view of the management, ought to be ideally in evidence in one and the same production. One is shock effects, the other is pandering to public taste. Get them worked up or give them what they want—this recipe can be served up with sophistication or vulgarity, subtlety or triviality, giving the theatre as I have experienced it up and down the country an appearance of crash, bang and wallop. At any moment the impossible can happen. The escalation of gimmicks can suddenly get out of control. The flouting of styles becomes the style itself. There is no consistency that I can rely on. As a member of an audience I am completely in the hands of the people running the theatre. There is no limit to the contrasting experiences, sudden changes of atmosphere and surprises that they can impose upon me if they so desire. They do not treat me as an intelligent and critical partner, they only want me as a consumer; they are less concerned with communicating something to me than with spellbinding and titillating me. I am supposed to sit in open-mouthed amazement rather than be open to understanding. Whether the play is called *Nathan der Weise* or *Who's Afraid of Virginia Woolf?*, whether it is by Lars Noren or Goethe, Giraudoux or Sophocles, makes no difference at all. The main thing is that the audience has a titillating experience. The result is that the audience

4. 'Ich sah da hervorragende, aber gleichsam von oben vergiftete Schauspieler: ohne Zuhause in einem Ensemble, ohne Mitteilungswillen für ein Publikum. Nach Aufführungen, die oft noch sorgfältig, ehrlich, ja wie durch einen Unfall vital und glanzvoll gerieten, saßen die Darsteller bei der Premierenfeier wie beim Leichenschmaus: sie stierten in eine Bierlache in der schütter beleuchteten Kantine und brummten vor sich hin, daß nichts mehr geht. Einen solchen Zustand finde ich verbrecherisch, weil lebens- und theaterwidrig.' Interview with Peter von Becker and Henning Rischbieter, *Theater Heute*, Jahrbuch 1985, p. 7.

soon grows bored. Today's sensations become yesterday's news. The public yawns, and the theatre producers have to think of something new all over again. There is no way out of this vicious circle of stimuli other than by a return to a consideration of the subject matter itself: theatre not as a circus but as a political act, the production of Shakespeare, for example, not the taking up of theatrical arms but a clear and sober demonstration that there is something rotten here and now in the state that is represented on the stage by Denmark. The play's the thing that puts the powerful on the stage in the same way that Hamlet presents his players before the king and usurper. The advice that this amateur director gives to the company—if we courageously translated it into the contemporary German context and took it to heart—would be sufficient to save us: 'Suit the action to the word, the word to the action; with this special observance, that you o'erstep not the modesty of nature.'

2

Blacking Up—Three Productions by Peter Stein

David Bradby

'ONE evening an actor asked me to write a play for an all-black cast. But what exactly is a black? First of all, what's his colour?'[1] With these words Genet introduced his play *The Blacks*, adding a further note in which he insisted that the play must be performed to an audience of whites. If by chance there were to be no white person present, a white dummy or white masks would have to be used.

The reasons for Genet's insistence are clear enough: blackness is a social construct, something culturally determined, having its origin in the colonial encounter. Biological factors such as ethnic origins and skin colour are quite unimportant by comparison with the power of one group of people to impose an identity on another group. Genet, who has always identified with the outlawed and criminal classes, has described himself as 'a black whose skin happens to be pink and white'.[2]

Genet wrote *The Blacks* for a group of black actors mostly from West Africa who called themselves 'Les Griots' (poet-musicians) and since its first production (by Roger Blin in 1959) the play has rarely been revived in Europe, though it is regularly performed by black theatre groups in America. The reason for this is simple: it is written in such a way as to demand performance by an all-black cast. So it was a bold move by Peter Stein and the Schaubühne to decide that they would undertake a production.

Bold, but not altogether surprising. Many of Stein's productions have involved his company identifying with a group quite different from themselves and spending a great deal of time and effort getting

---

1. Jean Genet, *The Blacks*, trans. Bernard Frechtman, London 1960, p. 5.
2. 'Jean Genet talks to Hubert Fichte', *The New Review* 37 (1977), 9–21.

into their skins. They did this for the revolutionary sailors of Vishnevski's *Optimistic Tragedy* in 1972 and for the idle *datshniki* of Gorki's *Summerfolk* in 1974. In 1976 they spent a year transforming themselves into inhabitants of Elizabethan England for *Shakespeare's Memory*. If Stein did experience any doubts about the wisdom of getting his cast to transform themselves into blacks, he may have felt it was no different in kind from these earlier experiments. Stein has always claimed that he has no set working method, that he shapes his methods according to the demands of the plays he tackles. The one constant factor in his working practice is a preference for working as part of a collective: clearly ensemble work of a high order is needed for Genet's dramatic ritual to find adequate expression on stage, but is it the kind of ensemble work developed by Stein and his company? Does it in the end matter whether Genet's prescription about black actors playing for a white audience is or is not followed?

In order to answer this and to understand Stein's work in 1983 and 1986, it is necessary to consider briefly the nature of Stein's early work as a director of the Schaubühne in the early 1970s.[3] The strength of this work lay in the way he confronted the contradictions it involved, contradictions which may be reduced schematically to two: one internal to the company and the other external. The internal contradiction was that of having to impose his role of director within the structure of a democratically self-governing collective. The external contradiction was that of performing revolutionary works (such as *The Optimistic Tragedy*) in a West Berlin theatre heavily subsidised as a showcase for capitalist values. Stein's work at this time prompted questions about the relationships between the individual and authority, private satisfactions and the public good. These questions were not confined to the subject matter of the plays he produced (such as *Prinz Friedrich von Homburg* or *Peer Gynt*); they permeated the processes of his work at every level. His role in the German theatre was not only to question all established practices, but openly to advocate the overthrow of the institutions that paid him. He was able to do this partly because of the peculiar state of cultural politics in West Berlin and partly because of his own qualities of vision, determination and commitment. One of his exceptional qualities was a sharp awareness

3. For a full discussion of Stein's work in the 1970s see Michael Patterson, *Peter Stein, Germany's Leading Theatre Director*, Cambridge 1981, and David Bradby and David Williams, *Director's Theatre*, London (Macmillan) forthcoming.

of the contradictions involved in his own and his company's work, and his ability to turn this awareness into a significant element of his productions.

Stein at first appeared to welcome both contradictions, not seeking to eliminate them but harnessing the dynamic process of challenge and counter-challenge that they entailed. Where the 'external' contradiction was concerned, he could point to a successful record of exploiting his favoured position without being exploited by it. For a time, during the early 1970s, he consistently presented material that challenged the expectations of his audiences and could not be accused of selling out to his paymasters. With respect to the 'internal' contradiction, Stein's success with the Schaubühne company appears to have stemmed from his total commitment to the collective process, even when it worked to his own inconvenience, and his ability to command the loyalty of first-rate actors. He was able to do this because the group was united by a sense of political purpose. The discussion of their contradictions was made to fuel a learning process. From the outset Stein's working methods involved a strong element of research and discovery by all members of the company. In order to raise the general level of political consciousness and to inform the managerial discussions within the group, political seminars were arranged, which everyone attended in working hours. The artistic aims of the group were also defined in terms of a learning process:

We wanted to concern ourselves with subjects not normally dealt with in the theatre, that is to say the history of revolution or revolutions and of the working class movement. That was our firm intention. And we were conscious of everything that implied: raising our political consciousness, studying the historical facts, etc. In short our need to learn not only about aesthetic matters, but also and especially about historical matters. That can only be a long-term undertaking. The other direction concerned the past and the history of the bourgeois class. There again, it seemed important to us to know more about it and to deal with it in our productions.[4]

This is unusual as a declaration of intent by a director of a theatre company because of its emphasis on what is to be learned rather than what is to be shown, on process rather than on product. It was informed by a clear belief that learning of this kind served a useful purpose: to understand and hence to be able to change. Significantly, Stein expressed the company's project in terms of alterna-

4. Interview in *Travail Théâtral* (Paris) 9 (1972), 16–36.

tives: history of revolutions on the one hand, history of the bourgeois class on the other. Together with this political aim went an aesthetic ambition to research and experiment with the alternative modes of representation available in a theatre such as his. In 1972 Stein talked about a planned production concerning the Paris Commune of 1871 (this never reached fruition). He explained that he had rejected both the existing plays on the subject by Brecht and Adamov and had sketched out a new idea in which the subject was to be 'the end of the bourgeois conception of revolution and the emergence of a different form of revolution, a different aesthetic, a different mode of representation and different metaphors since the Commune. That, I believe, is an interesting subject for the theatre'.[5]
It can be seen that the focus of Stein's work was not just historical or political alternatives, but a reflection on the alternative modes of representation available for depicting historical events, and this in turn is closely connected to the nature of the raw material with which the director works—that is, a company. Speaking fifteen years later about his production of Verdi's *Otello*, Stein said: 'You have to persuade people you are right to be on stage—and that for me is always the central problem. That we can only achieve if everybody on stage knows exactly what is going on, what the play or opera is about, of course, but also *what the staging in itself means*.'[6]
It is in this spirit that Stein's production of *The Blacks* must be examined to determine how 'the staging in itself' became a bearer of meaning. Stein stated clearly that the choice of play corresponded to the Schaubühne's desire to work collectively and to pursue its reflection on modes of dramatic representation:

We chose *The Blacks* because it opened up a subject having to do with the activity of theatre and one which we thought we could usefully explore and learn from. The subject was Africa, the European-African relationship, of course, as the play describes it. Moreover the actors were keen to work as a chorus and they are all on stage all the time.[7]

He added that the play also fitted the company's desire to follow up experiences not normally available to actors—in this case getting to know Africa. They made a brief trip to Africa, where they learned

5. Ibid.
6. Interview in the programme for the Welsh National Opera production of *Otello*, 1986. All subsequent quotations by Stein concerning *Otello* come from this interview.
7. Interview in *Théâtre en Europe* (Paris) 1 (1984), 24–9.

some basic African dance steps and these were put to good effect in the performance.

Genet's plays present any director with an unusual challenge since they are more ceremonies than stories, while nevertheless retaining close links to political realities. *The Blacks* presents not a story at all in the traditional sense, but a struggle between two languages. By imposing the French language on the Africans the colonisers have forced them to adopt all the hidden judgements enshrined in the European language. In the play a group of blacks face a white court, also played by blacks, wearing white masks. Beneath the horrified gaze of the court, the blacks re-enact the rape and murder of a white woman. The court appeals to Racinian purity, metaphoric whiteness, images of light and spotlessness, the white man's civilising mission. The blacks respond with a 'litany of the livid', exploiting the unpleasant associations of pallor, then they begin to develop a new set of value associations in which positive values are linked with notions of blackness. Genet's strategy here is not that of Senghor who, in developing his concept of negritude, used metaphors of blackness to which positive values have traditionally ascribed: mystery, fertility, power. Instead, Genet picked on all those things that have traditionally been used as insults by whites: smells, savagery, cannibalism. This is the language through which the white colonisers oblige the Africans to represent themselves—the only self-image available to them once they have adopted the French language. And so they develop and extend it, they celebrate it to a point of extremism, revel in it grotesquely. Genet's text prescribes the precise details of this ritual: the movements, the music, the use of masks, costumes and props. For example, he specifies a raised gallery running round the back of the stage from which the court looks down on the action, so that the ceremony of the blacks is caught between the facing ranks of white audience and white court: the gaze of one is reflected in the other. He also specifies that the play opens with the blacks dancing a minuet to a tune by Mozart.

Stein's production gave an extremely brilliant and very faithful representation of all this, adding very little that was not explicitly mentioned in Genet's directions. This in itself was remarkable since it had frequently been a hallmark of Stein's earlier works that he would reorder the text or add in extra material, the better to convey the kind of critical reflection on the play and its modes of representation alluded to in his remarks quoted above. In *The Blacks* scope for such additional work was reduced since the play is itself a reflection on modes of representation. The only changes or additions made by Stein appeared to be governed by political rather than aesthetic motives: they served to stress solidarity with the blacks rather than to reflect critically on representational images. But in so doing they undermined the very basis of Genet's theatrical ceremony. In order to understand how this happened it is necessary to consider the organisation of the performance in some detail.

The performance began with the audience viewing the process of blacking up by the actors. It was clearly important for Stein that the spectators should witness this complete transformation—i.e. should realise that they were to be faced, as nearly as possible, with a real group of blacks performing for them. After this, the play unfolded almost exactly as specified by Genet. The opening minuet was exquisitely performed by the group, humming in Swingle-singer style and waltzing round the stage as they did so. This was dramatically interrupted by a detail not of Genet's invention: an African spear which fell from the flying gallery to embed itself with a splintering crash in the beautiful varnished black wood of the stage. The members of the court, all blacked up like the others, wore white masks over their black faces as specified by Genet. They watched the ritual from a balcony set above and behind the action, much as in Blin's original production, and their pale gaze was supplemented by hundreds of other white masks which descended on strings as Village protested his love for Vertu—a mass of white voyeurs gloating in their power over the blacks. This addition helped to underline the fact that in Genet's ceremony the blacks have to refuse love as something polluted by the way it has been annexed by white civilisation. Instead, the only hope for the blacks is in the cultivation of hatred and the difficulty of this was demonstrated with great clarity in the dialogue between Village and Vertu (performed by Peter Simonischeck and Jutta Lampe) as they tried to develop a verbal language of hatred while all their body language expressed desire for one another.

The production was remarkable for the intelligence and faithfulness which Stein brought to the realisation of Genet's intentions. Particularly successful was the chanting of Félicité's 'Dahomey, Dahomey' speech in which Miriam Goldschmidt (the only black member of the cast) built up an atmosphere of tremendous power. The ensuing sequence, too, in which Neige accuses Village of having been attracted to the white woman was performed by Martina

Krauel as a wild possession dance with everyone on stage joining in. The use of movement and gesture was constantly illuminating and there were various ingenious *coups de théâtre*, such as the point where Diouf (dressed up as a white woman) and Village go behind the screen, ostensibly for the re-enactment of the rape and murder. When Ville de St. Nazaire folded up the screen, Diouf had disappeared: he was no longer on the same level as the other blacks but entered, suspended on a wire, flying like a grotesque angel above the head of the queen. Yet despite the faithfulness and clarity of the production, its overall effect was not to disturb and challenge the audience as Genet had intended. The reasons for this can be adduced from an examination of Stein's additions, modest though they were.

The one aim of all his additions seemed to be to increase the political punch of the show, as if, to make up for the fact that they were not real blacks, the cast had to demonstrate special energy and commitment. This aspect of the production became progressively clearer towards the end. At the point where Ville de St. Nazaire re-enters to announce the execution of a traitor off-stage in another place, Genet's stage direction specifies the sound of firecrackers going off and, on the black velvet of the set, the reflections of fireworks.[8] Not content with mere reflections, Stein provided a complete firework show which dazzlingly filled the whole stage space and led into a mood of common celebration as the court descended, removed their masks and pressed round Ville de St. Nazaire eager for information about the 'real' action taking place off-stage. For there are references throughout Genet's play to the effect that what we are being shown is not in itself of central importance: it is merely a diversion to keep its audience's mind off the 'real' action, taking place elsewhere, and involving the trial and execution of a black freedom fighter who has betrayed the cause, together with the commissioning of a new man to work in his place. Ville de St. Nazaire says: 'He's on his way. He's going off to organise and continue the fight. . . . As for you, you were only present for the display.' To which the one who played the valet replies curtly: 'We know. Thanks to us, they've sensed nothing of what's going on elsewhere.'[9] As this exchange makes quite clear, the function of Genet's play is somehow to disguise the reality of armed

8. *The Blacks*, p. 84.
9. Ibid., p. 85.

struggle, not to mobilise the audience for it. What is shown on stage can never have the force of an active revolt. Indeed, there are constant references to the suicidal nature of the enterprise the blacks are engaged on. In accepting the world of theatre, they have entered a de-realising space which robs them of any impact they might have had on the real world. This is spelled out by Archibald near the beginning of the ceremony: 'They tell us we're grown-up children. In that case what's left for us? The theatre! We'll play at being reflected in it and we'll see ourselves, big black narcissists, slowly disappearing into its waters.'[10] When Village protests that he wants to live Archibald snaps back at him:

ARCHIBALD. You're no exception! Nothing will remain of you but the foam of your rage. Since they merge us with an image and drown us in it, let the image set their teeth on edge!
VILLAGE. My body wants to live.
ARCHIBALD. You're becoming a spectre before their very eyes and you're going to haunt them.[11]

The necessary condition for transforming subservience into domination is first to cease to exist in the real world and turn into a spook, an 'image to set their teeth on edge'.

The political function of Genet's theatre is a subject on which he has spoken out forcefully. He has constantly said that the stage should not be used as a vehicle for resolving social problems. He insists that problems shown on stage should never be resolved on the imaginary plane because this will leave the audience with the comforting sense that the problem has been overcome and requires no further action: 'On the contrary, let evil explode on stage, let it show us naked, leave us haggard if possible, and with no other recourse than to ourselves.'[12] He wrote in a similar vein about *The Maids*: 'This is not an apologia on the lot of domestic servants. No doubt there exists a Trade Union for them—that does not concern us.'[13] The consequence of this attitude is that Genet's plays are not satirical in the common sense. Rather than cutting their characters down to size, they exalt them. The maids, the blacks do not represent the reality of servility or colonialism, but its image. They are reflections of images in the minds of their audiences. In so far as

10. Ibid., p. 31.
11. Ibid., p. 32.
12. (My translation) Jean Genet, *Oeuvres complètes IV*, Paris 1968, p. 35.
13. Ibid., p. 269.

they represent social relations as they exist in the real world, Genet's *dramatis personae* become simple figures onto which the audience is invited to project its familiar images. Hence the importance for Genet of the play being performed *by* blacks *for* whites: what takes place on stage is created by the spectators as much if not more than by the actors. The play is a ritual designed solely to undermine and dissolve the status of the actors as 'blacks', i.e. people whose being is defined by 'whites' as being non-white, other, alien, inferior. The function of Genet's play is not to appeal to the spectators' sympathy for the plight of the oppressed but rather to trap them in an act of imaginative complicity that can then be turned against them. It aims to disturb, challenge and upset them—it cannot at the same time win their sympathy for the cause of black freedom fighters. Yet this was exactly what the last stages of Stein's production pointed towards, moving on from the celebratory fireworks and concluding with the display of an enormous map of Africa divided into those territories that are independent and those still under the colonial heel. In front of this, the cast performed not a Mozart minuet (as in Genet's stage direction) but an aggressive dance to African drums.

Stein was criticised by some reviewers for having introduced an excessively political note into his production.[14] This is surely wrong. The mistake was not to suggest a political dimension but to misunderstand the force of the work's political thrust, presenting it as a call to action instead of a play of image and reflection. It is perhaps surprising to find Stein slipping into this error in view of his earlier emphasis on modes of representation. But at the same time it is not difficult to see why Stein's production developed in this way: it was a natural consequence of his emphasis on the group process and on a theatrical form that allowed for exploration of group identity. Once having undertaken the almost impossible task of performing a play written for black actors, it is clear that the whole company found itself identifying strongly with the oppressed group they were trying to portray. It was this same emphasis on group work that lent such power to Stein's production of *Otello* in 1986. He had been attracted to the Welsh National Opera Company because of the outstanding quality of its chorus work.

This production was the story of far more than just the relation-

14. E.g. Michael Stone in *The Guardian*, 24 June 1983: 'Genet did not really write a play about racial discrimination and its effects on its victims. *The Blacks* is only another expression of Genet's love of Mayhem.'

ship between Otello and Desdemona. It was the account of a ruler's relationship with his people and the key to this was Stein's use of the chorus. In the first act, he explained, 'the microcosm of Cyprus society and the macrocosm of the universe are both threatened by chaos.' Theatrically, this was conveyed by the chorus filling and swirling around the stage. Otello entered and both the storm and the citizens of Cyprus were stilled. Later, when a drunken brawl erupted, Otello again restored order. Stein described Otello's relation to the chorus as that of a good father to his children and the first act successfully established the sense of a community governed on old-fashioned paternalist principles: so long as Otello was among his people, all was well. In the second act, as Iago began to poison Otello's mind, he drew across the stage an enormous red curtain, half shutting out the brilliant light of the Mediterranean exterior, symbolically separating Otello from the public life of his people. This in turn built up to the catastrophe of the third act when Otello, crazed by suspicion, rounded on the chorus and attacked them: in Stein's words, 'the head turns against the limbs'. Here Otello's private tragedy, as he accepts the apparent proof of Desdemona's guilt was expressed in public disintegration as he hurled himself at the chorus, scattering them in all directions. The fourth act followed, as Stein put it, 'like a sad private consequence of a public crime, like ritual fulfilment of its implications' and the logical conclusion to his production would have been to bring the chorus back on stage at the end, opening the tragedy out once more to show its double dimension, extending beyond the destruction of Otello's love for Desdemona to the destruction of the bond between Otello and his people. He did in fact plan to introduce something of this kind but, in the end, found that he was unable to make it work and so left the focus on the bodies in the bedroom.

Stein himself expressed what gave his production its force when he said that 'Verdi and Boito's great invention, which they do not find in Shakespeare's tragedy, is the sense of community on the stage participating in the action. The chorus themselves create the space for the protagonists to act in . . . They construct the stage.' It is striking how aptly these words would also serve to describe what happened in Stein's 1986 production for the Schaubühne of O'Neill's *The Hairy Ape*. In both productions the real centre of the dramatic action is located in the relationship between the hero (Otello or Yank) and the group which he both dominates yet longs to be part of. Like Otello's encounter with Desdemona, the meeting in O'Neill's play between the coal-black Yank and the dazzling millionaire's daughter only acquires meaning in relation to the social and political forces in play. Such stark contrasts emphasising how an individual's existence only acquires meaning in relation to larger groupings had been a feature of Stein's work at the Schaubühne since its beginnings, but had previously been fuelled by an urgent sense of the need to discover alternative modes of understanding or of action in order to reconstruct the social order. In Stein's 1986 productions however, that urgent search for alternatives seemed to give way to a crushing pessimism. His stage images repeatedly stressed the individual's inability to make sense of his life, either as an individual or as a member of society. *The Hairy Ape* revealed this *Weltanschauung* most clearly as it unfolded its powerful catalogue of alienation. Lucio Fanti's monumental set for the ocean liner placed Yank (the representative industrial worker) in a position literally squeezed between the vast voracious boilers that he had to stoke in the dark bowels of the ship and the inaccessible passenger deck where the light was bright and the rich were free to lounge. Although Yank began by proclaiming his faith in the liberating power of modern industrial progress, he gradually realised that his faith was misplaced and that for him there could be no source of pride or self-esteem, whether in class-consciousness or in personal strength.

The reasons for choosing this play were similar to those governing the choice of earlier Schaubühne work: the play has a strong choral or 'ensemble' element and it focuses clearly on working-class experience under capitalism. It is possible to go further and to interpret it as an anti-colonial play: the encounter between Yank and the millionaire's daughter reproduces exactly the terms of the colonial encounter underlying Genet's *The Blacks*. Stein explained in an interview that he had always sought out plays about working-class experience but that 'Brecht, who was so terribly keen on the working class, scarcely wrote *anything* directly about them', so that after *The Mother* in 1970 the Schaubühne had turned to other authors, such as Vishnevski.[15] But, unlike *The Mother* or *The Optimistic Tragedy*, *The Hairy Ape* offers no political solution to the troubles of the modern world. Instead it presents, in spectacular fashion, a series of images of exclusion, imprisonment and failure. For this play, written in 1921-2 at the height of the Expressionist

15. 'The Theatre of Peter Stein', Interview by Roy Kift, *Drama* 2 (1987), 5-7.

Movement, Stein made unashamed use of the whole arsenal of Expressionist production methods. But in so doing, and in complaining that Brecht failed to write plays of this kind, he was overlooking the reason why Brecht (and other political dramatists) turned their back on Expressionist depictions of the working class. This was because Expressionist art favoured the presentation of stark images of alienation, tending not towards movement or analysis of alternatives, but rather towards fixity and fatalism. The more effectively group movement and stark visual contrast were employed, the more an image of hopelessness was reinforced, so that what might appear to be an art form sympathetic to mass experience in fact had the effect of suggesting that the lot of the working class was irremediably awful: sympathy tipped over into fatalism.

This experience is at the heart of O'Neill's play and was crystallised in one of the most successfully realised moments of the production. Travelling on the great ocean liner which forms the setting for the first part of the play is Mildred, the daughter of the millionaire president of the Steel Trust. Having trained as a social worker, she wants to visit the boiler hall in the depths of the ship and observe the conditions in which the stokers work. After a magnificently choreographed scene, in which the coal-blackened stokers shovel real fuel into the fiery furnaces, she appears, descending the ladder all in white, an alien being from a different world. The confrontation destroys both her and Yank. For her it is an experience of despair, since she was already aware of her superfluousness in her own world ('I'm a waste product in the Bessemer process') but had imagined that she might be able to enter sympathetically into the world of the exploited workers. Faced with the 'naked and shameless brutality' of the world of the stokers, she falls into a faint, muttering 'Oh, the filthy beast!'

Yank is destroyed because he suddenly sees himself through her eyes as nothing more than a beast of burden. His pride in himself has been destroyed and so he sets out to get even with Mildred and her class. In the second half of the play Yank is brought face to face with a circle of capitalists, a circle of union activists and finally a circle of apes in the zoo. With an equal lack of success, he tries to break into each of these circles in turn. His descent into a subhuman category is complete when he releases a gorilla from its cage; the animal crushes him to death before ambling off to enjoy a doubtless all-too-brief moment of freedom.

The strength of this production was in the extraordinarily powerful ensemble playing that Stein drew from the company, combined with the spectacular settings designed by Lucio Fanti (also the designer for *Otello*). At each point in the drama Yank's experience was echoed or contrasted with that of the whole group, who were on stage for most of the evening. This production confirmed the outstanding talent of Stein, who must rank as one of the most brilliant directors at work in the theatre today. But it also confirmed the reasons for the ultimate failure of *The Blacks*: Stein's willingness, in the early 1970s, to embrace contradictions, to mobilise them in the analysis of a social problem has given way in the 1980s to a coldness, even a fatalism, that finds expression in overwhelmingly beautiful images of irremediable alienation. In 1985 Stein resigned his post as artistic director of the Schaubühne without giving any very clear reason for this unexpected decision. He had only recently moved into a new theatre, built to his own specifications; he could call on a virtually limitless budget and an ensemble of outstanding actors who had worked together for nearly two decades. What cause could he possibly have for discontent? It seems likely that both he and the company felt that they had reached the end of their abilities to produce work that was new and challenging. The production of *The Hairy Ape* was a near-perfect realisation of O'Neill's text, but its very perfection stressed the death of the belief that had fuelled the company's early work: that a process of learning could lead to the discovery of social and political alternatives strong enough to mount a real challenge to the status quo. *The Hairy Ape* suggests that for Stein this belief may have turned into despair.

3

Myth and Mythology in the Drama of Botho Strauss

Irmela Schneider

MYTHICAL themes occupy a central position in three of Botho Strauss's plays—*Kalldewey Farce* (1982), *Der Park* (1983) and *Die Fremdenführerin* (1986). Undoubtedly, talk of myth is now something of a boom industry: it acts as an antidote to a technological world, as an escape from rational thought, and as the mark of an age that, fearing the future, prefers to make itself at home in the past. The way in which myth is discussed today leads to a polarisation: it has not only lost its ancient function of bringing people together, but it has turned into the opposite. The current discussion of myths and mythology above all reveals the distance between the ancient myths and the present; it reflects not only the reception of and the search for meaning in ancient myths but continues to produce new meanings for the concept of 'myth' itself. Myth is proving a protean problem; any attempt to define it is virtually an impossible task.

This state of affairs can be illustrated by juxtaposing some of the passages in which Strauss himself uses the term. On one occasion in *Paare, Passanten* he writes: 'Hitchcock's *The Birds* will live on in us longer than Brecht's *Mother Courage*. One belongs to our myths, the other to our studies.'[1] Here myth refers to stories which address elemental fears such as the threat of nature, and relate an event that cannot simply be explained away rationally or causally. Modern myths do not consist of something accessible to reason but something that acts as a stimulus and is taken in emotionally.

The quotation from *Paare, Passanten* suggests that myths associate terror with the uncanny. They tell of a power over human beings

---

1. 'Hitchcocks *Vögel* werden länger in uns lebendig bleiben als Brechts *Mutter Courage*. Das eine gehört zu unseren Mythen, das andere zu unseren Studien.' *Paare, Passanten*, Munich-Vienna 1981, p. 118.

threatening them from outside. Myths are not only stories from the past; stories from the present can also become myths. Perhaps it is not a coincidence that Strauss takes a film as an example of this since nowadays there is much more talk of myths in the cinema than in the theatre. A second passage from *Paare, Passanten* gives an explanation inspired by psychoanalysis of why people return again and again to myths: 'Human sexuality and its culture were the reservoir of myths—the silent world of the gods, these submerged, mysterious beings. A listless desire to love and at the same time to remain in a state of listlessness occasionally bore them up to us.'[2] The association of myths and sexuality already points to the plays in which attempted and failed love affairs are confronted and contrasted with reminiscences of ancient myths telling of the love of gods, admittedly something that is nowadays neither a source of power nor of terror.

The third passage from *Paare, Passanten* recalled here links just this relationship between myth and sexuality to the act of writing:

One does not love somebody, one loves the idea of love. It is the meeting of lovers with its radiance of the desire to return, with its myth of the dissolution of the personality. Writing indicates the state of absence. Everything is missing where the letter is. To desire that which has passed on, bodies which are no longer with us, is the original eroticism of human language which only produces understanding by means of meanings and symbols rather than by immediate stimuli.[3]

Here myth points to something lost and gone, indicates something original, the loss of which is compensated for by writing. Writing as a sublimated erotic act can claim a long, in fact an ancient, tradition, a tradition to which Strauss's protagonist Martin refers at the end of *Die Fremdenführerin*. Myth as something original, the loss of which is regretted, is a dimension of Strauss's plays, but equally so is the significance of myth as a surrogate for ideology as analysed by Roland Barthes in his *Mythologies*. Strauss too presents modern

2. 'Die menschliche Sexualität und ihre Kultur waren das Mythenreservoir—die stumme Götterwelt dieser untergetauchten, geheimnisvollen Wesen. Ein müdes Bedürfnis zu lieben und dabei müde zu bleiben, hob sie dann und wann zu uns empor.' Ibid., p. 128.
3. 'Man liebt nicht jemanden, man liebt sie (die Liebe). Die Liebesbegegnung mit ihrem Strahlkranz der Rücksucht, mit ihrem Mythos von der wiedereingeschmolzenen Persönlichkeitsmasse. Das Schreiben deutet die Sachlage des Fehlens. Alles fehlt, wo der Buchstabe ist. Die entschwundenen Dinge, den entschwundenen Leib zu begehren ist die ursprüngliche Erotik der menschlichen Sprache, die nur über Sinn und Symbol Verständigung schafft statt durch unmittelbare Reizauslöser.' Ibid., p. 102.

myths in the sense of ideologies or beliefs that people cling to in order to avoid an analysis of their own situation, and he goes back to ancient, mainly Greek, myths or what remains of them, making reference to them, to a certain extent re-enacting them, and in fact—according to my thesis—parodying them by demonstrating how the everyday reflects the mythological.[4] This approach indicates among other things the distance that separates the present from the myths of the past. Looking back is an act of mourning, rather than an expression of the hope that the salvation of the present might lie in myths. The mythological references are material to play with; they are allegorical in that they appear to represent something but this tentative allegorical meaning breaks down in the course of the play. There is a search for new theatrical images rather than for new relevance. Strauss's plays belong to the tradition of mythical drama but they cannot be stereotyped as either criticising or salvaging myth.[5] They form a variation in many respects reminiscent of the work of Aragon, Vitrac and also Godard. What characterises them is not a neo-Romantic search for the 'coming God'[6], but the insistence that while the search may be something meaningful in itself, it can no longer produce any meaning.

Two further quotations from *Paare, Passanten* can serve to broaden the question and illustrate the direction a consideration of the plays may take: 'The earth', according to Strauss, 'is also inhabited by angels, devils and gods. We are probably not alone. . . . And could it not be that we will soon be possessed by a new desire for allegory? A desire for the sublime incarnation, for the many ideas dreamt up in our century to become flesh.'[7] Are the plays of recent years an expression of this desire for allegory? Many scenes and images seem to suggest this. The following passage from *Paare, Passanten* shows how the desire for allegory indicates a return to the humanistic tradition and at the same time a radical break with this

4. See Volker Hage, 'Schreiben ist eine Séance: Begegnungen mit Botho Strauss', in *Strauss lesen*, ed. Michael Radix, Munich-Vienna 1987, p. 192.
5. The problem of myth in drama is extensively discussed in Manfred Fuhrmann, 'Mythos als Wiederholung in der griechischen Tragödie und im Drama des 20. Jahrhunderts', in *Terror und Spiel: Probleme der Mythenrezeption*, ed. Fuhrmann, Munich 1971.
6. See the discussion of the meaning of myth in the Romantic period in Manfred Frank, *Der Kommende Gott: Vorlesungen über die neue Mythologie*, Frankfurt 1982.
7. 'Die Erde ist gleichermaßen bevölkert von Engeln, Teufeln und Göttern. Wahrscheinlich sind wir nicht allein. . . . Und, könnte es nicht sein, daß uns bald eine neue allegorische Lust packte? Eine Lust zur großartigen Inkarnation, zur Fleischwerdung der vielen ausgeträumten Ideen unseres Jahrhunderts.' *Paare, Passanten*, p. 193.

tradition:

The passive, over-informed consciousness, no longer in a position to produce its own desires, ideas or memories, instead experiences a convergence (usually only revealed to madness) of the irreconcilable, and *thinks* a jumble of arbitrarily acquired data. By now nobody is immune to this. How taken aback one quite often is at what one's own personal filing system comes up with: images from a film of Glauber Rocha and quotations from Gotthold Ephraim Lessing. One looks for a motivation, tries to grasp the force of the heterogeneous—but in vain. It was only the free play of a would-be mechanical memory. A cultural egalitarianism that attaches the same superficial value to everything is the waste-land of consciousness: and it is on the advance, fast approaching the idiotic . . .[8]

Is the desire for allegory the caricature of a would-be memory? Is the devastation of consciousness reproduced and simply accelerated by the references to myth? Or is myth, the memory of ancient patterns of legitimation, the attempt at a new greening of the desert? These questions cannot all be dealt with in detail, let alone answered. We are concerned here only with Strauss's variations on the traditional mythological drama and I will try to show that he does not wish either to salvage mythology or to criticise it. The parody of myth in Strauss's plays is the result of his view of the present.

The fact that *Kalldewey Farce* as a new departure represents a break in Strauss's work for the theatre, has been put very clearly by Reinhardt Baumgart in his essay 'Das Theater des Botho Strauss':

Whether this 'tour de force' in the shape of a 'tour de farce' marks an end or a beginning: it heralds Strauss' farewell to an art of subtlety, an impressionistic precision of dialogue, a perspective of gentle amusement and melancholy in his last two plays. If he still refers to the contemporary scene, be it punk slang, psycho-babble or lib-speak, then it is with the sharpness of caricature. Now he turns statements into roles, he no longer observes or describes people according to their exact social features. In other words, Strauss here bids farewell to the 1970s of which he was an

---

8. 'Das tatenlose, überinformierte Bewußtsein, das nicht mehr in der Lage ist, Wunsch, Idee, Erinnerung zu produzieren, erlebt statt dessen eine (sonst nur dem Wahnsinn bekannte) Gleichzeitigkeit des Unvereinbaren und *denkt* einen wahllos aus den Beständen zugespielten Datensalat. Davon bleibt jetzt niemand verschont. Wie erschrickt man doch häufig über die bizarren Ausstöße des eigenen Archivs. Bilder aus einem Film von Glauber Rocha und Worte Gotthold Ephraim Lessings. Man sucht den Beweggrund, die Kraft des Heterogenen zu fassen. Es ist vergebens. Es war nur das unbrauchbare Spiel eines die Maschine nachäffenden Gedächtnisses. Eine kulturelle Egalität, die jedem Ding gleichen Erscheinungswert zubilligt, ist die Wüste des Bewußtseins; und sie wächst, sie drängt an den Rand des Idiotismus . . .' Ibid., p. 196.

unrivalled observer for our theatre.[9]

Strauss's plays are characterised neither by dramatic conflicts nor by a linear development of action. The works, particularly *Der Park*, are constructed episodically; they are plays that no longer refer to reality but to the theatre itself. Strauss's theatre is no longer a theatre of consciousness but a kind of *séance* with literary traditions and mythological situations into which present-day characters are introduced as types.[10] Dramatic situations or dramatis personae are no longer what matter but the play of themes, motives, effects and stimuli. Peter Stein and Luc Bondy are right therefore to warn against applying an interpretive yard-stick to his plays and puzzling out associations 'that wander too far from the stage'.[11] In this direction lies, as the critics have indicated, the danger of 'decorative theatre going round and round in circles'.[12] However, the danger also points to the source of inspiration and to what makes Strauss's plays so peculiarly attractive: their involvement with a game of interpretation that looks not for coherent structures of meaning but for the source of the irritation.

I come now to the more concrete observations. *Kalldewey Farce*, first performed on 4 November 1984 at the Berlin Schaubühne and directed by Luc Bondy, is a play in which the pattern of a plot unfolding chronologically without interruption is broken. We are faced with a clever combination of tragedy and satyric drama, and a short outline of the plot may make this clear. The first scene shows the parting of a man and a woman. The woman speaks of the 'wonderful time together' and the man bids farewell with the

9. 'Ganz gleich aber, ob diese *tour de force* als *tour de farce* eher ein Ende oder einen Anfang markiert: mit ihr verabschiedet sich Strauß von der Nuancen-Kunst, der impressionistischen Dialoggenauigkeit, von der zart belustigten und zart trauernden zuschauerhaltung seiner beiden letzten Stücke. Wenn er noch Zeitzeichen zitiert, ob den Punk-, den Therapie-, den Emanzenjargon, so tut er das mit karikaturistischer Schärfe. Er montiert nun Sätze zu Rollen, er beobachtet und beschreibt also nicht mehr Menschen mit genauem sozialen Umriß. Das heißt: Strauss verabschiedet sich hier auch von den siebziger Jahren, als deren Chronist er auf unserem Theater ohne alle Konkurrenz geblieben ist.' In *Botho Strauss*, ed. Heinz Ludwig Arnold, Munich 1984, p. 17.

10. For the concept of 'séance' in Strauss see Volker Hage in *Strauss lesen*, ed. Radix.

11. Peter Stein, 'Ein Autofahrerfaun. Das ist doch etwas schönes: Ein Gespräch mit Peter Krumme (1986)', in *Strauss lesen*, ed. Radix, pp. 172f; Luc Bondy, 'Die haben einen Regisseur gesucht für "Kalldewey": Ein Gespräch mit Peter Krumme (1986)', ibid., pp. 217f.

12. 'eines in sich leer kreisenden, ornamentalen Theaters', Peter Iden, 'Passanten in Bewegungen unteswegs. *Der Park* von Botho Strauss in der Inszenierung Peter Steins an der Schaubühne', *Frankfurter Rundschau*, 7 Nov. 1984.

cliché-turned-paradox: 'See you soon, eternally soon!'[13] The play thus begins at the end of a story, with a farewell.[14] The dark, almost subterranean, stage area, the dark clothes both are wearing, their gestures taken from the famous relief showing Orpheus and Eurydice on their way out of Hades, awaken memories of the ancient myth. This is reinforced by their profession: they are musicians. There is a music stand in the middle of the stage, the woman is holding a violin, the man a flute. Fragments of the sparse dialogue likewise summon up the myth: 'I love you. Look at me' and 'Sleep, sleep. Don't call!'[15] If this first image recalls the myth of Orpheus and Eurydice, Strauss here situates himself in a long literary tradition going back to the Romantic period which saw the great renaissance of Orpheus and a tradition that received a new variation at the beginning of the twentieth century above all in Rilke's *Sonnets to Orpheus*. In Rilke Orpheus is the archetypical representative of the opposing forces of aesthetic existence and historical fact.[16] In Strauss's variation on the theme, Orpheus is transformed in the course of the play and appears at the end as the director dismissing his fellow actors. He leads not an aesthetic but a ludic existence, one that is not, however, opposed to the world of fact but is its result. Role-play is training for survival.

The background to the parting becomes clear in the following scene through the eyes of the woman. In a lesbian bar she meets 'K' (Katrin) and 'M' (Meret) who discuss women, men and work in the slang of the radical scene. It is a dialogue of clipped phrases referring to the women's liberation movement and its hostility to men. The exchanges are, however, not reproduced as a naturalistic set-piece but stylised. It is never a question of representation but of theatrical transformation. This scene forms a sharp contrast to the first. There is a switch from tragedy to farce: the controlled gestures of the first are opposed by the more strident manner of the second. The dark colours of the stage set at the beginning have given way to loud colours and lighting effects. After a period of caricatured dialogue

13. 'Bis bald, ewig bis bald!' *Kalldewey Farce*, Munich-Vienna 1981, p. 8.
14. Henriette Herwig's *Verwünschte Beziehungen, verwebte Bezüge. Zerfall und Verwandlung des Dialogs bei Botho Strauss*, Tübingen 1986, discusses the importance of the farewell-motif in the work of Botho Strauss. In her view the moment of separation for Strauss is what 'conflict' was for classicism.
15. 'Ich liebe dich. Schau mich an' and 'Schlaf, Schlaf. Nicht anrufen.' *Kalldewey Farce*, p. 8.
16. See Peter Pfaff, 'Der verwandelte Orpheus. Zur "ästhetische Metaphysik" Nietzsches und Rilkes', in *Mythos und Moderne*, ed. Karl Heinz Bohrer, Frankfurt 1983.

which presents the two women as mere types, they are joined by Lynn, the woman from the first scene (played by Edith Clever). Now she is wearing a brown trench coat in the style of the 1970s. She has come to ask the help of the two women: her husband beats her and rapes her, so she wants to leave him. The two women, the audience discover indirectly, appear to run a sort of agency that offers help with marriage and relationship problems. Even this area has not escaped marketing. All the elements of the plot that relate to contemporary reality refer to 'ideologemes', to modern myths: consumerism, the solution of conflict by means of agencies, faith in therapy and hostility to men as a philosophy.

After Lynn has repeatedly insisted in answer to their question that she cannot live with her husband any longer, the three women go to the couple's flat occupied by the husband. The man and the woman chat about inconsequential things: bananas, biscuits, trades-men and the telephone. Then all three women tear the man to pieces like the maenads dismembering Orpheus. The scene contains elements of burlesque—these are kitchen-sink Furies.[17] It parodies the myth of the Amazon Penthesilea and radicalises the Orpheus story by having Lynn/Eurydice herself joining the other two in tearing Orpheus apart. (His remains are disposed of in the washing machine, a whim that appeals to the women.) The free play of associations which has thus been generated is not, as one might expect, channelled or directed along a certain path but merely held in check. The following scene reveals this game as being of no consequence: Lynn, who in the meantime is living in another flat, is expecting her husband, Meret and Katrin as guests on her birthday. All three have been to see a film together. The myth, whether Orpheus and Eurydice or Penthesilea, has lost its normative power—it is material for acting, containing elements of the fantastic. The people who act it out do so inaccurately. There is clearly an element of parody in this but parody devoid of rational motives. The point here is not emancipation from myth to the advantage of reason; parody, in this instance, merely indicates the absurdity of the present.

The third scene, Lynn's birthday, does not itself contain any new references to the Orpheus myth. Its motto 'Life is a Course of Therapy' provides a variation of Calderón's baroque play *Life is a Dream*. Thus it introduces as a modern myth the belief in therapy. This surrogate ideology is likened to a fairy-tale motif: not only the

17. See Luc Bondy in *Strauss lesen*, ed. Radix, p. 221.

invited guests come to Lynn's birthday celebration but also a man whom it appears nobody knows. He is the only one to have brought a present—a miniature bottle. Asked to identify himself he replies with an obscene couplet: 'I am the invisible bee sting/ that stings naughty women in their tits.'[18] When the women and Lynn's husband Hans come to the conclusion that this man—whose name defies etymological decoding[19]—has gatecrashed, they try to get rid of him, but as for some inexplicable reason the door will not open any more they order him under the table where he promptly disappears for good. Kalldewey leaves in the same miraculous way that Hans has reappeared. For the rest of the proceedings he simply serves as an object of projection: the absentee could have been a bringer of good fortune.

Who Kalldewey is, the audience find out from the husband in the following entr'acte which takes place years later in the mountains. The husband declares him to be the Pied Piper of Hamelin who had abducted them—like the children of the story. Kalldewey provides the play with carnivalesque elements and it is out of the carnivalistic situation created through his presence that a discussion relating to the present develops. The characters converse in the language of the 'me' generation about therapy, the positive and the negative, harmony and finding oneself, but the carnivalesque backdrop turns the discussion into a parody. The satirical edge undercuts the dialogue and reveals the hope the characters invest in the idea of therapy as being an act of self-deception.

In the course of the entr'acte conversation what has happened so far is declared to be a play (the actors are still visible on the horizon). The entr'acte becomes a play within a play that simulates a chronological development but this is revealed as a red-herring: the characters have aged but after this scene the earlier play continues from where it left off. The central point of the conversation between the man and the woman, in which the man has again taken over the leading role, is the almost tautological description of the modern age as all ages rolled into one: 'It's one great rag-bag, the store of information is infinite: everything is there to be drawn upon. A ready supply of material is available from the "repertoire of

18. 'Ich bin der unsichtbare Bienenstich/der bösen Frauen in die Titten sticht!', *Kalldewey Farce*, p. 53.

19. There has been much speculation about the name Kalldewey. Marie-Luise Bott, 'Spuren dieser Zeit: Zu "Kalldewey Farce" in *Strauss*, ed. Arnold, p. 35, relates it to the Grips Theatre's play *Alles Plastik* and sees it as a reference to the KADeWe. See also Herwig, op.cit., pp. 95f.

the ages".'[20] The text can be read as a summary of contemporary trends: the eclectic plundering of traditions, historical material and styles. It is an age in which style is noted for its arbitrariness. The term 'repertoire of the ages', which puts history onto the stage[21], reminds one of the baroque concept of the 'theatrum mundi', and secularises the notion of 'vanitas mundi' by turning it into a belief in the Pied Piper Kalldewey:

With his flute he tore the vermin from our soul and drowned it in the river of oblivion. But then he thought he had been cheated of his just reward and he abducted our little band like the children of Hamelin and imprisoned us in this mountain. There on the rock headland—can you see?—on the edge of the cliff with a sheer drop beneath us, we are held captive and there we remain damned to a never-ending comedy, condemned to the horror of hearty enjoyment. So our life goes on—and on ad infinitum.[22]

Another play within a play is presented in the next scene that continues the birthday party. Everyone apart from Kalldewey is waiting for the therapist in the corridor where they engage in a therapy game called 'TV-treatment', a brilliant parody of television quiz shows. As the saviour who is not recognised as such until it is too late, Kalldewey is the permanent topic of conversation. The motif of the Pied Piper of Hamelin who abducts the children by playing his flute is replaced by the introduction of the music from Act II Scene 5 of *The Magic Flute* in which Tamino learns from Sarastro of the trials he must undergo in order to win back Tamina.[23] This motif brings the one version of the story to a close, whereas the other ends with a double farewell. The man does not bid farewell to his fellow actors: 'It was only a play with other plays underneath / Not really magic: therapy picked from a catalogue / A

20. 'Diese Zeit, die sammelt viele Zeiten ein; da gibt's ein Riesensammelsurium, unendlich groß ist das Archiv, und ist zuhanden. Viele brauchbare Stoffe noch in den Beständen, im Fundus der Epochen', *Kalldewey Farce*, p. 63.
21. See Walter Benjamin, *Ursprung des deutschen Trauerspiels*, Frankfurt 1963, p. 89: 'Dem trostlosen Lauf der Weltchronik tritt nicht Ewigkeit, sondern die Restauration paradiesischer Zeitlosigkeit entgegen. Die Geschichte wandert in den Schauplatz hinein.'
22. 'Mit seiner Flöte zog er uns das Ungeziefer von der Seele und ertränkte es im Vergessensfluß. Doch dann glaubte er sich um seinen gerechten Lohn betrogen und er entführte uns, die kleine Schar, wie in Hameln einst die Kinder, und schloß uns ein in diesen Berg. Dort auf vorgeschobenem Fels, du siehst, über steiler Wand und leerem Grund, hält eines uns gefangen und bleiben wir erhalten, verflucht in eine ewige Komödie, verbannt ins Grauen heftiger Belustigung. So überleben wir und wiederholen uns und werden's wohl für alle Zeiten tun.' *Kalldewey Farce*, p. 26.
23. Marie-Luise Bott in *Strauss*, ed. Arnold sees the Magic Flute motif as the key to the meaning of *Kalldewey Farce*. As the oblique references in Strauss's plays cannot be read as paradigms, this approach does not seem to me to be legitimate.

rooting around in the bran-tub called soul / Remnants, old desires in all colours / The whole lot a bargain, so we get in on it / on occasion, half greedy or half bored / And end up with something we don't need anyway.'[24] This version ends as the play began: for the second time the man and the woman part with mutual affirmations of love. The myth of Orpheus and Eurydice is referred to once more, the distance between myth and the contemporary play is emphasised. Myth and fairy-tale, the traditions of tragedy and satyric drama, farce and parody all combine in *Kalldewey Farce* to form a script that radically promotes a ludic impulse by turning the various traditions into the material of play. Listeners who think that Orpheus may be resurrected as a singer find themselves severely disappointed.

In *Der Park* mythological forms are no longer simply referred to but appear directly and become flesh and blood. In the introduction Strauss asks the reader to imagine that: 'A down-to-earth society about as remote from sacred things as from immortal poetry (and by now a little weary) falls—not for a myth or an ideology—but for the genius of a great work of art. Seen from this vantage point the characters and the plot of the new play are taken over and motivated, elevated and made fools of by the spirit of Shakespeare's *A Midsummer Night's Dream*.'[25] Myth and ideology are here used interchangeably. Sacred things and immortal poetry are on the same level. The intention is that the 'spirit' of Shakespeare's *Midsummer Night's Dream* permeates the plot and the characters. It is precisely this return to Shakespeare that shows the liberating power, that for Shakespeare lay in the return to mythological stories, to be no longer relevant. Shakespeare's fairies and heroes do not bring enlightenment but reveal human beings in their full mediocrity and banality and themselves become mediocre and banal in the process. As is well known, since the eighteenth century Shakespeare's plays have been treated like myths. The somewhat nebulous German term

---

24. 'Es war dies nur ein Spiel mit tieferen Spielen/Nicht wirkliche Magie: nach Katalog bestellte Therapie/Ein Wühlen in der Krabbelkiste namens Seele/Restposten, alte Wünsche grün und blau/Spottbillig der Krempel/man wühlt sich durch Gelegenheiten, halb gierig, halb interesselos/und bringt bestimmt was Überflüssiges nach Haus,' *Kalldewey Farce*, p. 10.

25. 'eine tüchtige Gesellschaft, beinahe gleich weit entfernt von den heiligen Dingen wie vom zeitlosen Gedicht (und ein wenig ermüdet schon) erläge statt einem Mythos oder einer Ideologie dem Genius eines großen Kunstwerks. So gesehen sind die Figuren und ist die Handlung dieses neuen Stücks besetzt und bewegt, erhoben und genarrt durch den *Geist* von Shakespeares *Sommernachtstraum*.' *Der Park*, Vienna 1983, p. 7.

Geist, which is frequently used in this context reflects this mythological treatment. Its tendency towards the pseudo-archaic is in marked contrast to the events of the play.

The question I should like to pursue is: what image of Shakespeare's *A Midsummer Night's Dream* emerges in Strauss' play? What sort of effect does the myth of this Renaissance play have on the present? Shakespeare's play is generally known to combine four strands of plot and two worlds: 'At the court of Athens the clear, manly reason of Theseus holds sway while in the nearby forest foolishness, dream and fantasy rule the fate of human beings and fairies', according to the *Shakespeare Handbuch*.[26] The triangular development from order into the dream world and back into order is totally absent in Strauss's play. As the title indicates, everything in *Der Park* takes place in an area opposed to nature and though reminiscent of Shakespeare merely parodies his pastoral counterworld. The forest of Athens has become a city park in which the roaring of the bull competes with the sound of police and ambulance sirens. 'The stage set,' as Henriette Herwig writes, 'transports the audience into an artificial landscape: it is a replica of the modern world, a comment on the act of representation and a variation on a literary reference.'[27] The Park is not only from the topographical point of view a mixture of city park, fairy-land and Hades, it is also a place of synchroneity where our own times, antiquity, Renaissance, and, in the shape of Cyprian, the Romantic age are simultaneously present. Around its borders live the city people, within it dwell Titania and Oberon, Daedalus and Pasiphae and Shakespeare's Puck who becomes Hoffmann's Cyprian. Strauss therefore not only brings together a contemporary love story and Shakespeare's comedy of love but he also turns present-day characters—Helen and Helma—into characters from Shakespeare's *Midsummer Night's Dream* and ancient myth. Shakespeare's fairies become like ancient gods and, at the same time, they resemble characters from the Romantic period. Strauss has helped himself to the 'repertoire of the ages'. The play thus refers to quite different mythological and literary traditions, different conceptions of art and the artist but what is left in it of the present is only one caricatured version of the 1980s. Here are a few details: as in Shakespeare and the Oberon

26. Ed. Ina Schabert, Stuttgart 1978, p. 462.
27. 'Das Bühnenbild versetzt den Zuschauer in eine Kunstlandschaft, und sie ist Abbild der modernen Welt, Kommentar der Abbildung und variiertes literarisches Zitat.' *Verwünschte Beziehungen*, p. 187.

legend in general, Titania and Oberon are jealous of one another and fall out. The motif of jealousy has, however, changed somewhat: no longer are they jealous because Oberon has had a love affair with Hippolyta and Titania with Theseus; their jealousy is merely about the estimation in which they claim to be held by others. The argument between them is therefore caused by human beings: as a god-like figure Oberon is following a 'mission': he wants to promote 'sensible pleasure' rather than the 'lewd rending of bodies'.[28] Oberon's mission fails. From this point of view the play is about 'different forms of the inability to love and desire', revolving around Peter Stein's question 'whether love has now been abolished or not'.[29]

Unlike Oberon, right from the outset Titania considers her divine status to be a restriction which is painful to her. She attempts to draw the attention of human beings to herself by asking them the time. This question is a recurring set-phrase in the early scenes, a pervasive comment on the concept of time: Bergson used the clock as a symbol for the representation of time recurring irrespective of quality. Titania's desire to go by the clock shows that she is accepting a cyclic conception of time.[30] The last scene of the play once more reinforces the power of this 'eternal return of the same': on the occasion of a silver wedding an attempt is made to turn an ordinary Tuesday into a special festival. The enterprise is a complete failure: the guests do not turn up. The players of the game are left on their own. The look into the future represented by the last scene shows that the future will bring no change except that the characters—as in *Kalldewey Farce*—have grown older.

The strand of the plot which is about the present—demonstrated by the language, manner and clothes of the characters—is reminiscent of the numerous stories concerned with love and relationships in the literature and the theatre of the last few years: Helen, an American trapeze artist who after a fall has never been back up on the trapeze, and Georg, a lawyer and clearly left wing, meet in the first scene and marry in the third. Wolf, a friend of Georg's, falls in love with Helen and his wife Helma gets jealous. She wants to remain a good wife to her husband and so she buys an amulet from Cyprian, the artist whose artistic production is dictated by the

28. 'Kluge Lust nicht geiles Leiberreißen', *Der Park*, p. 83.
29. 'verschiedene Formen der Unfähigkeit zu Liebe und Lust'; 'ob die Liebe abgeschafft ist oder nicht.' *Strauss lesen*, ed. Radix, p. 184.
30. Henri Bergson, *Zeit und Freiheit*, Jena 1911, pp. 84f.

42

market. The effect this amulet has is to captivate not only her husband but also Georg. When she has made her husband give up this 'tangle of love' with Helen, the amulet is reduced to a piece of jewellery which is no longer in fashion.

The only thing the two couples have in common with Hermia and Lysander, Helena and Demetrius, apart from the similarity of the women's names, is that they demonstrate by means of magic the arbitrary nature of their choice of partner. Their conversations are about their relationships combining a critique of the present with a nostalgia for the world of fairy-tale: 'Take me into good company! Good company, Wolf! I can't stand it here with these beasts in human form any more! I'd rather live with trolls and elves than with efficiency experts and people besotten with prosperity. I'd rather be a little ichneumon fly than a human being among psychologists, judges and educationalists.'[31] When the magic spell takes effect, when the transformation as in Shakespeare's *Midsummer Night's Dream* takes place, Helma struggles against it—as she realises: 'My popularity may have increased all of a sudden but so has the awful suspicion that prompts me to uncover every rottenness. I don't want to be infected with the truth to that extent! I'd rather deceive myself and be deceived.'[32] The result of the transformation is that the characters become 'sick with truth', and that they can now see the entirely arbitrary nature of their choice of respective partners, whereas Shakespeare's characters were mercifully allowed to experience the events in the forest of Athens as a dream and fantasy. In *Der Park* Shakespeare's flowery juice has become a talisman that one can buy, the accidental metamorphosis has become a means to an end, to win back the husband, and the dream of tranformation has turned into 'sickness of truth'. The action of the play demonstrates on this level that the attempt to evoke *A Midsummer Night's Dream* in a contemporary setting does not work. 'Whoever sees *Der Park* atones and makes amends for a society that has betrayed the *Midsummer Night's Dream*', writes Helmut Schödel in his critical review of the play.[33]

31. 'Bring mich in gute Gesellschaft! Gute Gesellschaft, Wolf! Ich halt's nicht mehr aus unter diesen Menschenbiestern! Will lieber unter Trollen und Elfen leben als unter Leistungsexperten und Wohlstandssäufern. Lieber ein Schlupfwesplein als ein Mensch unter Psychologen, Richtern und Erziehern.' *Der Park*, p. 61.
32. 'Wohl hab ich Zulauf plötzlich, doch mit ihm schwillt der Argwohn schmerzlich an und zwingt mich, jede Faulheit zu entdecken. So wahrheitskrank will ich nicht sein! Lieber täusche ich mich und laß mich täuschen.' Ibid., p. 75.
33. 'Wer den *Park* sieht, tut Buße, Abbitte einer Gesellschaft, die den *Sommernachtstraum* verraten hat!' 'Das Paradies, mein Sohn, die wahre Uraufführung: Peter

The second level of the play, the strand of the plot concerning
Oberon and Titania, links Shakespeare's fairy world to the ancient
myth of Pasiphae, who as punishment for some offence of her
husband's was afflicted with a desperate love for a bull; to help her
Daedalus made a cow so life-like that the bull was deceived, and
Pasiphae wooed and mated with him in this disguise. Strauss's
Titania is not changed into the lover of a donkey by Cyprian,
Strauss's Puck who is at the same time the hedonistic artist and
homosexual. She receives a drug to tranquillise her, slips into the
role of Pasiphae and wishes to turn Cyprian into Daedalus. Cyprian
insists that he is the servant of Oberon and wants her to swear to
remain 'Titania of the moon', by which he refers to the leitmotif of
the moon in A Midsummer Night's Dream and at the same time to
the relation that can be made between Shakespeare's Titania and the
Cretan legend of Pasiphae: Pasiphae is a moon goddess.[34] Cyprian
fulfils Titania's wish after she has given him an assurance that she
will stop chasing after the black boy desired by him, and translates
her into a 'bloody myth'.[35] Strauss takes the Shakespearian world of
fairies back to the doom-laden world of myth. By agreeing to the
amorous bargain—whereby he gets the black boy, Titania the
cow—Cyprian brings Oberon's mission to an end. Oberon dismis-
ses him from his service—'I disarm you and all your works'—and,
himself 'a bird of ill omen like all the others', he plunges into this
'sorry tale'. 'Love has lost' is Oberon's conclusion.[36] The power
struggle between the gods and the times the characters have become
involved in is resolved—not because the characters have allowed
themselves to be disarmed by a more enlightened world but because, like Cyprian, they have betrayed their masters and slipped
into mythical roles thus exposing Shakespeare's pastoral to the
terror of myth.

Cyprian is the most complex character in the play. He is an artist;
Wolf admires his statuettes. But he is a calculating artist who goes
by the laws of the market place and produces whatever sells. He is
the Puck of Shakespeare's Dream who has lost his innocence. He is
also, to judge by his name, the narrator of E. T. A. Hoffmann's

Stein inszeniert an der Berliner Schaubühne den *Park* von Botho Strauss', *Die Zeit*, 9
Nov. 1984.
  34. See W. H. Roscher, *Ausführliches Lexikon der griechischen und römischen
Mythologie*, Hildesheim 1965, vol. III. i, Col. 16666f.
  35. 'eine blutige Mythe', *Der Park*, p. 82.
  36. 'und ich entmachte alle deine Werke'; 'ein Unglücksrabe unter Gleichen';
'trauriges Geschehen'; 'Die Liebe hat verloren', Ibid., p. 83 and p. 94.

44

cycle of tales *Die Serapionsbrüder*. In Hoffmann, Cyprian tells the story of Count P. . ., one time celebrated man of the world who sees himself as the martyr Serapion. Cyprian tells this story in order to convince his friends that their attempt to establish a seamless connection with the past is absurd. At the same time, in his meeting with Serapion Cyprian attempts to convince him with rational arguments that he, Serapion, is Count P. . . and not the martyr—but without success. Cyprian, as Henriette Herwig points out, thus represents not only different conceptions of art but also the counter-argument to the play's claim to evoke Shakespeare's *Midsummer Night's Dream*. When Oberon has dismissed him, he rehearses *A Midsummer Night's Dream* with Titania. But when he calls for the fairies Cobweb, Moth, Peaseblossom, Titania gives the abrupt answer: 'Not here.'[37] The role of Bottom who is turned into a donkey has become equally impossible. Cyprian, in the end, is the artist killed by the black boy who filled him with love and desire.[38] His failure marks the true point of convergence of the various periods referred to in the play.

Strauss therefore does not simply draw a parallel between the present and Shakespeare's fairy-tale world. Rather he brings together in one place characters from various historical, mythological and literary contexts and shows their helplessness confronted with the present. Of course they are not helpless because reason and rationality are now dominant, but because modern myths have assimilated the power of the old ones, and because human beings can see the gods as human beings and have therefore created new gods for themselves: racism, chauvinism, stereotyped ideas of a good marriage and conventional behaviour. The sphere of belief in gods and tales of the gods is otherwise engaged. The fairies and gods of antiquity are helpless in face of this new belief. Oberon becomes Herr Mittenzwei who works as a salesman in a video shop. Titania tries to get a wife for her son, the Minotaur, born of her union with the bull, but he reacts in a helpless and boorish fashion. The 'spirit' of *A Midsummer Night's Dream*, the histrionic and at the same time ambivalent representation of love—if it is to become the stuff of drama nowadays—appears to turn cynical. The characters may play the roles from *A Midsummer Night's Dream* for a while, but then

37. 'Nicht da.' Ibid., p. 87.
38. Cyprian's death reminds one of the end of Pierre Paolo Pasolini an extract from whose novel *Vita Violenta* is included in the printed programme of the Berlin performance.

they are forced into the world of myth and legend and the 'vita violenta'.[39] The gap between *A Midsummer Night's Dream* and *Der Park*, between Shakespeare's play about love and the bankruptcy of love, forms the structural principle of Strauss's play. The lay of courtly love that Titania performs with three uniformly dressed and equally strange men, is now nothing but show.[40] Strauss does not join the chorus of regret at the loss of the past—instead he recalls the past and shows that one cannot expect any salvation from it.

Die Fremdenführerin is a play for two persons first performed on 15 February 1986 at the Berlin Schaubühne and directed by Luc Bondy. Its subject matter can be quickly related: Martin, a teacher of around forty (played in the Berlin production by Bruno Ganz) goes to Greece, to Olympia, to work out in his own mind whether or not he wants to continue in his profession. On a tour of the Olympic stadium he meets Kristine, a tourist guide twenty years younger than he, and starts a relationship with her. After her boy friend, the alcoholic Vassili, has died the pair go and live in a grotto in the Greek mountains. In the end Kristine leaves Martin who in his turn takes his leave of the audience with a quotation from Ovid's *Metamorphoses*. So much for the bare structure of the action. As usual with Strauss it is lacking in drama: at first sight what we have is a conventional story of a relationship in which the main characters do not emerge clearly as individuals but remain types. While the woman completely gives in to the pleasure principle, the man seeks to reconcile feeling and reason. Thematically the play is related to Strauss's story *Die Widmung*; Peter von Becker has said of it that it is 'as up-to-date (and trivially mythical) as the film 'Paris Texas'.[41] Only on a higher level does the play become a 'mythical drama in everyday clothing'.[42] Kristine and Martin—particularly in the second act—are related to the Pan myth whose complicated spectrum of signification, developing from an instinctive nature god into a civilised universal god, has already produced some well known representatives in literature.[43] One only needs to think of Goethe's

39. Not only the figure of the black boy but also the cynical resignation of the characters of 'The Young Girl' and 'The Young Boy' are reminiscent of Pasolini's *Vita Violenta*.

40. *Der Park*, Act IV, Scene 5.

41. 'Platos Höhle als Ort der letzten Lust. Das Motiv der Liebe, am Abend der Aufklärung–Zu den neueren (Theater-)texten von Botho Strauss', *Strauss lesen*, ed. Radix, p. 33.

42. Rolf Michaelis, 'Die Liebe? Kein Spiel. Botho Strauss: *Die Fremdenführerin*', ibid., p. 162.

43. See. Reinhard Herbig, *Pan: Der griechische Bocksgott*, Frankfurt 1949.

Satyros in which the story of the god Pan is reflected as in a distorting mirror.

From a topographical point of view the first and the second acts are significantly distinct: from ancient Olympia the couple move out into the realm of nature. The topography refers to two different stages of Greek mythology: at the beginning the site of the Greek games and of the Olympian gods, in the second act the Arcadian idyll. On stage Olympia with its many temples and altars has become a barren, hilly landscape through which Martin is led by the tourist guide. The description of the Olympic stadium couched in guide-book language contrasts sharply with the quotation from Ovid at the end. The tourist guide, who is only doing the job to help out, endeavours to deliver the text like an advertising slogan: 'For the people of Classical antiquity this place was the embodiment of supreme glory . . . notice first of all the overwhelming simplicity of the whole lay-out. You can see with what harmony it fits in with its natural surroundings.'[44] Olympia is a tourist attraction. Terms like simplicity and harmony, characteristic of the humanistic view of antiquity, have become clichés.

The two characters look lost in this region, they do not rightly belong. The tourist guide is wearing punk-like clothes, the tourist Martin, initially shy and insecure, is later on more interested in the woman than in what he can learn from her about Olympia. After the official part of the tour is over, Kristine asks out of the blue: 'What do you think about the Greeks now that you have done the tour?' and Martin's answer is not at all that of a tourist who is impressed: 'What do I think? Oh, I think the Greeks were obsessed with the love of glory. I think many of them were extremely vain and arrogant people—unbearable show-offs.'[45] This view based on simple rationalist psychology represents a cliché no less than the search for origins which, Martin explains a little later, is the reason why he has come to Greece: 'Because everything was going wrong, I thought I should go back for a while to the roots, to the place where our intellectual world was born. The place where everything

44. 'Für den Menschen des Klassischen Altertuns war dieser Ort der Inbegriff höchsten Ruhms . . . Beachten Sie zunächst die überwältigende Einfachheit der gesamten Anlage. Sie sehen, wie harmonisch sie an ihre natürliche Umgebung angepaßt ist.' *Die Fremdenführerin*, Munich-Vienna 1986, p. 9.
45. 'Was denken sie jetzt über die Griechen, nachdem Sie die Führung mitgemacht haben?'; 'Was ich denke? Oh, ich denke, die Griechen waren von Ruhmsucht zerfressen. Ich denke, viele von ihnen waren außergewöhnlich eitle und hochmütige Menschen. Unerträgliche Angeber.' Ibid., p. 13.

was joyous and straightforward in its originality. Harmonious. Reasonable. Simply to feel that spring, to feel the elements.'[46] Nostalgia for the original, the simple, the harmonious and the reasonable is an escape from the here and now into the world of the Greeks that does not exist any more in its original form—as the first scene has graphically shown. In Greece Martin is in search of the place that the Romantics also yearned for in which human consciousness dwells 'safe as in an impregnable fortress'[47] in its primeval state, but the introductory scene shows that this search will be in vain. The contradiction, clear in the first two scenes, between respect for and parody of the image of the Greeks defines the structural principle of the play including even details of the dialogue. As Peter Iden emphasises in his review: 'The characters' words and phrases take flight, venture up into the sublime and then plummet into the trivial, the ridiculous even. Many may call this fall a weakness: it is, however, precisely the strong point of the text: it does not pretend that its author knows it all already, we are taking part in an investigation that is full of twists and turns.'[48]

The fall from the heights into the depths is of course less an investigation than a reference to different discourses. Phrases that could be from the popular press are to be found next to ambitious quotations. The characters in their dialogue make use of different fields of reference, they draw from the stock of ready-made formulas either from the tabloid press or the humanistic tradition. The relationship of the couple to one another is as contradictory as the linguistic orientation of the play as a whole. While Kristine is spending a night with Martin, she informs him that she has just fallen in love with another man. When he sends her away she camps in front of his holiday bungalow or on the roof. Each remains a stranger to the other since they both set out with different expectations. He sees her as his tourist guide, she sees him as a teacher.

---

46. 'Weil mir manches schiefging, dachte ich, ich sollte eine Zeitlang zu den Quellen gehen, dorthin, wo unsere Ideenwelt entstanden ist. Wo ursprünglich alles heiter und gerade war. Harmonisch. Vernünftig. Einfach nur die Quellen spüren, die Elemente spüren.' Ibid., p. 21.
47. 'Wie geborgen in einer unzugänglichen Burg', Schelling, *Sämtl. Werke*, Vol II. 2, p. 159 quoted from Frank, *Der Kommende Gott*, p. 20.
48. 'Die Wörter und Sätze der Personen schwärmen aus, versteigen sich in beträchtliche Höhen und fallen in triviale, sogar lächerliche Niederungen. Dieses Gefälle mag mancher eine Schwäche nennen: es ist indes gerade eine Stärke des Textes: Er tut nicht, als wüßte sein Dichter altklug schon alles, wir nehmen teil an einer windungsreichen Erkundung.' 'Das unbetretene Land, viel betreten. *Die Fremdenführerin* von Botho Strauss, uraufgeführt an der *Schaubühne*', *Frankfurter Rundschau*, 17 Feb. 1986.

There is a confrontation not of human beings but of different systems of discourse. She is the one who leads him into foreign parts if he gives in to her—and she can only see in him what he is by reason of his professional role. He warns her against her boy friend Vassili, the name refers to Basilius the king, and calls him 'dirty Bacchus'.[49] With this insult Martin passes judgement on his own subsequent development since in the second act he becomes for a while just as degenerate as Vassili. Kristine, who worshipped Vassili even in his state of degeneracy, leaves Martin to his decline. She is transformed from Selene, with whom the god Pan was united in love in the grotto, into the nymph Syrinx who flees from Pan. Martin no longer has in his possession the reed that he can make into the Syrinx-flute, only the quotation that ends this story. Martin himself wavers between two patterns of behaviour. When he sees that 'the story of Martin and Kristine' is about to begin he declares that 'experience and common-sense' will no longer be in control.[50] Nevertheless he remains the pedagogue. In the last scene of the first act before they turn their backs on the civilisation of the holiday bungalow, he comes out with his homilies once again: 'One cannot live for stimulus and pleasure alone. One day you find your life empty and lacking in form, reduced to idiocy by your feelings. Sooner or later everybody's life must take on some sort of form. Of course one has to watch out that it does not turn out too petty and narrow.'[51] Here we seen even in the choice of words within the sentence the bathos that situates the text somewhere between banality and the sublime.

The second act represents a new beginning. Above all there is a change of location: the action now takes place in a 'simple mountain hut. A window in the back wall. On the right an entrance without a door. On the left the way into a bedroom.'[52] The house is surrounded by a few olive trees that provide little in the way of shade. One is reminded of the grotto of Pan but it is a far cry from the Arcadian idyll: they are both mercilessly exposed to the heat of the midday sun. Basically it is a run-down place, the stage-set leaving

49. 'dreckiger Bacchus', *Die Fremdenführerin*, p. 22.
50. 'die Geschichte von Martin und Kristine'; 'Erfahrung und Verstand', ibid., p. 27.
51. 'Man kann nicht nur nach Reizen und Gelüsten leben. Eines Tages stehst du leer und formlos da.Verblödet von Gefühl. Zu irgendeiner Form muß aber jedes Menschenleben gelangen früher oder später. Allerdings muß man aufpassen, daß sie nicht zu klein und eng ausfällt.' Ibid., p. 41.
52. 'Im Kargen Berghaus. Ein Fenster in der Rückwand. Rechts türloser Eingang. Links Durchgang zu einer Kammer.' Ibid., p. 49.

one free to recall not only the grotto of Pan but also the love grotto of Tristan and Isolde. The place awakens memories of the Arcadian idyll and shows how far away it is. While in the first act the topography and the individual fragments of dialogue recall Greek myth, the references become clearer in the second act: at the end of every scene, according to the stage directions, Pan's shouts ring out and the voices merge together in an echo. The couple speculate whether their grotto is a shepherd's hut and Pan finally appears causing Kristine to panic. Kristine, although she herself in her instinctiveness embodies elements of Pan, chases him away, failing to recognise him. For her he is an intrusion. Pan defends himself with a fool's sword taken over from the world of the carnival. Rather like in *Kalldewey Farce* and *Der Park*, here again the different levels, the historical strata are mixed up. Everything gets jumbled up. When after chasing Pan away Kristine asks who that was, Martin replies confidently 'me'.[53] It is he who wishes to slip into the role of Pan. In this way the dichotomy between the myth of Pan and the abortive love story shown here is exacerbated. The couple have thrown away the favour of the god Pan, his grotto— refuge and love-nest rolled into one—is not respected. However, Pan has also relinquished his power. When he has gone the couple act as though nothing has happened. Kristine packs her things and leaves as she had earlier planned to do. Martin will continue to wait for her. The noontime slips by without the two of them being able to enjoy the midday calm that plays an important role in the Pan myth. Here noon is just hot and sticky.

When the play is over and Kristine has left the grotto Martin looks out Ovid's *Metamorphoses* and recites the passage where Mercury tells of Pan who no longer holds the nymph Syrinx but only the reed in his hands that he makes into a flute and in whose name he keeps alive the memory of the nymph. The story becomes one of reminiscence, thus returning to the impulse which gave rise to it in the first place.[54] It ends with a parable of the translation of instinct and feeling into poetry. Today this is nothing but a quotation. The road leads from the tourist attraction of Olympia to Ovid. If one wishes to speak of a development, then it is the development from an ancient site literally laid bare—to a poetic quotation as the only surviving remnant of the distant original. The notion of

53. Ibid., p. 66.
54. Iden, in his review cited above (n. 48).

reduction and the disappointment inherent in it demonstrates that any attempt in our day to repeat the sublime transformations of antiquity is doomed to failure. The gods cannot be reinstated, they turn out to be, like Oberon, mediocre people, or, like Pan, foolish and malicious. They allow themselves to be driven out by humanity.

The tradition, in which mythical dramas are a salvaging or a criticism of myth, is punctured by Strauss as in other contemporary plays. A salvage operation is attempted but it does not come off. Rationalist criticism is referred to but also rejected. In this area between lies the parodistic element, slightly sentimental and aggressive at the same time.

4

'Dramatisches Talent hat sie nicht, doch viele schöne Worte'—Friederike Roth as a Playwright

Lucinda Rennison

THE opinion expressed in the title of this chapter, taken from a review of *Klavierspiele* in the *Westdeutsche Allgemeine Zeitung* of 21 February 1981, is one shared by many theatre critics in their assessment of Friederike Roth's work as a dramatist. Not only is *Klavierspiele* seen as 'illustrated poetry';[1] *Die einzige Geschichte* is said to be concerned with 'the universal lyrical themes',[2] while *Krötenbrunnen* stands on 'dramatically shaky legs'[3] according to the theatre critic of *Die Zeit*. The title of this chapter clearly implies that Friederike Roth is essentially a poet, in full command of the niceties of lyrical language, but lacking when faced with the need to create dramatic situations and development suitable for the stage, a deficit which puts into question the relevance and accessibility of her works for the stage.

Another aspect usually stressed by critics is Friederike Roth's status as a woman dramatist, and part of this emphasis may be traced to her use of language. It is surely no coincidence that the words used to describe her language are words which in traditional terms are associated with the feminine ideal—'gentle', 'unobtrusive', 'sensitive'[4] and so on. Clearly even the most enlightened of

1. 'bebilderte Lyrik'. Klaus Wagner in the *Frankfurter Allgemeine Zeitung*, 21 Feb. 1981.
2. 'die universalen lyrischen Themen'. Georg Hensel in the *Frankfurter Allgemeine Zeitung*, 19 June 1985.
3. 'dramaturgisch wackligen Beinen'. Rolf Michaelis in *Die Zeit* 2 Nov. 1984.
4. 'zart': *Der Tagesspiegel*, 24 May 1986, *Der Spiegel*, 16 Feb. 1981; 'unaufdring-

critics find it difficult to escape their preconceived ideas of what constitutes 'female' language. Of course the undeniable fact that most of Friederike Roth's stage characters are women is the main reason for classifying her dramatic works as 'women's plays'. These characters inevitably employ language and approach their topics of conversation in a 'female' way, for linguistic research shows that whether we like it or not men and women express themselves differently, but this difference does not lie in quietness or lyricism. Anna, in *Ritt auf die Wartburg*, is far from both, as some of her fairly aggressive responses indicate. One is certainly on shaky ground, therefore, if the supposed difference in language is extended to apply to the themes of the play and if these themes are judged to concern only, or even predominantly, women.

To return to the extent to which the plays are undramatic in consequence of their language—it is interesting to note that Friederike Roth's main interest during her university studies was in linguistics and that her doctorate was concerned with the aesthetic evaluation of literary texts.[5] This serves to underline above all her early consciousness of literary language as a phenomenon in its own right and her interest in its analysis and criticism. Directly influenced by this linguistic work, she produced, in 1970, her first published prose text—*minimal erzählungen* of which she later says, in an interview with *Theater Heute*: 'These texts emulated Concrete Poetry. I wanted to know how to arrange linguistic material, that is, words, so that they had their own fascination.'[6] This experimental use of language, the arrangement of words and sounds to produce something with its own phonetic attraction, has been retained in her later work, though her language is no longer dominated by pure concentration on the sound and feel of linguistic material. As she herself says, she later became concerned not only with the material of language, but also with its communicative value: 'It was Jandl who led me away from the dead end of Concrete Poetry. He too was once a "concrete" poet in the strict sense. The same thing happened to him, he too wanted content.'[7]

---

lich': *Frankfurter Allgemeine Zeitung*, 21 Feb. 1981; 'zartbesaitet': *Die Welt*, 4 July 1984.

5. *Semiotische Analyse der ästhetischen Untersuchung Georg Simmels*, phil. Diss. Stuttgart 1975.

6 'Das waren Texte in der Nachfolge der Konkreten Poesie. Ich wollte wissen, wie man Sprachmaterial, also Wörter, so anordnen kann, daß sie reizvoll werden.' *Theater Heute*, 1981, 3.

7. 'Aus dieser Sackgasse des Konkreten herausgeführt hat mich Ernst Jandl. Jandl

So after a fairly abstract prose text and two volumes of poetry, Friederike Roth went on to write *Klavierspiele* which appeared in the 'Verlag der Autoren' in 1980. The change of medium, which may have surprised critics who had greeted her arrival on the literary scene as a promising poet, was an inevitable development for the author herself: 'I always knew that I wanted to write dialogue. I had already written a few radio plays. It has something to do with the way my mind works, the way I hear sentences and store them.'[8] Dialogue, surely one of the most vital aspects of successful theatre, is something with which she feels confident—to such an extent that she uses the word to describe the structure of her own thought. Undoubtedly, her work as a dramatic producer for 'Südwestfunk' in Stuttgart has also added to her understanding of what will and will not prove effective as a dramatic text. Radio and stage obviously call for separate skills. It is well known that Friederike Roth continues to write successful radio plays (*Der Kopf, das Seil und die Wirklichkeit* (1982), *Nachtschatten* (1985), both of which won awards) and that many of her stage plays were originally performed on radio. The stage versions have frequently been criticised for lacking the visual element: 'But the audience—to help their concentration—can shut their eyes. They will miss nothing of the action on stage.'[9]

It is for all these reasons that opinions on Friederike Roth's stage plays remain very divided. Her reception as a playwright has most certainly been mixed. Yet, amid much criticism of her plays' shortcomings, it must be remembered that she has also been hailed as a promising young dramatist and that she was awarded the Gerhart-Hauptmann prize in 1983 when *Ritt auf die Wartburg* was also voted play of the year by *Theater Heute*. A closer examination of *Klavierspiele*, first performed in Hamburg in 1981, gives some insight into why this is the case.

The play centres around one character, a woman, known only as 'She'. The most important relationship in her life has come to an end and the text is concerned with her reactions and emotions in the face

war auch einmal ein streng konkreter Dichter. Ihm gings ähnlich, auch er wollte Inhalte.' Ibid.

8. 'Mir war immer klar, daß ich Dialoge schreiben möchte. Ich habe ja auch früher ein paar Hörspiele gemacht. Das hängt mit der Art meines Kopfes zusammen, mit der Art wie ich Sätze höre und speichere.' Ibid.

9. 'Doch kann der Zuschauer—zur besseren Konzentration—auch die Augen schließen. Von der Bühnenhandlung verpaßt er nichts.' Claudia Duchrow in *Der Südkurier*, 19 June 1985.

of this crisis. The concentration on the main figure is such that other characters scarcely exist outside her mind and reflections. There are several monologues, during which, as can be seen in the following example, the language becomes allusive and lyrical. 'The heavens should have turned and turned around the earth. But the fires of heaven were dying and a white sun had risen some time ago. White suns bring nothing but rain. I don't want it up there any longer. A lightheaded wildness goes humming through my mind.'[10]

The largest part of the play, however, consists of a series of brief dialogue scenes between 'She' and the people who inhabit her world before and after the breakdown of the significant relationship. Each scene remains isolated. While it is true that Friederike Roth does little to create a dramatic whole from this series of 'pictures', the dialogue within each scene is frequently sharp-edged and fast-moving:

CUSTOMER. I'm a piano teacher in a musicians' association . . .
SHE (venomously). I could certainly hear that.
CUSTOMER. An' I'm looking for a second-hand piano for a pupil.
SHE. It's second-hand alright. There's no denying that.
CUSTOMER. If it was only out of tune. But the pedals are completely gone.
SHE (still hostile). You weren't half stepping on it just now.[11]

The balance between these two elements of the play is admittedly a precarious one. On occasion the dialogue scenes, particularly those between She and the second female character, Friend, run the risk of breaking down into lyrical reflection which a theatre audience will certainly find difficult to follow. On the other hand, in the case of the scenes in the 'pub' and involving the sale (or attempted sale) of the piano, the snappy dialogue can appear little more than cliché-ridden and banal.

Directors of *Klavierspiele* have been compelled to walk a tight-rope and have frequently lacked the sensitivity required to combine

10. 'Der Himmel hätt sich drehen müssen und um die Erde gehn. Aber der Himmel hatte ein wegsterbendes Feuer, und längst war eine weiße Sonne aufgezogen. Die weißen Sonnen bringen ja doch nichts als Regen. Jetzt will ich's nicht mehr oben. Leichtfertig schwirrt's mir wild im Kopf.' *Ritt auf die Wartburg / Klavierspiele*, p. 131.
11. KÄUFER. Ich bin Klavierlehrer im Tonkünstlerverband . . .
SIE (giftend). Man kann es deutlich hören.
KÄUFER. Und such für einen Schüler ein gebrauchtes Klavier.
SIE. Gebraucht isses. Dagegen läßt sich nix sagen.
KÄUFER. Wenns bloß verstimmt wäre. Aber auch's Pedal ist völlig unbrauchbar.
SIE (weiter feindselig). Sie haben aber vorher mächtig Gas gegeben.
Ibid., p. 103.

these two dimensions effectively.[12] Yet, charmed by Friederike Roth's use of language, directors are still trying to establish the right balance, not an easy task as the very nature of this language seems a positive hindrance in the search. Despite a nearness to cliché, to kitsch and to exaggerated pathos, Friederike Roth's writing retains a certain brilliance. To comprehend this achievement fully, it is necessary to consider the dramatic themes which most concern her. At first glance it seems that Friederike Roth's chief concern is human relationships. The plots of her dramatic works, in so far as they can be described as having plots, centre around relationships, and in particular, sexual relationships. Even *Die einzige Geschichte*, on the surface about the long-drawn-out death of an elderly woman, has sexuality at its centre, both in the antics of those waiting for her death and in the last words of the dying woman. Viewed from another standpoint, one can say that death is ever present and lurking beneath the surface of vitality and sexuality in the other plays, as the following quotation from *Klavierspiele* indicates: 'I might see old women, the way they shamelessly lift their skirts to show their legs with blue violet veins and the ingeniously wrinkled old men with their sharp, lustful glances. All of it leads who knows where, and that's where I want to go.'[13] Sexuality and mortality are inextricably linked in all these texts. The widespread belief is that Friederike Roth is concerned with sexual relationships from a woman's point of view, that her theme is the 'fixation of woman upon man'.[14] In this context, however, the validity of this supposition becomes irrelevant. When the emphasis lies on mortality and its inevitable presence, gender is forgotten— man and woman are both subject to death and to fear of death. Even when life appears to be asserting itself to the full, in sex, mortality is the true reality. It is to a man that She says, in *Klavierspiele*, 'there are coins lying on your eyelids.'[15]

12. *Klavierspiele* has been and still is attempted in numerous established theatres in the Federal Republic—despite several productions, conspicuous in their mediocrity, which have taken place since 1981. (Stuttgart, Elke Lang, Oct. 1981; Freiburg, Matthias Fontheim, Oct. 1984; Zürich, Peter Schweiger, Sept. 1985.) Obviously few have been deterred by the débâcle at the première in Hamburg, when the slap in the face given to the publisher's representative Karlheinz Braun by the director Christof Nel, rather than the play itself, was the talking point of the evening.

13. 'Unter Umständen seh ich dann alte Weiber, wie sie ungeniert ihre Röcke heben, um ihre Beine zu zeigen mit den blauen, violetten Adern, und die knifflig gefälteten Greise mit dem raschen, gierigen Blick. Das alles führt wer weiß wohin, und dahin will ich.' *Ritt auf die Wartburg / Klavierspiele*, p. 121.

14. 'die Fixierung der Frau auf den Mann' *Kölner Stadtanzeiger*, 22 Oct. 1984.

15. 'Dir liegen Münzen auf den Augen', *Ritt auf die Wartburg / Klavierspiele*, p. 111.

A closer examination shows what Friederike Roth sees as the link between death and sexuality. It is firstly the repetitive nature and secondly the apparent inevitability of the two forces which mark their similarity. As far as love and sexual relationships are concerned, all Friederike Roth's plays question the extent to which feelings are genuine and unique rather than reflections of past relationships and received impressions. Such impressions may include the written and spoken word or personal observations and fantasies and they culminate in a level of expectation that influences and limits sexual relationships, not only in their progress, but also in the emotions which are experienced. We are constantly reminded of the fact that the progress of a relationship or an affair is predictable, almost inevitable: 'Good heavens, I was young in those days and I had run away to Paris—you know how it is. He wanted to save me. You always want to save people when you are young and in love.'[16] Once this form of recurrence has been recognised, the quality of the emotions experienced is necessarily thrown into question—in simple terms, doubt begins to make itself felt about the reality of personal feelings. In this context, the moment of death becomes the only moment in which the reality of the experience leaves no room for doubt. On a personal level, despite the fact that death is a recurrent human experience, the individual can be certain of a moment to which there is no return. In *Die einzige Geschichte* The Strange Woman speaks of 'the sweetest dream, that nothing will be repeated. You dream it as you die.'[17]

Many lyrical passages in the plays of Friederike Roth can be seen to reflect and allude to the doubts which surround accepted reality. Dreams and flights of the imagination are evoked to underline the characters' tenuous grip on the real world. A new, lyrical world is created, in which images from the 'real' world are combined with images reflecting Friederike Roth's dramatic themes. The fact that her lover is married and has a young child becomes, for example, lyric fantasy in the imagination of She in *Klavierspiele*. At this point the realistic text is overlaid with images reflecting sexuality, innocence and death. It is because Friederike Roth wishes to emphasise the impossibility of ever defining anything as 'real' that many of her

16. 'Lieber Himmel, ich war damals jung und weggelaufen nach Paris—wie das so ist. Er wollte mich retten. Man will immer retten, wenn man verliebt ist und jung.' *Krötenbrunnen*, Frankfurt 1984, p. 14.
17. 'DIE FREMDE FRAU: Der schönste Traum, daß nichts sich wiederhole. Im Sterben träumst du ihn.' *Die einzige Geschichte*, Frankfurt 1985, p. 85.

scene-settings are ambiguous in their conception: the dance scene in
Ritt auf die Wartburg 'should, in its reality, convey the impression
of a dream', the penultimate scene of *Die einzige Geschichte* is
intended to appear in its entirety as a 'slightly grotesque circus'.[18]
Clearly, these stage directions are vague and extremely difficult to
realise—a further, and this time a valid, reason to criticise the
author's dramatic sense. They will, however, prove a sheer impossibility if the production as a whole overlooks the need for a constantly ambivalent atmosphere. The 1986 production of *Das Ganze
ein Stück* by Günter Krämer at the Concordia Theatre in Bremen
surely indicated that the task is not insurmountable. An excellent
balance was maintained between apparent realism, in the dialogue
and the effects, and the sheer absurdity which forms a vital part of
Friederike Roth's play. The fantastic scenery of Xenia Hausner
drew the audience into a labyrinthine shell, which underlined for
them the proximity in their own world of the real and the questionable, the apparently logical and the absurd. This approach to
Friederike Roth's work emphasises the dialectic within it.

Let us return briefly at this point to the idea of Friederike Roth as
a woman dramatist, writing about women for women. It is fair to
say that the play which has probably done most to earn her this
reputation is *Ritt auf die Wartburg*. It is scarcely necessary to read
more than the titles of some press reviews in order to recognise the
general tendency—'Witches' ride to place of pilgrimage', 'Four
women fall from the saddle', 'Scarcely more than an excuse for a
giggle'[19] and so on. It is clear that many critics are inclined to share
the view of Hans Jansen, that this is 'above all a play by a woman
about women',[20] an interpretation which overlooks one of the
play's main concerns. It is of course four *women* who leave home,
men, and the tedium of everyday life in order to spend some days
together, and their search for emancipation from their present social
roles is indeed, on a certain level, one of the themes of the play.
However, if the characters were four men, or even a mixed group,
the critics might perhaps have had less difficulty in seeing *Ritt auf*

18. 'sollte in seiner Wirklichkeit sich doch vermitteln wie ein Traum', *Ritt auf die
Wartburg / Klavierspiele*, p. 38; 'ein leicht grotesker Zirkus', *Die einzige Geschichte*,
p. 58.
19. 'Hexenritt zum Wallfahrtsort', *Frankfurter Allgemeine Zeitung*, 6 Oct. 1982;
'Vier Frauen fallen vom Pferd', *Theater Heute*, 1983, 12; 'Kaum mehr als eine
Kicherpartie', *General-Anzeiger*, 31 July 1984.
20. 'ein stück nämlich vor allem von einer Frau über Frauen', *Westdeutsche
Allgemeine Zeitung*, 27 June 1983.

die Wartburg as a play about emancipation in general, about breaking away from reality, however brief the escape may be. The women
do not know exactly what they are searching for, but their main
concern is to reject, temporarily, what they see as real. The trip is
often referred to as a dream and it is with regret that they later
realise that the dream is impossible to fulfil: 'Back home I shall rave
about this trip and exaggerate a lot. Yet really I will have nothing to
show for it.' [*To Anna in the room*] 'When I think about home from
here, it seems as if I deceived myself all along.'[21]

In this context the choice of the GDR as their destination is
logical—as a result of the political system to which they themselves
belong they have a wealth of preconceived ideas about life there.
Their conversation is riddled with references to the vision and the
reality of Eisenach. What exactly did they expect in the East? This
they cannot specify or articulate, but they are aware that their
expectations, just as those of the journey in general, have not been
met. Even the history and legend surrounding the Wartburg fits
into this pattern of imagination and reality, expectation and disappointment. The charms of the imagined evaporate with Anna's
weariness. 'From here a beautiful castle. The most beautiful. Perhaps. Up there, crumbling walls. I'd rather wait here and imagine it
to myself.'[22] It is obvious that the desire to escape everyday existence, the desire to realise a dream and experience at close hand
something which has always appeared distant and exotic is a *human*
desire, by no means confined to women. There is sufficient evidence
in the dialogue of *Ritt auf die Wartburg* to suggest that this
universal desire is one of Friederike Roth's main themes in the play.
This hypothesis is supported by the indications in the other plays
that she is interested in the concept of reality and its complex
relation to the imagined and the preconceived.

Just as the quality of experience is thrown into question, the
quality of language and the reality of meaning are also doubted in
Friederike Roth's work. Here too we are conscious of repetition and
inevitability. Words which have been repeatedly used to describe
situations, emotions and visions have been 'used-up', stripped of
any actual meaning. Even if it were possible to have a genuine

21. 'Zu Hause werde ich von der Reise schwärmen und viel übertreiben. Dabei
stehe ich mit leeren Händen da.' [*Zu Anna ins Zimmer*] 'Wenn ich von hier aus an zu
Hause denk, kommts mir so vor, als hätt ich mich von Anfang an getäuscht.' *Ritt auf
die Wartburg / Klavierspiele*, p. 86.
22. 'Von hier aus eine wunderschöne Burg. Die Schönste. Vielleicht. Und oben
bröckelnde Mauern. Ich warte lieber hier und denk sie mir.' Ibid. p. 71.

experience or feeling, therefore, it would still prove impossible to describe and communicate it. Since our consciousness is largely dependent on language, this inability to articulate the original is tantamount to a lack of original experience. It is important in this context to take a look at Friederike Roth's prose work, and in particular her most unusual text—*Das Buch des Lebens*, which bears the rather curious subtitle, *Ein Plagiat*. Friederike Roth explains here that in her understanding language and through it poetic art, is a constant act of plagiarism. The writer continues trying to be original—his position as an artist and in an extended sense as a unique individual is at stake, since the desire for original experience is an existential concept. The honest conclusion which must be drawn, however, is that reached by the Actress in *Krötenbrunnen*: 'Whenever I feel like writing, nothing occurs to me. [Pause] I just go on saying what others have already said.'[23] It is no coincidence that the title *Das Buch des Lebens* makes the connection between art, in the form of literature, and life. This connection lies not in the accepted view that art is a reflection of life, but in the fact that both are plagiarised—necessary reflections and repetitions of that which has gone before. A similar association is made in Friederike Roth's most recent play *Das Ganze ein Stück* (1986). Here life and the art form become completely entangled in each other because of this common factor. The progress of the play is discussed within itself by two of the characters, a Man and a Woman. In a similar way the play is a discussion of reality, its central action is copied from the repetitive and in turn imitative actions of those attending a cultural gathering. If the image is extended still further, the action of the play reflects those watching it as they watch it. *Das Ganze ein Stück* in a double sense—reality and drama so entangled that they seem in their entirety to be no more than a play, or the play itself only one piece of a whole far more complex than even this complicated work.

Given her understanding of language and its limitations, an understanding already evident in her phase of experimentation with 'concrete' art, Friederike Roth is naturally aware of the constant influence of past works, her own included. She accepts the consequences of this recognition and consciously uses the cliché, for example, because it reflects the clichés of experience and of art in an

---

23. 'Immer wenn mir nach Dichten zumut ist, fällt mir nichts ein. [Pause] Dauernd sage ich nur das, was andere schon gesagt haben.' *Krötenbrunnen*, p. 36.

easily recognisable form. The cliché is not only used, but drawn
attention to, as we can see in this example taken from *Krötenbrunnen*.
Repeated so-called clichés of the experience of love, spoken by the
Actress and the Sculptress, are exposed by the cynical figure, the
Exhausted Woman:

ACTRESS. I thought, completely normal love would be wonderful, I
thought, that his eyes would be alight when he looked at me, I hoped, to
be able to sense that someone feels good when I'm near.
SCULPTRESS. Then he even began to come to terms with the fact that you
can't have everything. It really tore me apart. I so much wanted, so much
wanted, to be everything for him.
ACTRESS. The way you could run, as a child, rejoicing, against the wind.
EXHAUSTED WOMAN (smiling). That's a good number you've got there.
Where does it come from? Would you lend me the text? I'd like to read
the whole thing.[24]

It is a mistake, therefore, to criticise Friederike Roth's language as
too close to cliché, since this closeness is entirely intentional.
Through the active use of the cliché, feelings are, as in this example,
clearly called into question as no more than received and repeated
ideas. The connection is once again made between life as it is
experienced and the written word. The border between the two is
rendered uncertain, since both lack true originality.

Friederike Roth also re-uses her own language in different works.
This form of self-plagiarism is particularly interesting and immediately obvious in *Das Buch des Lebens* and *Die einzige Geschichte*.
Several passages which originally appeared in *Das Buch des Lebens*
are transposed, without modification, as dialogue into the play *Die
einzige Geschichte*. Why should an author so obviously, and therefore so intentionally, copy the exact words of an earlier work in this
way? This is once more an attempt to extend the idea of doubt in the
originality and genuineness of real life and of the written word to
cover art itself. Since art and its quality is usually judged in terms of

24. DIE SCHAUSPIELERIN. Ich habe gedacht, so eine ganz normale Liebe wäre
schön, habe ich gedacht, daß es in seine Augen leuchten soll, wenn er mich ansieht,
hab ich gewünscht, daß ich bloß einmal spüren könnte: einem tut meine Nähe gut.
DIE BILDHAUERIN. Dann fing er sogar an, sich damit abzufinden, daß man
nicht alles haben kann. Es hat mir fast das Herz zerissen. Ich wäre doch so gern, so
gern wäre ich alles gewesen für ihn.
DIE SCHAUSPIELERIN. Wie man jauchzend gegen den Wind rennen konnte als
Kind—
DIE ERSCHÖPFTE (schmunzelnd). Ihr habt da eine gute Nummer drauf. Woher
ist das? Bitte leiht mir den Text. Ich würde gern das Ganze lesen.'
Ibid. pp. 54f.

originality, this is a courageous standpoint to take—particularly as it condemns, in a certain sense, the author's own productivity. This idea of art as 'second-hand' is a constant theme in *Das Buch des Lebens*. It is made most clear in the figure of Else. Else, whose aim is to create something absolutely original for the stage, is described with irony and a certain amount of pity:

Our lovely friend wanted to create something for the stage, and it—what It was remained airily vague—was to be more than, and above all, different from everything which had gone before; it was to be everything in a certain sense—and on the other hand nothing, both at the same time of course; it was to encompass the past and the future and in this simultaneity of past and future it was to be be a mirror held up to the here and now, giving a clear picture of the present, which no-one truly grasps, without being too obviously topical. A sort of simplicity itself in a nutshell. Poor Else.[25]

There is of course an element of self-irony in this treatment of Else. Self-awareness as a writer is an essential part of Friederike Roth's language. Although she has long since left the phase in her writing where phonetic material was the only basis, linguistic experimentation is not the only legacy of that period. She has also retained a lack of faith in the true communicative value of language. With this in mind, it is natural that she views the literary efforts of others and of herself with ironic amusement. Contradictory as it may seem, much of her linguistic originality is born of this awareness that absolute originality is an impossibility.

To sum up, therefore, let me return to the critical statements referred to at the beginning of this chapter and examine the extent to which they have been refuted. The first of these criticisms was that Friederike Roth's language is lyrical and that as a result the plays lack the dramatic element necessary to the theatre. Her language certainly has lyrical and experimental qualities, but the plays also contain successful, swift moving dialogue alongside the associative passages and the direct monologues. It is also important to remember that a large part of the lyrical, associative language becomes

---

25. 'Unsere schöne Freundin wollte nämlich etwas auf die Bühne stellen und es—was Es war, blieb schwimmend unbestimmt—sollte mehr und vor allem anders sein als alles bisher Dagewesene; Es sollte gewissermaßen Alles sein und andererseits auch wieder Nichts, und zwar beides gleichzeitig; Es sollte alle Vergangenheit und alle Zukunft enthalten und in der Gleichzeitigkeit von Vergangenheit und Zukunft ein Spiegel des Hier und Jetzt sein, ein präzises Bild unserer Gegenwart geben, die keiner zu fassen mag, ohne vordergründig gegenwartsbezogen zu sein. Es war eine Art Ei des Kolumbus in des Pudels Kern. Ach arme Else.' *Das Buch des Lebens*, Darmstadt 1983, p. 34.

much less obscure once we are aware of the various themes which preoccupy Friederike Roth. These themes have been mentioned above and include originality and repetition, imagination and reality, and sexuality and mortality. They are, for their own part, all to a greater or lesser extent interconnected. Their presence provides an underlying structure in the plays, a structure which may seem to be lacking at first glance. The separate scenes in *Klavierspiele*, for instance, appear to have little in common in terms of dramatic action, but the themes remain constant throughout. It cannot be denied that this pattern is complex and perhaps not quite what we expect when we speak of dramatic structure. The development in Friederike Roth's work tends to be circular rather than linear. In keeping with her awareness of the repetitiveness of life, the plays have a tendency to return to their starting points. We are given the impression that the whole thing, like the love affairs, the conversation, the attempts at self-discovery, could begin all over again. As is said in *Das Ganze ein Stück*, 'the old box in a box construction'.[26]

The second charge against her work, that it is of limited content, banal, and at best relevant only to a few, mostly women, can easily be refuted. Friederike Roth's plays are constructed on several levels, and critical observations of this type can stem only from a reading of the most obvious of these levels. The numerous themes in her work are relevant to a much wider audience. The mistaken view of Friederike Roth as not only a 'woman playwright', but also a 'woman's playwright', evolves from the preconceptions aroused by her at times lyrical and quiet language and by the continuing fallacy that female dramatic characters (as is all too often the case in traditional drama) are moved by less central and less comprehensive issues than those faced by men.

It can fairly be said that the plays of Friederike Roth are not easily accessible. Perhaps, to male actors and directors, they are not wholly acceptable either. The unprecedented aggression shown at the première of *Klavierspiele* in Hamburg would support this view. The writer herself provides only limited visual possibilities and a great deal of responsibility is put on the producer to draw out not only the dramatic qualities in the dialogue, but also to convey to the audience sufficient of Friederike Roth's themes and concerns to render the quieter episodes of the drama equally relevant and logical.

26. 'die alte Schachtel-in-der-Schachtel-Konstruktion'. *Das Ganze ein Stück*, Frankfurt 1986, p. 81.

5

The Anxiety of Influence—Tankred Dorst's 'Deutsche Stücke'
Steve Giles

THE year 1985 saw the publication of the first volume of Tankred Dorst's collected works, but instead of being built around *Toller*, the play largely responsible for his international reputation, it contains a sequence of dramatic and non-dramatic texts brought together as *Deutsche Stücke*.[1] This might appear to be a surprising choice, but the *Deutsche Stücke* represent Dorst's most ambitious project to date, and one of the most enterprising in recent German literary history. Dorst worked on the *Deutsche Stücke* for more than a decade, in an attempt not only to come to terms with some fifty years of German history but also to exploit the resources offered by a variety of genres ranging from drama to narrative and to film. With the exception of *Die Villa*, all the texts in *Deutsche Stücke* have been realised in at least two media,[2] and a study confined to the three plays in the collection runs the obvious risk of reducing the diversity and complexity of Dorst's undertaking, and of ignoring the possibility that the very self-identity of the texts

1. Tankred Dorst, *Deutsche Stücke*. *Werkausgabe 1*, Frankfurt am Main, 1985. My account of particular texts is based on the versions published in this edition, as are the page references indicated in brackets below.
2. In order of first appearance these are: *Auf dem Chimborazo*: radio première 1974, stage première 1975, revised version 1977, TV film 1977; *Dorothea Merz*: TV film 1976, book publication 1976; *Klaras Mutter*: TV film 1978, book publication 1978; *Mosch*: TV film 1980, book publication 1980; *Heinrich oder die Schmerzen der Phantasie*: narrative version (*Die Reise nach Stettin*) 1984, stage première 1985. *Die Villa* was published in 1979.
   For further discussion of the multi-media aspect of the *Deutsche Stücke* see Karl Prümm, 'Das Buch nach dem Film. Aktuelle Tendenzen des multimedialen Schreibens bei Tankred Dorst und Heinar Kipphardt', in Helmut Kreuzer (ed.), *Fernsehforschung und Fernsehkritik*, Göttingen 1980, pp. 54–65 and C. Bernd Sucher, 'Ein Film: das ist eine Erzählung mit neuen Zeichen. Ergebnisse eines Gesprächs mit dem Buch- und Filmautor Tankred Dorst', *Der Deutschunterricht* 33.4 (1981), 76–82.

might be jeopardised through their insertion into differing modes of transmission and apprehension. Nevertheless the three plays—*Auf dem Chimborazo, Die Villa* and *Heinrich oder die Schmerzen der Phantasie*—were completed at crucial stages in the composition of the *Deutsche Stücke*, namely at the beginning, middle and end of the project, and they raise within the context of theatre the issues addressed by critics of the *Deutsche Stücke* as a whole: the effectiveness of Dorst's formal strategies, and his success in mediating the private and the political, the personal and the social, and the individual and the historical.

Dorst's involvement with the *Deutsche Stücke* dates back to the early 1970s. In an interview with Rudolf Vogel in November 1973[3] he indicates that he has been engaged for some time on a project dealing with the history of a middle-class family from the mid-1920s onwards, which he intends to produce as a series of television films. These remarks are made during a discussion of the role of writing and theatre which is of immediate relevance to his emerging conception of the *Deutsche Stücke*. Dorst is sceptical of theatre's capacity to have a direct political impact, but he feels nevertheless that it can affect people by provoking them to reflect actively on things in a more complex and differentiated fashion.[4] This conception of the theatre underlies Dorst's comments two months later, when he suggests that theatre can help people to understand each other better, and it is implicit in his early view of the *Deutsche Stücke*.[5] It is also reflected in his increasing emphasis on the presentation of the political and the social via the individual and the apparently private areas of human interaction, an emphasis which marks a fundamental shift in his position as a writer. Whereas previously he had tended to excise his own experiences and more intimate concerns from his work, and had been interested in history at the level of rather more grandiose themes and personalities, he now proposes to engage in an archaeological exploration of his own past and of his characters' preoccupations and perspectives as a way of gaining access to history.[6] This attention to the personal and the particular is complemented formally in the composition and struc-

---

3. Reprinted in *Werkbuch über Tankred Dorst*, ed. Horst Laube, Frankfurt am Main 1974. p. 220.
4. Ibid., pp. 213–14.
5. Ibid., p. 73.
6. See 'Abneigung gegen Dramatisches', *Süddeutsche Zeitung*, 23 Jan 1975 and 'Erkennen oder Wiedererkennen', *Theater Heute*, March 1975. The autobiographical basis of the *Deutsche Stücke* has been noted by several commentators.

ture of the *Deutsche Stücke*, which should not be seen as constitut-
ing an epic cycle or a Galsworthian family saga. Only three of the
texts are directly concerned with the affairs of the Merz family, and
the intertextual relations within the *Deutsche Stücke* underscore the
limited and fragmentary nature of the perspectives on reality embodied in each text, which is itself no more than a fragment or
Stück. There are clear gaps in the areas of German history that
Dorst deals with, and this overall sense of discontinuity is intensified by the fact that the texts were not written in their internal
chronological sequence, just as their provisionality is reinforced by
Dorst's propensity to revise and rewrite them.[7]

The approach to history and politics embodied in the *Deutsche
Stücke* is potentially fraught with enormous difficulties which, to
judge by the initial critical response, Dorst's essays in television and
narrative singularly failed to avoid. The negative reception of *Dorothea Merz* is typical in this respect: the television film was attacked
for its lack of sufficient political clarity and its banal and trivialising
'authenticity', while the published text tended to be seen as a
superficial and random reproduction of family affairs at the expense
of historical truth.[8] Dorst's narrative technique was crucially impli-
cated in these charges. The 200 or so pages of text consist of 85
numbered chapters or segments, some with titles, which are made
up of descriptive prose, scenic dialogue, diary entries, lists and
letters, interspersed with photographs and reproductions of paintings and documents. While this mode of presentation is supposed to
ensure that the reader engages with the text and its multiple perspectives in a productive and active fashion, its tendency to fragmentation and discontinuity entails the distinct disadvantage that
the reader might simply be lost in an undifferentiated disarray of
trivia. When applied to drama, Dorst's aesthetic of sequentiality has
been construed in more positive terms, as its dissolution of linear
causality leads to the story being presented 'as if in a cracked mirror'

---

7. The chronological sequence of the texts is: *Dorothea Merz, Klaras Mutter,
Heinrich oder die Schmerzen der Phantasie, Die Villa, Mosch, Auf dem Chimborazo*.
For further discussion of the revisions to *Auf dem Chimborazo* and *Heinrich oder
die Schmerzen der Phantasie* see below nn. 11, 18 and 34.
8. On the television film, see for example Heiko R. Blum, 'Die arge Unverbind-
lichkeit', *Deutsche Volkszeitung*, 10 June 1976 and Frank J. Heinemann, 'Köln auf
Dorst-Strecke', *Frankfurter Rundschau*, 22 May 1976; on the printed text see Günter
Blöcker, 'Der Geist des Familienalbums', *Frankfurter Allgemeine Zeitung*, 24 June
1976 and Stephan Reinhardt, 'Oberflächenrealismus', *Frankfurter Rundschau*, 24
Jan. 1977. *Dorothea Merz* is given a more sympathetic reading in Karl Prümm, ibid.

that simultaneously reflects its various and contradictory aspects.[9] It would not be difficult to relate this notion to *Heinrich oder die Schmerzen der Phantasie*, but it has even been seen as characterising such apparently naturalistic works as *Die Villa* and, in particular, *Auf dem Chimborazo*.[10]

Auf dem Chimborazo (1974) was the first of the *Deutsche Stücke* to be completed, though in chronological terms it is the final text in the sequence, its action taking place on a mountain near the border between the Federal Republic and the GDR in the early 1970s.[11] It received its first public performance on radio in 1974, but had no real impact until its stage première at the Schloßparktheater in Berlin on 23 January 1975. The critics' response was almost unremittingly hostile. The play was attacked for failing to exploit and thematise its location, for generally subordinating political and historical considerations to private and domestic matters, and for being theatrically derivative and old-fashioned—a hotch-potch of Ibsen, Strindberg and Chekhov.[12] This assessment was influenced in part by Dorst's own comments in an interview published on the day of the première in which he indicates that his main concern is with the characters and the theme of illusion.[13] The reviewers, however, were less inclined to take up Dorst's suggestion in the same interview that the play is also an epilogue on the bourgeois family, which he subsequently described as a social institution that had had decidedly negative effects on its members[14]—a point which might be made with equal force about the aesthetic institution of bourgeois drama. And, while it is true that Dorst does not systematically exploit either the play's geopolitical setting or the fact that three of its characters were resident for several years in the GDR, it does explore the relationship between the personal and the political by means of a devastating analysis of the family, the cornerstone of bourgeois society, and by attending in some detail to

9. 'wie in einem zerbrochenen Spiegel', Günther Erken, 'Nachwort', *Deutsche Stücke*, p. 609.
10. Ibid., p. 610.
11. Though the 1974 version dates the action of the play as 'um 1970', in both versions Dorothea refers to the 49th anniversary of her marriage. As she married not later than 1924/1925, the play must be set in the early 1970s.
12. See in particular Hellmuth Karasek, 'Ab ins Tal', *Der Spiegel*, 27 Jan. 1975; Georg Hensel, 'Luft aus der geplatzten Lebenslüge', *Frankfurter Allgemeine Zeitung*, 25 Jan. 1975; Friedrich Luft, 'Niobe im Zonenrandgebiet', *Die Welt*, 25 Jan. 1975; Rainer Wilken, 'Die bittere Lust, das Leben zu belügen', *Stuttgarter Zeitung*, 25 Jan. 1975.
13. See 'Abneigung gegen Dramatisches', *Süddeutsche Zeitung*, 23 Jan. 1975.
14. See 'Erkennen oder Wiedererkennen', *Theater Heute*, March 1975.

the part played by ideology in the constitution of the subject. *Auf dem Chimborazo* is centrally concerned with relationships within the family, in particular between the ageing middle-class widow Dorothea Merz and her two middle-aged sons Tilmann and Heinrich. The Oedipal implications of this scenario are present throughout, and are almost crassly exposed when Heinrich informs his mother that his elder brother Tilmann wishes to marry her. Both sons are in fact unmarried, and ultimately incapable of breaking with their mother, a circumstance which deforms their relationships to others and to themselves. Heinrich and Tilmann resemble 'Tschuas': as Heinrich explains, 'they're children, when they're born they're bandaged up in such a way that they're crippled. Their brains atrophy and their limbs are like whitish potato shoots.'[15] While Tilmann is pathetically incapable of articulating his deeply felt emotional and sexual needs and aspirations, Heinrich's simmering resentment underlies his now indifferent, now sadistic treatment of Tilmann, and ultimately explodes, first as Tilmann jovially mocks him for inadvertently eating ants, and then as he mercilessly strips away his mother's illusions about her two sons. Although at one level Heinrich's onslaught represents an attempt to resist and even undermine maternal hegemony, at another it expresses an astringent critique of the values and perceptions embedded in his mother's self-image. He is sympathetic towards the left-wing radical Frau Falk, insists on referring to the Eastern Zone of Germany as the GDR, questions the standard view that GDR citizens yearn to emigrate to the West, and debunks the ideology of freedom, individualism and self-development supposedly embodied in the social structures and practices of the Federal Republic. At the same time he appears to have nothing but the vain clichés of Baroque nihilism to put in the place of the vacuous liberalism he rejects,[16] and at the end of the play it is he who goes off to look for his mother in the enveloping darkness of the forest.

The role of ideology in sustaining a sense of personal identity is nowhere more clearly indicated than in the presentation of Doro-

---

15. 'Es sind Kinder, die werden als Neugeborene so bandagiert, daß sie verkrüppeln. Verkümmertes Hirn, und die Glieder sind wie weißliche Kartoffeltriebe.' (p. 579).

16. At the beginning of Scene 20, Heinrich quotes the final six lines of Gryphius's famous sonnet 'Ihr irrt, indem ihr lebt . . .', which is printed in full at the head of the text, together with an extract from W. H. Auden's long poem *The Age of Anxiety*. It is interesting to note that this piece was itself subtitled 'A Baroque Eclogue' and prefaced by an extract from the *Dies Irae*. Cf. W. H. Auden, *Collected Longer Poems*, London 1968, p. 253.

thea. While for much of the play she appears to be little more than a domineering and destructive egomaniac, whose strategies of domination repress and disfigure her sons and her friend Klara, it is also implied that she is profoundly insecure, and indeed needs others in order to establish herself and assert her construction of reality. It is crucial to Dorothea that her perceptions and preoccupations should define the conditions and parameters of discursive interaction, and she becomes increasingly anxious as Heinrich whittles away at her view of others and, by implication, of herself. Her fundamental insecurity underlies her scathing comments on her cousin Paul, whom she presents as her other—a lazy, egoistic good-for-nothing whose life is empty and meaningless—but who is in fact a projection of her own deep-seated fears about herself. Her indignant insistence to Heinrich that 'you've got to have a goal!'[17] is generated by the vacuum at the heart of her existence: she married in the hope that her husband Rudolf would explain life to her, that she would understand everything, but to no avail. Throughout the play her nostalgic reconstruction of the past[18] had been intimately associated with the Waldenesque idyll that was to have been the guiding principle of her life with Rudolf, but in the end this too collapses under the weighty banality of her late husband's aphorisms: 'If you throw stones in the water too close together the ripples are destroyed.'[19]

The inescapability of the past has been a key issue in discussions of the dramatic status of *Auf dem Chimborazo*. Though there has been a general tendency to indict Dorst with a clichéd *Epigonentum*, it has also been suggested that the play is rather more self-conscious in its assimilation of classic realism, and virtually Beckettian in its transmission of non-communication.[20] At first sight, the play presents us with a naturalistic slice of life. It strictly observes the unities of time and place, so much so that there is a rigorous correspondence between chronological time and the duration of the action, and the mind-numbing triviality of certain sequences of

17. 'Man muß doch ein Ziel haben!'(p. 589).
18. The 1977 version of Scene 4 cuts several statements made by Dorothea about the negativity of her past experiences which are present in the earlier version, together with her more explicit comments at the end of the scene on the significance of *Walden* in giving her life meaning. The earlier version of *Auf dem Chimborazo* is reprinted in *Theater Heute*, March 1975, pp. 40–48.
19. 'Wenn man Steine ins Wasser wirft, zu nah beieinander, dann zerstören sich die Wellenkreise', p. 596.
20. See for example Erken, *Deutsche Stücke* pp. 609–10 and Wilken, 'Die bittere Lust'.

conversation and behaviour could easily be legitimised in terms of a
naturalistic aesthetic, as could the fragmentation and discontinuity
of whole stretches of dialogue. At the same time, the text appears
intentionally and systematically to disrupt the linear causality of
classic realism, particularly in its scene breaks, which are occasionally signified by entrances or exits, but seem for the most part to be
quite arbitrary and are presumably influenced by techniques of
filmic composition. Now the text could be seen as self-consciously
problematising the conventions of theatrical illusionism, so as to
precipitate a crisis in the dramatic form Dorst has adopted. In his
Theorie des modernen Dramas, Peter Szondi identified just such a
breakdown in dramatic form because its crucial preconditions—
'present interpersonal happening'—were being eroded.[21] In Dorst's
play, too, present gives way to past as reminiscence plays a major
role in Dorothea's behaviour patterns, the interpersonal is in a state
of almost perpetual crisis, and happening decays into the surface
inconsequentiality of debates on broken shoes and bread-and-
butter pudding. The crucial difference is that Szondi was theorising
a crisis in drama at the turn of the century which was essential to the
emergence of Modernism; some seventy years later Dorst's epilogue
on bourgeois drama functions as a poignant reminder of the dilemma of the post-modern writer who wishes to problematise a
form whose resilience confounds premature reports of its demise.

The most striking difference between *Die Villa* (1979) and *Auf
dem Chimborazo* is that while the latter play has a mere five
characters and deals essentially with the affairs of the Merz family,
the former has double the number of characters, who represent a
much broader range of the social spectrum, such as worker, student,
factory owner, communist party functionary, black marketeer,
aspiring actress. As in *Auf dem Chimborazo* the action of the *Die
Villa* takes place near the border between East and West, but it is set
in the Soviet zone in 1948, and one might be tempted to conclude
that Dorst had taken heed of the criticism of his earlier play, and
had built a much firmer socio-political dimension into the later
work. Dorst, however, has seen *Die Villa* as a play about theatre,
about characters trapped in bourgeois preconceptions, about
communication—as a play whose significance transcends its histori-

21. 'gegenwärtiges zwischenmenschliches Geschehen', Peter Szondi, *Theorie des
modernen Dramas* (1880–1950), Frankfurt am Main 1971, p. 74. For further discussion of the viability of Szondi's categories see Steve Giles, 'Szondi's Theory of
Modern Drama', *British Journal of Aesthetics* 27. 3 (1987).

cal location.[22] The reviews of the Stuttgart première on 20 September 1980 were all too ready to take up his suggestions and see *Die Villa* as a play not so much about history as about distorted communication, where crossing frontiers is more a metaphysical and metaphorical issue than a political dilemma,[23] and this concern with the existential import of the play was reinforced by the non-realist aspects of the Stuttgart production. The set was anti-illusionist, scene endings were indicated by blackouts, audience and auditorium were separated by a glass wall, and Tilmann's final words to Heinrich at the end of the play—'You simply stand outside and don't lift a finger! You just stand there and watch all the time! All the time you just watch!'[24] were provocatively addressed to the audience at the beginning. The Düsseldorf première, on the other hand, which also took place on 20 September 1980, was quintessentially realistic, and reviews of this production tended to see the play as an authentic piece of history presented from a position of ideological neutrality.[25] Dorst was impressed by both productions, even though he had construed the play in broadly realist terms, and there is certainly a strong case for presenting it in this way. It adheres to the unities of time and place—albeit less strictly than does *Auf dem Chimborazo*, in that there is a two-hour gap between Scenes 14 and 15—and, notwithstanding the alterations to the scene breaks in the Stuttgart production, which Dorst subsequently approved,[26] all the scene changes in the printed text are marked by entrances or exits and the action tends to flow from one scene to the next. The set is described in naturalistic terms, characters perform everyday activities such as taking the washing down and putting wood on the stove, and their language is differentiated on a class and regional basis. This is not to say, however, that the text lends no support to the employment of anti-illusionist production techniques. The relationship between drama and reality is thematised on several occasions, in particular through Herzog's

22. Cf. 'Ich weiß nicht, ob das Stück pessimistisch ist', *Süddeutsche Zeitung*, 13 Sept. 1980 and 'Es geht um Leute, die sich verfehlen', *Theater Heute*, Nov. 1980.
23. Cf. for example Susanne Ulrici, 'Eine deutsche Geschichte von 1948', *Saarbrücker Zeitung*, 25 Sept. 1980; L. Schmidt-Mühlisch, 'Der Letzte Tango an der Zonengrenze', *Neue Zürcher Zeitung*, 23 Sept. 1980.
24. 'Du stehst einfach da draußen und rührst dich nicht! Du stehst nur da und siehst immer nur zu! Immer siehst du nur zu!', p. 450.
25. Cf. Gerd Vielhaber, *Saarbrücker Zeitung*, 25 Sept. 1980; Georg Hensel, 'Zwischen den Zonen anno 1948', *Frankfurter Allgemeine Zeitung*, 22 Sept. 1980; 'Wie in einem Spiegel', *Rheinische Post*, 22 Sept. 1980.
26. Cf. 'Es geht um Leute, die sich verfehlen', *Theater Heute*, Nov. 1980, and compare the discussion of this issue in Erken, *Deutsche Stücke*, pp. 609–10.

various comments on art and theatre, and illusionist convention is foregrounded when Heinrich and Elsa move into the kitchen in Scene 7 so that they won't be overheard, and again when Tilmann describes a piece of modern theatre in the penultimate scene. Similarly, the Dussek scene functions as a sudden and unmotivated hiatus in the action of the play, whose self-conscious moment reaches its culmination in the penultimate scene in the extended dramatised reading from Diderot's *Rameau's Nephew*, a text which Dorst had himself adapted in 1963. At the same time, I would argue that, as in Hauptmann's *Die Ratten*, a play which Dorst admires and which may well have influenced *Die Villa*, ultimately the realist element predominates, and not simply in theatrical terms.[27] There is a strong sense in *Die Villa* of the interconnection between the individual and his or her social and historical position, so much so that it could almost be seen as a classic instance of realism as defined by Erich Auerbach in *Mimesis*, in providing 'a serious representation of contemporary social reality against the background of a constant historical movement'.[28]

The situation of all the characters in the play is one of coming to terms, for good or ill, with the realities of life in the Soviet zone in 1948, and their responses are deeply marked by their own history, whether social, economic, psychological or sexual. To this extent at least, the play questions the very notion of a zero hour, stressing the underlying continuities of past, present and future. Kurt Bergk, the owner of a small factory under threat of appropriation, seems to be incapable of grasping such concepts as class difference or class conflict as he emphasises the paternalistic organisation of his business which, despite the protestations of worker Rebhahn, he feels cannot be tarred with the brush of capitalist exploitation. Indeed, his very identity is enmeshed with his rootedness in tradition, variously embodied in his birthplace, his family inheritance, and his patriarchal view of the relationship between man and wife. This confluence of past and present is equally significant for those committed to the process of communist reconstruction. Rebhahn's violent altercation with the young student Robert Scharwenka in Scene 11 throws into sharp relief long-standing differences within the

27. Compare the account of the conventionality of *Die Villa* in relation to the work of Heiner Müller, Botho Strauss and Thomas Bernhard in Volker Canaris, 'Die Tage nach der Stunde Null', *Der Spiegel*, 29 Sept. 1980.
28. Erich Auerbach, *Mimesis: The Representation of Reality in Western Literature*, trans. Willard R. Trask, Princeton, NJ, 1968, p. 518.

working-class movement between its agricultural and industrial sectors, and while Scharwenka himself may come across as a cynical and heartless ideologue, it is equally clear that his political attitudes are fuelled by a legitimate and deep-seated resentment at the privations suffered in particular by his mother. The suggestion that ultimately *Die Villa* is ideologically neutral is apparently confirmed by the multi-faceted presentation of its characters, and reinforced by the gradual de-emphasising of political and economic factors in the final scenes; but its implied critique of Germany's fascist past, together with its intimation of an ethos based on compassion, invites a more positive reading of the play as tacitly endorsing a humanitarian socialism.

Heinrich oder die Schmerzen der Phantasie (1985), the last of the *Deutsche Stücke*, is a reworking of *Die Reise nach Stettin*,[29] a text excluded from the Suhrkamp collection. It was published in 1984, one year before *Heinrich oder die Schmerzen der Phantasie*, and is written in the scenario narrative form associated with *Dorothea Merz* and *Klaras Mutter*. Although the bulk of the material used in *Heinrich oder die Schmerzen der Phantasie* is taken directly from *Die Reise nach Stettin*, there are crucial differences in its mode of presentation. *Die Reise nach Stettin* consists of twenty-five chapters which follow one another in chronological sequence, and although it is narrated from Heinrich's point of view and concerned with his inner world, inner and outer are always clearly delineated.

Heinrich oder die Schmerzen der Phantasie, on the other hand, is a highly disrupted text written in an explicitly anti-realist fashion strongly reminiscent of late Strindberg and early Toller.[30] Unlike the previous two plays in *Deutsche Stücke*, it makes no concessions to the conventions of the illusionist stage. The set is a large empty space, where particular locations are to be indicated swiftly and economically in different parts of the stage, individual scenes may merge into one another or be played simultaneously, and precise causal and temporal links between scenes are sometimes impossible to determine. The text's anti-realism is intensified by the insertion

29. Tankred Dorst, *Die Reise nach Stettin*, Mitarbeit Ursula Ehler, Frankfurt am Main 1984.
30. The opening stage direction in *Heinrich oder die Schmerzen der Phantasie* is clearly reminiscent of Strindberg's note on dream theatre at the beginning of *A Dream Play*, and Dorst's techniques throughout *Heinrich oder die Schmerzen der Phantasie* appear to be influenced by Expressionist practice as exemplified in Toller's *Die Wandlung* and *Masse Mensch*, which were themselves heavily indebted to Strindberg's later work.

of surreal fantasy sequences, and by its systematic blurring of the distinction between dream, fantasy and reality. In his classic account of the principles of montage in cinema, Eisenstein wrote that 'by combining these monstrous incongruities we newly collect the disintegrated event into one whole, but in *our* aspect';[31] the 'monstrous incongruities' of Dorst's play are not so much refocused as diffracted through the medium of its central character's consciousness, whose exploration is one of its main concerns.

The action of the play is set in 1944, when Heinrich was a sixteen-year-old schoolboy, and the audience is confronted throughout with the permeation of individual and social experience by National Socialism. Visually this is achieved through a succession of images presenting Nazi insignia—gymshirts imprinted with swastikas, Hitler Youth and SS uniforms, the school flag—and is reinforced by Hitler salutes and the singing of patriotic songs. Much of this activity is associated with life at school, that essential site of ideological transmission, whose militarisation is confirmed by the headmaster's advocacy of the virtues of Discipline and Duty, and by the schoolchildren's preoccupation, reminiscent of Günter Grass's *Katz und Maus,* with the bric-à-brac of war. The Fascist colonisation of the cultural sphere is indicated through references to Schubert's *Unfinished Symphony*, Rilke's poetry, and Fridericus Rex films,[32] and the ideological entrapment of the individual appears to be complete.

This pervasion of consciousness is elaborated through the presentation of Heinrich. Although his personal problems are partly determined by family relationships, especially to the dead father he barely knew and to his narrow-minded and domineering mother, in crucial respects they are rooted in his attempts to establish a sense of identity within the particular constraints of National Socialist society: his profound anxieties concerning race, sexuality, love, women and shame are intertwined with the structuring of masculinity in a militaristic social order. Heinrich yearns for immediate combat duty at the front, and his initial determination by and incipient dislocation from the psychic symbolism of National Socialism are mediated particularly effectively through his shifting relationship to

---

31. S. M. Eisenstein, *Film Form: Essays in Film Theory*, ed. and trans. J. Leyda, New York 1957, p. 34.

32. For further discussion of the relationship between Fridericus Rex films and the development of National Socialist ideology see Julian Petley, *Capital and Culture: German Cinema 1933–45*, London 1979, pp. 106–11.

the figure of Frederick the Great of Prussia. It is this aspect of Heinrich's development that brings out the full significance of the play's fantasy sequences. They involve a subconscious processing of experiences and images which forms an integral part of his distanciation from National Socialist ideology, most strikingly in the episode in Berlin in Scene 10 when his sea cadet uniform bursts into flames. The incompleteness and provisionality of his supposed 'inner liberation'[33] are tellingly exposed, however, in his accounts of the incident in Stettin that led to his expulsion from the 'Admiral Trotha' in Scene 7. The incident in question—he was caught reading while on watch—is itself sufficient evidence of a fissure in Heinrich's consciousness, and he has enormous problems in connecting his mode of action and his internalised norms. In Berlin he can only relate his misdemeanour to others in the now problematic idiom of the military establishment, and even on his return home in Scene 12, when he claims that he has been fundamentally changed by his experiences of the past few weeks, his assertion of the intentionality underpinning his actions in Stettin is thrown into sharp relief by his critical assessment of them as sabotage and sedition.[34]

An important stage in Heinrich's developing dissociation from National Socialism is reached when he notices a group of silent people at a railway station after leaving Berlin. They first became visible, to the audience at least, when Heinrich departed for Berlin at the end of Scene 6, but it is only now in Scene 11 that their identity becomes clear. Some are Jews, but they all await transportation, and their role in the play is central to its overall perspective on Fascism. Huddled together in winter clothes, marginal to the action of the play yet ever-present, they remain in view to the end and constitute the final image the audience perceives. They function as a constant, if almost subliminal reminder of National Socialism at its most abhorrent, acting as a focus for references in the play to Nazi policies on race and sex. Any questioning of the play's anti-fascist credentials would seem to be outrageous, yet reviews of

33. See Georg Hensel, 'Tage und Tagträume aus jener Zeit', *Theater Heute*, Aug. 1985, p. 36.
34. The revised version of *Heinrich oder die Schmerzen der Phantasie*, reprinted in *Theater Heute*, Aug. 1985, pp. 42–52, makes fundamental changes to the ending of the play. The final four scenes of the first version are condensed into a single scene which cuts several long speeches showing Heinrich still trying to come to terms with the incident in Stettin. The comments of one reviewer (Hans Martin Frese, 'Die ewig gleiche Krankheit Jugend', *Rheinische Post*, 19 June 1985) imply that the première was based on this revised version, but it is worth noting that in both versions, the function of 'Die Schweigenden' remains the same.

the première, in Düsseldorf on 16 June 1985, did just that.[35] Crucially, in this production the 'silent ones' did not appear until the very end of the play, and one cannot but concur with the judgement of the reviewer who criticised the première in the following terms: 'The neutralisation of Dorst's text makes it unnecessary for the audience to mobilise their own guilt feelings.'[36] On the evidence of *Heinrich oder die Schmerzen der Phantasie*, the accusation of noncommitment which has so often been laid at Dorst's door might be better directed at the institution within which he works rather than at the last of the *Deutsche Stücke*, which engages in a politicisation of the stage certainly less strident than that of the 1960s, but arguably more complex and more subtle.

35. Cf. for example Hermann Lewy, 'Jugend im Getriebe der NS-Maschinerie', *Jüdische Allgemeine Wochenzeitung*, 8 July 1985 and Ulrich Schreiber, 'Leiden in und an Deutschland', *Frankfurter Rundschau*, 19 June 1985.
36. 'Die Verharmlosung von Dorsts Textvorlage enthebt den Zuschauer der Notwendigkeit, eigene Schuldgefühle zu mobilisieren', Ulrich Schreiber, 'Realität und Traum', *Handelsblatt*, 21 June 1985.

6

Subject, Politics, Theatre—Reflections on Franz Xaver Kroetz

Moray McGowan

ON 3 April 1971, the controversial twin premières of *Heimarbeit* and *Hartnäckig* at the Munich Kammerspiele catapulted the hitherto unknown Franz Xaver Kroetz into public prominence. Since then the forty-odd plays he has had performed in countless productions throughout the world have made him the most successful German dramatist since Brecht. The sheer volume of his work, his delight in vociferous public pronouncements and the attentions of the scandal-hungry media have created misunderstandings which have often obscured both the continuities and the real developments both in his work and in his political and aesthetic position. This analysis, focusing on the inter-related themes of subject, politics and theatre, will try to establish these continuities and developments.

In the earlier 1970s Kroetz's public statements expressed a radical rejection of subjectivity, self-reflection and formal considerations in literature in favour of social criticism.[1] This appeared to be con-

---

1. See: Moray McGowan, 'Das Objekt entdeckt seine Subjektivität: "Innerlichkeit" in den neueren Kroetz-Stücken?', in *Subjektivität—Innerlichkeit—Abkehr vom Politischen? Tendenzen der deutschsprachigen Literatur der 70er Jahre*, ed. K. Bullivant and H.-J. Althof, Bonn 1986, pp. 263–76; here p. 263.
Kroetz's works and related essays, statements and interviews published in book form, are referred to by the following abbreviations plus page number:
BS '*Bauern sterben*', Frankfurt 1987
FH *Furcht und Hoffnung der BRD*, Frankfurt 1984
FXK *Franz Xaver Kroetz*, ed. Otto Riewoldt, Frankfurt 1985
GS *Gesammelte Stücke*, Frankfurt 1975
MM *Mensch Meier / Der stramme Max / Wer durchs Laub geht*, Frankfurt 1979
NF *Nicht Fisch, nicht Fleisch; Verfassungsfeinde; Jumbo Track*, Frankfurt 1981
WA *Weitere Aussichten*, Cologne 1976.

firmed by his work. He gained fame initially with plays, such as *Heimarbeit*, that seemed to be grim records of the material and linguistic poverty of the outsiders and the underprivileged behind the glittering facade of the *Wirtschaftswunder*; part, like the plays of Martin Sperr or R. W. Fassbinder, of the fashion for 'new realism'. Even after the decline of documentary literature critics and audiences in the early 1970s still expected 'authenticity', an imitative relationship to social reality, and believed that they saw it in Kroetz's early work, whereas the contemporaneous early plays of Botho Strauss such as *Die Hypochonder* (1972) which consciously subverted such expectations, initially left them mystified.[2] At the time, Kroetz insisted that his early work was drawn from newspaper reports and from observation: 'Invention, I hope, has little to do with it', he remarked in 1972.[3]

Kroetz's later work in the 1970s, from *Oberösterreich* (1972) to *Nicht Fisch, nicht Fleisch* (1981), established him as the dramatist of the West German everyman, the *Kleinbürger* and his habits of thought, speech and consumption. The socially critical orientation of these plays seems at first sight to confirm Rolf-Peter Carl's judgement of Kroetz's work as one, 'which is in no sense a place for the author to write about himself'.[4]

However, the fundamental change in Kroetz's self-conception as a writer that emerged around 1980 has altered the perspective on his earlier work. In this respect his resignation from the German Communist Party (DKP) in that year is of more than political significance. Kroetz had joined in 1972, very shortly after his breakthrough, to escape the role of court-jester to the bourgeoisie. For a time his party commitment reflected his bad conscience about his political powerlessness as a writer: 'I'd rather sit in Bonn in the *Bundestag*', he announced in 1973.[5] He would, he said, abandon writing altogether, or write only agit-prop plays in future. But in fact only *Globales Interesse* (1972) and *Münchner Kindl* (1973) fit this category. Initially Kroetz echoed, and with the enthusiasm of the convert often outdid, the party's rhetoric. But as the decade

2. See Moray McGowan, 'Unendliche Geschichte für die Momo-Moderne? Rezeptionskontexte zum märchenhaften Erfolg von Botho Strauss', *TheaterZeit-Schrift* 15 (1986), 88–106, here pp. 90–3.
3. 'Erfindung ist—hoffentlich—wenig dabei', *Theater Heute: Jahressonderheft* 1972, p. 65.
4. 'Das überhaupt nicht zum Ort wird, über sich selbst zu schreiben', R. P. Carl, *Franz Xaver Kroetz*, Munich 1978, p. 17.
5. 'Ich sässe lieber in Bonn im Bundestag', *WA* 585.

progressed, and his analytic insight, sharpened by Marxist dialectic, grew, he rejected both this rhetoric and the party's East European model of socialism. He became equally disillusioned with the DKP's dogged adherence to progress in the Marxist sense. This pessimism, which Kroetz shares with so many of the once-optimistic West German left, has since increased, as his diary for 1982–3, reproduced in the Suhrkamp edition of *Furcht und Hoffnung der BRD*, confirms. He continues, however, to reject that nihilistic gloom which can be used to justify inaction (e.g. *FH* 228–9). Since 1980 he has given support to the SPD, the Greens and the DKP, choosing camps according to issues from a position of sceptical independence which he had previously damned as élitist.[6]

This move from dogmatism to pluralism is reflected in the transformation of Kroetz's aesthetic theory. In the essay 'Kirchberger Notizen' (1980), a major re-examination of his attitudes to subjectivity, art and politics, he still rejected the search for individual meaning or eternal truths at the expense of social reality and social solidarity, but he also argued that political art, *above all*, should not neglect form: 'Art without teeth is no art. But nor is art without form.'[7] He now also accepted the role of subjectivity in literature; indeed he acknowledged that his work had always concerned 'my own autobiographical, existential ship-wrecks, which I try to understand and portray as social phenomena'.[8] His work is full of 'injury, severance, despair, depression, loneliness, indignities, inferiority complexes, wounds'.[9]

This catalogue of psychic maladies evokes the 'new subjectivity' of the 1970s with which it at first sight seemed so out of step. In his plays of the 1970s, however, Kroetz insists on the right of ordinary working-class characters to the identity crisis which, whether in Goethe's *Werther* or in Botho Strauss's *Die Widmung*, has customarily been reserved for the sensitive bourgeois intellectual. Arguably, this rehabilitation of an archetypal bourgeois theme in

6. Kroetz, 'Sozialismus aus Liebe zum Vernünftigen', in *Warum ich Marxist bin*, ed. F. J. Raddatz, Munich 1978, p. 34.
7. 'Kunst ohne Zähne, ist keine. Kunst ohne Form, auch nicht', 'Kirchberger Notizen', *FXK* 172.
8. 'Meine eigenen, biographie-immanenten, existentiellen Ruinen, die ich versuche, als gesellschaftliche Phänomene zu begreifen und darzustellen', 'Ich schreibe nicht über Dinge, die ich verachte', Interview with Manfred Beetz, *Theater Heute 7* (1980), p. 18.
9. 'Verletzungen, Brüche, Verzweiflungen, Depressionen, Einsamkeiten, Demütigungen, Minderwertigkeitskomplexe, Wunden', 'Rede an den Wiener Literaturtagen', unpublished manuscript 1980.

socially critical guise contributed to Kroetz's success with a public whose disillusionment with the political demands made on literature in the late 1960s was advanced but still not complete. But despite his increasing emphasis on subjectivity, during the 1970s Kroetz held to the rationalistic goal of portraying existential crises as social, therefore man-made and changeable, phenomena affecting representative figures whose problems have concrete social and economic origins.

Nonetheless, an exclusively social realist reading of Kroetz's plays does not do full justice to his work in any of the three phases which the following analysis identifies. In the first phase, Kroetz's early plays *did* coincide with the realisation, expressed in such books as Jürgen Roth's *Armut in der Bundesrepublik* (1974), that in West Germany the outsiders and the socially disadvantaged (the *Randgruppen*), formed a very substantial minority beneath the affluent surface. But in fact these early plays are not solely concerned with social outsiders (a misunderstanding indicative of the narrow social experience of many theatre critics). Erwin in *Wildwechsel* is a lorry driver, for example; Rustorfer and Ertl in *Hartnäckig* are publicans, Otto in *Lieber Fritz* is a market garden owner, Fräulein Rasch in *Wunschkonzert* is a clerical worker, *Männersache* concerns a factory worker and a shopkeeper. In any case these plays are more than social reportage: they are also imaginative restatements of personal experience. The motif of *Heimarbeit*, piecework labour performed in the home, which occurs in *Heimarbeit*, *Geisterbahn*, *Sterntaler*, *Das Nest*, *Heimat* and *Agnes Bernauer*, is not only a social fact, a metaphor for exploitation and an effective piece of stage business. It also articulates the socially isolated and insecure world of Kroetz himself in the late 1960s, drifting between unskilled casual jobs, rare engagements as an actor, and unsuccessful attempts as a writer.

The same applies to the motif of handicap in *Heimarbeit*, *Hartnäckig*, *Stallerhof* and *Lieber Fritz*: it is both a social reality and a metaphor for the rejection Kroetz experienced before 1971. The tenderness of the early plays reflects his sensitivity and compassion; their aggression reflects his sense of personal as well as social injustice. In fact though, the motif of handicap recurs obsessively as a metaphor of a humanity denied and denying its own ideal nature, from his earliest experimental texts of the 1960s to his novels *Der Mondscheinknecht* (1981) and *Der Mondscheinknecht: Fortsetzung* (1983) whose central character is a polio victim, and the play *Der*

Nusser (1986), his adaptation of Ernst Toller's *Hinkemann*. 'I believe we are all handicapped', remarks Kroetz on the dustjacket of *Der Mondscheinknecht*.

Many critics saw the early plays as epitomising the 'Sprachlosigkeit', the 'speechlessness' or 'inarticulacy' of a linguistically, spiritually and materially deprived sub-proletariat, a critical oversimplification for which Kroetz was partly responsible (his foreword to *Heimarbeit* declares: 'The language of my characters does not work).[10] Kroetz's plays were linked with the rediscovered work of Ödön von Horváth under the banner of the 'neues Volksstück'.[11] Kroetz himself in fact first subtitled a play (*Das Nest*) a 'Volksstück' in 1974, when most directors and critics were already bored with what was for them a passing fashion; by 1980 Kroetz himself rejected the term as having outlived its political usefulness. However, in the early 1970s Kroetz was seen as continuing Horváth's demonstration of a whole class's linguistic dispossession. So closely did Kroetz's work seem to fit Basil Bernstein's then fashionable models of language competence—of a middle-class 'elaborated code' and a working-class 'restricted code'—that one analysis declared, unjustifiably, in view of Kroetz's ignorance of sociolinguistic theory, that he 'unmistakably bases his work on the current discussion about language barriers and class-specific language use'.[12]

Moreover, just as Bernstein's theories were criticised for unintentionally confirming the hierarchy of class by measuring working-class speech by middle-class norms and neglecting the former's creative and affective potential, so too Kroetz came to reject the label of 'speechlessness' both for the fatalism it implied and for the way it neglected the elements of humour, struggle and

---

10. 'Die Sprache funktioniert bei meinen Figuren nicht', *FXK* 64.
11. A near untranslatable term: 'folkplay' misleadingly suggests rustic amateur festivities, 'popular drama' begs numerous questions about the genre's reception. See e.g. Jürgen Hein, 'Formen des Volkstheaters im 19. und 20. Jahrhundert', in *Handbuch des deutschen Dramas*, ed. Walter Hinck, Düsseldorf 1980, pp. 489–505. On Kroetz as a *Volksstück* author see Michael Töteberg, 'Der Kleinbürger auf der Bühne. Die Entwicklung des Dramatikers Franz Xaver Kroetz und das realistische Volksstück', *Akzente* 2 (1976), 165-73. So long as Kroetz accepted the term *Volksstück* for his work, he defended it against the apparent paradox of *Volkstheater* (popular theatre) being played before the largely bourgeois audience of the West German public theatres by pointing to the mass television audience for his work, notably for *Oberösterreich*.
12. 'Dieser Autor geht unverkennbar aus von der gegenwärtigen Diskussion um Sprachbarrieren und Schichtenspezifischen Sprachgebrauch', Harald Burger and Peter von Matt, 'Dramatischer Dialog und restringiertes Sprechen. Franz Xaver Kroetz in linguistischer und literaturwissenschaftlicher Sicht', *Zeitschrift für germanistische Linguistik* 2 (1974), 270.

solidarity present even in the bleakest of his plays.[13]
But the early plays are in any case as much theatrical experiments
as social documents. In 1985 Kroetz argued that these plays had
begun as only one direction of formal exploration among many in
his writing of the late 1960s, before their success determined his
concentration in the 1970s on this kind of 'realistic play'.[14] The 'new
realist' *Wildwechsel* was written in 1968, the same year as *Oblomov*,
an ironic study of crippling self-awareness which, four years before
Strauss's *Hypochonder*, anticipated 'new subjectivity', and the same
year as *Hilfe, ich werde geheiratet (Help, I'm being married off)*, a
farce which lives up to the dire promise of its title, and these three
very different plays are sandwiched between formalistic experimental prose texts such as *Tiroler Elegien* (1967) and *Koreanischer
Frühling* (1969). Even among the plays which actually appeared in
the early 1970s—those which we see as archetypal Kroetzean neo-
realism—there is considerable formal variety, and the starkly reduced dialogue itself represents a radical formal innovation. Despite
parallels with the social realism of Edward Bond's *The Pope's
Wedding* and *Saved*, Kroetz's distillation of intensely dramatic
interactions out of apparently banal, naturalistic exchanges punc-
tuated by pauses is often closer to the early Harold Pinter, though
Kroetz's characters rarely demonstrate the manipulative control of
language employed by some figures in, say, *The Birthday Party*.[15]
Kroetz's language is certainly artificial: his transcribed interviews
with Bavarians which were published in *Chiemgauer Gschichten*
(1977) and might have confirmed the much-praised 'exactitude' of
his dramatic dialogue, share some syntactic features with the plays
but are noticeably different.[16] Kroetz's work is not 'exact' in the
sense of exact reproduction of reality; the 'exactitude' lies in his
dialogue's economy, its precise adherence to the central dramatic
purpose, and is thus a formal quality.

Michis Blut, stripped of all the reassuring trivia of naturalist
milieu or dialogue, carries 'speechlessness' to a formal extreme. For
Wunschkonzert Kroetz makes the naturalist demand that 'real time

13. See e.g. *FXK* 117.
14. 'Ich habe immer nur von mir geschrieben', *Theater 1985*, Velber 1985, p. 76.
15. See Moray McGowan, 'Sprache, Gewalt und Gesellschaft: Franz Xaver
Kroetz und die sozialrealistischen Dramatiker des englischen Theaters', *text + kritik*
57 (1978), 37–48.
16. See Anne Betten, *Sprachrealismus im deutschen Drama der siebziger Jahre*,
Heidelberg 1985, e.g. p. 253; Ernest W. B. Hess-Lüttich, 'Neorealismus und sprach-
liche Wirklichkeit. Zur Kommunikationskritik bei Franz Xaver Kroetz', *FXK*
297–302.

and stage time should be the same'.[17] But the unrelenting intensity of this famous one-person play completely devoid of dialogue creates an alienation effect like that of photo-realist paintings (Kroetz explicitly admires environment artists such as Kienholz, *FH* 126, 256). *Dolomitenstadt Lienz* also employs a naturalist *Sekundenstil*; but it is broken up in Brechtian manner by 'Songs'. The prisoners' dreams of flying, a motif echoed in *Sterntaler* (1974) and in *Mensch Meier* (1977) and notably in Kroetz's comments on the staging of *Furcht und Hoffnung der BRD* (1984)—'I often have the feeling that all my characters are standing at the window and want to fly away'[18]—indicate that incarceration is not only a social reality or a restatement of autobiographical experience (Kroetz was once briefly imprisoned in Lienz on a drunken driving offence) but is also, like handicap, a metaphor for repressed human potential. Many conscientiously social realist productions reduce Kroetz's work by underplaying the transcendental longings behind the characters' halting fantasies, their dreams, even the ache of their silences. In a different way the bizarre black comic shootout that ends the original version of *Männersache* anticipates the Kroetz of *Nicht Fisch, nicht Fleisch* onwards in departing from imitative naturalism to express the essential dynamic of a relationship or psychological state.

Kroetz has always been a man of the theatre—actor and director as well as writer—for whom the documents of despair, such as the knitting needle abortion scene in *Heimarbeit*, are also powerful stage images. This point is reinforced by the return of *Bauern sterben* (1985) to the drastic stage imagery of the early plays. Though anchored in the social context of a decaying, economically marginal peasantry, it concentrates human experience into its own metaphorical transcendence. In one scene, while mother and daughter lay out grandmother's corpse, daughter has a miscarriage and lays the stillborn foetus in the worm-eaten stomach of the dead grandmother: an image of life as bleak circularity (a visual echo of the 'Born astride a grave' speech in *Waiting for Godot*) that leaves naturalism behind.

The early plays are thus not—or not just—social reportage. They are restatements of lived subjective experience; they are metaphors

---

17. 'Reale Zeit sei gleich Bühnenzeit', *GS* 187.
18. 'Ich habe oft das Gefühl, alle Figuren stehen am Fenster und wollen wegfliegen', *FH* 8.

for the human condition, both social *and* existential; and they are radical theatrical experiments.

Subjectivity plays a central role in Kroetz's work in another sense: his plays explore the relationship between the human being as object of social forces and the human being as conscious subject struggling for self-determination, and in so doing trace a process from object to subject.

Kroetz's work is a debate with itself, in which he continually reshapes certain essential dramatic constellations as his own political and aesthetic views and intentions develop. The characters of many of his plays are unfree objects, pinballs in a pin-table of social forces. Their attempts to fulfil wishes which their social situation simply does not permit only confirm the social processes which have blocked their way out of object existence. The aggressions that the society generates in them are not turned back on the society, but directed inwards, at members of their family, at the unborn child in the womb, at themselves. Thus in *Heimarbeit* Willi murders his wife Martha's child by another man (after her own abortion attempt fails), when the real root of his frustration is his own social rejection. Hanni in *Wildwechsel* shoots her father, loses her unwanted child and sinks back into a cow-like indifference. 'Like animals these people project their desperate situations in their silent behaviour', as Kroetz puts it.[19]

Kroetz's early plays are *not* unremittingly negative. In *Stallerhof*, for example, Sepp and Beppi attempt, despite their disadvantages and despite the taboos on their relationship, to realise their needs for tenderness. Sepp's abuse of Beppi is a helpless, misdirected step, perhaps, but at least a step *undertaken*, out of the apathy characteristic of the early plays. The Stallerin's decision not to abort Beppi's child may too be seen as an assertion of her humanity against the pressure of social norms.

However, the process of self-discovery and self-assertion of the subject really begins with *Oberösterreich* (1972). The mainstream of Kroetz's work in this second phase from *Oberösterreich* to *Nicht Fisch, nicht Fleisch* addresses the pressures and contradictions of West German—capitalist—society as manifested in the nuclear family: the married couple, with or without children. These people—van and lorry drivers, factory workers, skilled, highly paid typesetters—are, as C. D. Innes puts it, 'integrated in the super-

---

19. 'Wie Tiere projizieren diese Menschen ihre Notsituationen in ihrer Haltung im Stummsein', *GS* 185.

market society of a modern economy'.[20] From the deprivation of *Heimarbeit* it is a long way to, say, *Der stramme Max*, where Anna and Max send their daughter Sabine to an expensive boarding school to compensate for her working-class origins. From play to play the characters become increasingly aware of, and able to articulate, the problems they face. Both their language and their horizons open out. But their economic, social and linguistic growth (compared to the early plays) is accompanied by what Kroetz calls *Verkleinbürgerlichung*, the largely unquestioning adoption of petit-bourgeois and middle-class attitudes and aspirations by working-class people.[21] Anna and Max's ambitions for Sabine are symptomatic, as is Otto's refusal in *Mensch Meier* to let his son Ludwig become a worker like himself. These attitudes, like the linguistic deprivation of the earlier plays, prevent the characters from knowing themselves and their true interests. But the closed circle of plays like *Heimarbeit* is not repeated. Typically, in the plays of the second phase, the later 1970s, the male protagonists experience a socially grounded threat to their petit-bourgeois existence—unemployment, or the economic consequences of a pregnancy, for example—a threat which disorientates them sufficiently for them to recognise their lack of individual identity. This alienation permeates their whole existence, from the workplace into the marriage bed, as Heinz explicitly remarks in *Oberösterreich* (*GS* 400). The motifs of manifest handicap used in the early plays to portray alienation have gone; but Kroetz now observes more subtle deformations of the thinking and behaviour even of capitalist society's average and apparently well-integrated members.

Up to this point, Kroetz may seem to share the pessimism of other contemporary authors like Botho Strauss or Thomas Bernhard, who also portray the human subject as an object of larger determining forces.[22] However, the Kroetz of the later 1970s remained a humanist, concerned with 'a return to human values'.[23] And, as he says on the dust cover of *Der Mondscheinknecht*, 'You have to stand up for yourself, if you want to be a human being'. This contrasts markedly with Strauss, for example, whose *Rumor*

20. *Modern German Drama*, Cambridge 1979, p. 232.
21. 'Ich kann nur schreiben von dem, was ich sehe', Interview with Donna Hoffmeister, *Modern Language Studies* 11.1 (1980/81), 45.
22. Cf. Dieter Kafitz, 'Die Problematisierung des individualistischen Menschenbildes im deutschsprachigen Drama der Gegenwart', *Basis* 10 (1980), 93–126.
23. 'Das Zurückfinden zu menschlichen Werten': Kroetz, 'Der lebende Mensch ist der Mittelpunkt', in *Als Schriftsteller leben*, ed. H. L. Arnold, Reinbek 1979, p. 39.

(1980) challenges the humanist faith in the human being as an active subject, seeing it as long disproved by science and by the universe's indifference. Kroetz's characters, in contrast, initially degraded into objects, struggle to become self-determining subjects, and precisely this struggle establishes their identity as human beings.[24]

These plays of the second phase of Kroetz's work can therefore be seen as a sequence of steps towards awareness of self and social reality. Kroetz portrays the impact of manifestly political phenomena, rationalisation, industrial safety, real or threatened unemployment, on fundamentally apolitical individuals. They take at most small, but real, steps away from apolitical consciousness towards a modest awareness, founded on experience and not on theory, of their political and social reality.

This can be observed most clearly in *Das Nest*. The modestly affluent *Kleinbürger* Kurt and Martha inhabit a deceptive idyll, shattered when Kurt, to meet the consumption targets on the fulfilment of which his breadwinner identity depends, accepts a special assignment to dump poisonous chemicals and in doing so almost kills his own son. This unleashes an identity crisis in Kurt, deepened by Martha's accusation that he is just a 'dressierter Aff', a 'trained monkey' (*WA* 241). Kurt realises how much he and Martha have been unthinking objects of social forces. He reports himself to the police and confronts his boss, who scorns him as a 'Würstl', a little worm (*WA* 249). The once self-satisfied, deferential Kurt now knows this to be true in capitalist society, but precisely at this point when his boss's affable mask drops, because he has challenged him, Kurt becomes less of a 'Würstl', because he is asserting himself. The human being degraded to an object is thus here given the possibility of regaining the capacity for action and so of becoming a self-determining subject.

The socio-economic analysis has a Marxist basis: both Kurt, who fails to see the connection between his 63-hour-weeks and his boss's new 60,000 Mark car (*WA* 231), and Martha, who is exploited as a *Heimarbeiterin*, create surplus value for the owners of the means of production. Modern consumer capitalism creates inherently destructive contradictions: even those who like Kurt identify with its values cannot fulfil the expectations it awakes without dehumanising and endangering themselves or their families.

24. See Moray McGowan, 'Botho Strauss and Franz Xaver Kroetz: two contemporary views of the subject', *Strathclyde Modern Language Studies* 5 (1985), 59–75.

But beside *Das Nest's* modest plea for social solidarity in its suggestion that with trade union support Kurt will be stronger in his fight (*WA* 251), it also reaffirms the role of *individual* moral fortitude. The characters remain products of social circumstances as in Kroetz's other plays: Kurt and Martha's 'nonage', in Kant's terms, is thus not wholly 'self-inflicted'. But their progress towards enlightenment is very *much* a matter of individual integrity: now that they have recognised how their actions can influence circumstances it is their responsibility not to be the victims of circumstances. This may seem a surprising verdict from a playwright who was a communist at the time; here as elsewhere Kroetz's critique of capitalism combines with a christian-humanist concern for the individual and her or his moral integrity. More than once in Kroetz's work, his professed political position seems to conflict with underlying conservative attitudes.

The optimism of *Das Nest* is virtually unique in Kroetz's work; his later plays do not share its exemplary, morality play character. Kroetz's humanism gains dialectic subtlety: he now shows that the step out of object existence not only brings the awakening of consciousness and the beginning of self-determination, but also lays bare the painful conflicts between individual and social existence, conflicts which the progress from object to subject may intensify rather than resolve.

In *Mensch Meier*, for example, Otto's dissatisfaction with his identity, or lack of it, as a worker, is expressed in success fantasies (in which the Kroetzean hero's archetypal freedom dream of flying is perverted by Otto's internalisation of hierarchical social values into a dream of *owning* a model plane factory) and in his refusal to let his son Ludwig take a manual job like himself. Instead, the unemployed Ludwig becomes the target for the aggressions Otto accumulates at work.

This eventually destroys the family. Otto's wife Martha leaves, echoing exactly Martha's words to Willi in *Heimarbeit*.[25] But whereas Willi's wife returns, thus restoring, fundamentally unchanged, the fateful order of things, Martha Meier builds her own separate existence. Like Ludwig, who also leaves and becomes a bricklayer, Martha grows by asserting herself. By accepting her identity she is able to change it and, within her modest possibilities, begin to determine her own future.

25. 'Ich geh weg von dir, Otto, weil ich dich verlass', *MM* 48. Cf. *GS* 59.

Otto, in contrast, remains trapped in brooding fantasies, convinced that his real self is straitjacketed by his socio-economic status, yet unable to act to free it (*MM* 58). Life without the prospect of escape from a working-class identity he rejects seems senseless: 'Before you even begin, it's all over'.[26] This too echoes the 'Born astride a grave' speech in *Waiting for Godot*, but Otto draws this conclusion from the alienation of his specific material existence as an assembly-line worker, the sensation of being little more than a human robot (e.g. *MM* 45–6, 53). In the plays of the later 1970s, the crises that Kroetz's characters experience continue to have social causes.

By the late 1970s Kroetz himself was reaching a crisis. Behind the façade of party loyalty was increasing frustration with the DKP, behind his status as a world dramatist he agreed with those of his critics who said he was repeating himself: 'I find myself again and again producing kitchen-sink realism'. [27] After *Der stramme Max* (written in 1978), came a two-year gap, followed by Kroetz's resignation from the DKP, his next play *Nicht Fisch, nicht Fleisch* (1980; premièred in 1981) and his first published novel *Der Mondscheinknecht* (1981), which together marked the end of the second phase in Kroetz's work and the beginning of a third.

Nicht Fisch, nicht Fleisch is a play of ideas: it addresses the benefits, and the threat, of technological progress. But the social conflicts and contradictions of this issue are, as always in Kroetz's work, registered as they manifest themselves in individuals. At the time of writing the play, Kroetz was in the process of coming to terms with his own subjectivity (see especially 'Kirchberger Notizen'). In the sensitive brooding individualist Edgar and the rational trade union activist Hermann, two halves of Kroetz's own personality confront one another: the creative artist and the party worker.

Edgar and Hermann are articulate and well-paid typesetters. But when their firm introduces computer typesetting the craftsmen have to retrain as machine operators: technical progress robs them of their profession and so of their identity. This awakes in Edgar grim visions of a totally rationalised future in which the individual has no place (e.g. *NF* 43–4). Edgar responds with romantic, atavistic dreams of the wilderness, where man daily reasserts his identity in the struggle for existence. And should he die, he says, then let

26. 'Bevor man anfangt, is alles aus', *MM* 45.
27. 'Ich lande immer wieder beim Wohnküchen-Gasherd-Realismus', 'Die Erotik ist zerbrochen', Interview with Carna Zacharias, *Abendzeitung*, 22/23 Dec. 1979.

hyenas eat his corpse and carry it 'in their belly to the four winds'.[28] Instead of asserting himself by resisting the material causes of his loss of identity he dreams of Nirvana, of being dissolved and at the same time preserved in universal nature.

In contrast, Hermann's tenacious optimism is founded on the experience of struggle in the real world against real people. Hermann approves of progress in principle, fighting it only when it manifests itself as rationalisation in the exclusive interests of capital. He scorns Edgar's individualism and declares him a traitor to his colleagues and his class.

Nicht Fisch, nicht Fleisch marks the beginning of a new period of formal experimentation confirmed by the plays that have followed. By creating two complementary married couples as central figures Kroetz significantly widens his scope while retaining the strengths of the dramatic constellation that he has made his trademark. The play is Kroetz's most serious attempt to make drama out of the clash of ideas as well as the subtextual tensions of unarticulated desires and frustrations. The no man's land scene (*NF* 75–8), in which Edgar and Hermann, grotesquely distorted, wander a desolate, flooded stage, gives notice of a move away from 'kitchen-sink-realism' without subverting it completely, a move still more pronounced in the variety of form, physical and sociological setting of the fifteen fragmentary scenes of *Furcht und Hoffnung der BRD*, or in the Expressionist *Stationendrama* form of *Bauern sterben*. In 1982 Kroetz commented favourably on a revival of *Michis Blut*, typical of the 'extreme' early work he rejected in his middle phase. In 1985, invited to direct a revival of one of his earlier plays in Stuttgart, Kroetz's choice was *Agnes Bernauer*, one of his least 'socially realist' plays of the 1970s.[29] Ten years after the proud denial of the role of 'invention' in his writing, Kroetz, in an interview with Ulrike Prokop before the 1982 Frankfurt production of *Nicht Fisch, nicht Fleisch*, remarked: 'fantasy is much more real than life'.[30]

Again and again, in *Furcht und Hoffnung der BRD*, familiar Kroetzean scenes (the couple in the opening scene are even called

---

28. 'In ihrem Bauch in allen Himmelsrichtungen', *NF* 50.
29. Cf.: 'Ich habe immer nur von mir geschrieben', p. 80; in 1987 Kroetz directed productions both of Felix Mitterer's *Stigma*, steeped in the South German *Volksstück* tradition, and of Kafka's *Beschreibung eines Kampfes*.
30. 'Die Phantasie ist viel wirklicher wie das Leben', 'Ich meine, wenn, dann phantastischer Realismus', Interview with Ulrike Prokop, *Programmheft des Frankfurter Schauspiels zu 'Nicht Fisch, nicht Fleisch'*, Frankfurt am Main 1982, p. 10.

Willy and Martha) grounded in the material reality of ordinary West German working-class experience, are transformed into surreal, comic or disturbing stage images as Kroetz explores the dramatic potential of thinking them through to their extreme conclusion. A man bleeding psychologically from the unseen stigmata of his long-term unemployment in a society that defines a man's identity by his work, tries to crucify himself (*FH* 82–7). In a scene that Kroetz eventually rejected, Willy, forced by unemployment into a house-husband role which his sense of male identity cannot accept, dons housewife clothes and a female identity, carries household tasks to absurd extremes, simulates intercourse with a cylindrical Vim-packet, fantasises his impregnation first by a homecoming sailor and then by Christ on the cross (*FH* 165–7).

In his phase of party membership from 1972–80, Kroetz, the political radical, constrained perhaps by his initial eagerness to please and by the aesthetic conservatism of orthodox social realism, was actually writing the most formally conventional of his plays. Since 1980 the formal radicalism of his early work has re-emerged, but linked now to the understanding of social mechanisms provided by his study of Marxism and to the ability to portray them economically and with little trace of didacticism, a skill acquired through the *Kleinbürger* plays of the second phase. *Furcht und Hoffnung der BRD* is an aggressive, expressionistically energised cabaret of scenes, but scenes whose formal adventurousness relative to Kroetz's work of the later 1970s never obscures their attempt to address central social and political issues of the early 1980s, above all that of unemployment.

This later Kroetz has left naturalism far behind. In fact, there are many parallels with the Expressionists. Even the young Kroetz exhibited the artistic youth's revolt against parental pressure to conform, familiar from the biography of many Expressionists like Reinhard Sorge, and, in his early DKP phase, the longing to identify with and be subsumed into the masses. Kroetz's anger against society has an expressionist intensity. Hermann Bahr defined Expressionism as 'the soul's struggle with the machine ... Man is crying out for his soul, the whole period becomes a single urgent cry. And Art cries too, into the deep darkness, crying for help, crying for the spirit. That is Expressionism'.[31] Plays such as *Staller-hof* or *Michis Blut* have the intensity of this urgent cry. In all

31. Quoted in John Willett, *Expressionism*, London 1970, p. 100.

Kroetz's work humanity cries out against its dehumanisation; 'the soul's struggle with the machine' becomes explicit in the Huxleyan fantasies of Otto in *Mensch Meier*, Max in *Der stramme Max* and especially Edgar in *Nicht Fisch, nicht Fleisch*. In 1982, in a note on a variant of the latter in which Emmi ends the play pregnant, Kroetz remarks that she has 'the whole of future humanity in her belly', like the archetypal Expressionist woman-figure pregnant with 'the New Man'.[32]

Kroetz is not simply a latter-day Expressionist. Changed historical conditions and his grasp of Marxist dialectics militate against that. But expressionist forms seem to offer a possible way out of one-dimensional naturalism. Moreover, since he formally broke with the DKP and its faith in progress in 1980, another aspect of his complex make-up has become much more apparent, one which he shares with many Expressionists: the conservative rejection of modernity that is potentially part of 'the soul's struggle with the machine'. Edgar's stance in *Nicht Fisch, nicht Fleisch* echoes the revolt against technology which contributed in the 1970s to the growth of the land commune movement and the Green Party, and to the popularity of Eastern religions. The conservative tendency that forms one facet of these movements' critique of modern civilisation underlies much of Kroetz's work, as he himself has admitted (*FXK* 185–6).[33] It emerges in *Bauern sterben* as a daemonisation of urban society: 'The city is the butcher'.[34]

In the interview with Ulrike Prokop cited above Kroetz revokes *Das Nest*'s support for trade unions, attacking them now for their acceptance of untrammelled technological progress: 'It has long been the case that those things in this world which give me pleasure are more threatened than protected by technology and progress.' He further argues that 'breaking with tradition always leads to a loss of life quality',[35] reflected in *Nicht Fisch, nicht Fleisch*'s greater sympathy for the fecund, motherly Helga than the childless career-ist Emmi, and in *Bauern sterben*'s requiem for lost 'Heimat': 'Without soil, you die'.[36]

In another respect *Nicht Fisch, nicht Fleisch* points forward, in the

32. 'hat die ganze zukünftige Menschheit im Bauch', *FH* 260.
33. Cf. also Michael Töteberg, 'Ein konservativer Autor', *FXK* 284–96.
34. 'Die Stadt ist der Metzger', *BS* 91.
35. 'Es ist längst so, dass die Technik und der Fortschritt die Dinge, die mir auf dieser Welt noch Spass machen, mehr bedrohen als schützen . . . Bruch mit der Tradition führt auch immer zum Lebensverlust', Interview with Ulrike Prokop, p. 4.
36. 'Ohne Boden stirbt man', *BS* 104.

unresolved conflict between Edgar's pessimism and Hermann's optimism, to *Der Nusser*, Kroetz's last play to date. In the interview with Ulrike Prokop quoted above Kroetz indicates his interest as a dramatist in 'the seeking out of real conflicts that cannot be resolved with good intentions, leader articles and negotiations'.[37] Ernst Toller wrote of *Hinkemann* that no social system can eradicate every human pain: 'there's always a remainder. But *social* suffering is senseless, unnecessary, can be eliminated.'[38] Kroetz's *Hinkemann*-adaptation *Der Nusser* (whose German everyman protagonist has parallels in Kroetz's *Kleinbürger* plays but whose handicap motif brings Kroetz full circle to his very earliest extant work) focuses on this awareness of the tragic contradictions of life, but linked with the refusal to be blind to the social and therefore changeable causes of human suffering where they do exist: the expectation never to win but the determination to fight. This is Kroetz's position in his third phase.

If Kroetz's demands in the early 1970s for a social realism that championed the underdog were, as he has suggested, primarily motivated by the parallels to his own material reality, if, as he suggested in 1985, 'I've never been interested in "the people" . . . all my life I've only written about myself',[39] it was inevitable that material success would change his political and aesthetic priorities.[40] Alternatively, one could argue that the thirty-odd plays of the 1970s were a necessary step towards the multi-dimensional and differentiated view of the contradictions of life, both mutable and immutable, and their literary reflection which his work in the 1980s has begun to demonstrate. Certainly, the social realist studies of the West German *Kleinbürger* with which the name Franz Xaver Kroetz has become so closely associated may come to be seen as an interlude. Or perhaps they should be seen, certainly, as an expression of social commitment, but also as one direction of artistic experiment among many, and one not entirely free of opportunism, in the wider context of the theatrical work of an aggressively subjective, contradictory, experimental, radical playwright.

---

37. 'Das Aufspüren tatsächlicher, nicht mit gutem Willen, Leitartikeln und Tarifverhandlungen auflösbarer Konflikte', Interview with Ulrike Prokop, p. 7.
38. 'Immer bleibt ein Rest. Aber soziales Leid ist sinnlos, nicht notwendig, ist tilgbar', Toller, *Eine Jugend in Deutschland*, Reinbek 1963, p. 161.
39. 'Mich hat niemals das Volk interessiert . . . Ich habe mein Leben lang nur von mir geschrieben': Kroetz, 'Ich habe immer nur von mir geschrieben', p. 78.
40. One might see this confirmed by the male chauvinist posturings and comparisons of his genius with that of Goethe that Kroetz, possibly but not necessarily in self-mockery, displayed in an interview in the German *Playboy* 9 (1986), pp. 35–47.

7

The Child Grows up—Towards a History of The Grips Theater

Horst Claus

THE year 1987 saw the coming of age of the West Berlin Grips Theater, a company which has brought about one of the most radical changes in twentieth-century German theatre—the uncompromising break with the escapist fairy-tale Christmas plays, the *Weihnachtsmärchen*. In this process the *Jugendstück* developed, a genre written predominantly for young people between the ages of thirteen and eighteen which more than any other dramatic form in West German theatre addresses issues of immediate concern to its audiences. Rarely lacking popular appeal, the company celebrated its transition into adulthood with *Linie 1*[1] which has been hailed as the beginning of the new German musical. For Grips this seems to indicate a turn in yet another direction, but in many ways *Linie 1* also represents a summary of the company's work to date. Together with *Stokkerlok und Millipilli*[2] (the title refers to the names of the play's main characters) which Volker Ludwig, the theatre's founder, manager and main author, regards as the starting point of Grips, it is an ideal point of reference for an assessment of Grips' achievements.

Grips plays are the result of unique working practices and conditions which evolved over a period of seven to eight years and are determined by:

(1) The continuous presence and artistic development of a nucleus of key personnel who are fully aware of the restrictions their environment imposes on theatre activities designed to raise social awareness.

1. Berlin 1986. Here and elsewhere, where the place of publication of Grips plays is given as Berlin this refers to the edition sold at the theatre at the time of the play's run.
2. *Theater Heute* 4 (1970), pp. 37–44.

(2) The interaction of these people with a number of creative talents—particularly young actors—staying for shorter periods (but long enough to ensure the continuity of a specific Grips style which, with their help, remains in a state of constant development).

(3) The active response of these two groups to the social, political and economic issues of the day from a clearly defined ideological position.

(4) The concerned interest in and reaction to the needs and responses of the company's audiences.

(5) The advantages and disadvantages of working outside the state theatre system in the independent sector with a minimum of subsidies.

Though *Stokkerlok und Millipilli* stands at the beginning of the history of Grips, it did not come about overnight. It is the product of its authors' long years of experience in political cabaret, their experiments with plays based on fairy-tales, their critical reaction to existing plays for children, and their close identification with the aims and objectives of the anti-authoritarian student movement of the late 1960s. The roots of both play and company reach back to October 1965 when Volker Ludwig founded the West Berlin Reichskabarett, a political cabaret which through its name and the title of its first programme, *Kein schöner Land*, an ironic reference to a nostalgic folk-song contemplating sentimentally the beauties of Germany, expressed its rejection of restoration tendencies in West Germany. By the time the grand coalition marked the disappearance of parliamentary opposition in Bonn, the Reichskabarett company had responded to these developments by abandoning the common practice of West German cabaret of just criticising the symptoms of individual problems. Instead they concentrated on criticising the system. This shift forced them to replace the traditional format of a cabaret programme consisting of independent numbers with a more structured sequence of songs and sketches dominated by an overall theme. The 1968 programme *Der Guerilla läßt grüßen*—against global corruption and US involvement in Latin America—contained both plot and characters. By this time the Reichskabarett had established itself as the mouthpiece of the student movement, and had become so successful that actors and authors concluded that they were preaching to the converted. In their 1969 programme *Alles hat seine Grenzen* they recommended starting the revolution at home, organising rent-strikes, and developing solidarity (especially against those at the top).[3]

Audiences with open minds, still able and prepared to learn, were readily available in the Reichskabarett's own theatre, if not in the evening then during the day. For as early as 1966, Volker Ludwig had initiated a 'Theater für Kinder' which used the facilities of the Reichskabarett during the day. Under the imaginative guidance of a former member of the Reichskabarett, the children's theatre group developed fairy-tale-related plays which aimed to take a more critical stance than traditional plays for children, and to incorporate experiences relevant to the social environment of the audiences. Apart from contributing a fairy-tale musical, Ludwig was only marginally involved in this work. His real commitment to children's theatre did not come about until 1969 when the people mainly responsible for the children's plays left. Serious disagreement over the suitability for children of a parody on American Westerns had caused the split, and Ludwig, for the first time, articulated one of the key demands of Grips: that children's theatre has to avoid catering for the taste of adults and instead has to concentrate on what children like and enjoy. Since the gap left by the children's theatre group had to be filled, Ludwig and his brother Rainer Hachfeld wrote *Stokkerlok und Millipilli* within a period of only four weeks. It subsequently won two prizes, and more than sixty theatres in Germany and abroad added it to their repertory (making *Stokkerlok und Millipilli* the most widely produced Grips play).

The three main reasons for the play's popularity were its anti-authoritarian stance, which reflected the dominant mood of the time, its links with traditional fairy-tale plays, and a sudden interest in children's theatre which came from almost diametrically opposed sections of the community. On the one hand there were the subsidised state theatres. These had experienced a continuous decline in young audience numbers since 1965—reason enough for their managers to identify children as a special target group. On the other hand there were the socially committed or politically motivated groups who regarded children's plays as a means to educate young people and who introduced them to ideas and fostered their creative and communal spirit through entertainment. Their contributions to

---

3. For more detailed information on the Reichskabarett see Heinz Greul, *Bretter, die die Zeit bedeuten*, vol. II, Munich 1971, pp. 494–9; also Georg Zivier, Hellmut Kotschenreuther and Volker Ludwig, *Kabarett mit K—Fünfzig Jahre große Kleinkunst*, Berlin 1974, pp. 95–105.

preparing the ground for the new kind of children's theatre represented by Grips were considerable. The unique inter-relationship between the changes within the Reichskabarett and the parameters of the period was a precondition for the emergence of Grips as the movement's most prolific and influential exponent. *Stokkerlok und Millipilli* in particular is a referent for a decisive phase of development. It represents a watershed between the *Weihnachtsmärchen* tradition of children's plays and what came to be known as emancipatory children's theatre.

Until the late 1960s children's theatre in Germany was virtually identical with the *Weihnachtsmärchen*. Based on fairy-tales or using fairy-tale elements within a fantasy world, these plays were initiated in the middle of the nineteenth century to boost audience numbers during the notoriously slack pre-Christmas period. The bourgeoisie soon adopted the *Weihnachtsmärchen* as an indispensable ingredient of the Christmas ritual, like Father Christmas or the Christmas tree. Once a year grandmothers would take the children to the theatre in order to give their stressed, middle-class parents a break during the hectic weeks of Christmas preparations. With the carrot of Christmas gifts dangling on the horizon the glittering spectacle also served as a timely reminder to children of what their social environment expected of them in terms of decorum and proper behaviour.

The *Weihnachtsmärchen*, with their fairy-tale and allegorical characters who frequently communicate in an artificial, supposedly child-like language, are a prime example of the way the bourgeoisie excluded social realities from their nurseries in order to protect their children's innocence. Within a strict hierarchical order and clearly defined parameters of 'good' and 'evil' the plays offer easy answers to problems which in the real world are insoluble. The *Weihnachtsmärchen* is an adult's fantasy of how a child's imagination should work. As such it offers adults an escape route as well as a means to suppress children's real interests and to make them conform to established standards.[4] *Peterchens Mondfahrt*[5] by Gerdt Bernhard von Bassewitz-Hohenluckow (first performed in December 1912), up to the late sixties probably the best known and most widely produced *Weihnachtsmärchen*, exemplifies the aims, objec-

4. For a detailed analysis of the origins and ideological practices of the *Weihnachtsmärchen* see Melchior Schedler, *Kindertheater—Geschichte, Modelle, Projekte*, Frankfurt 1974, pp. 43–126.
5. Leipzig 1912.

tives, and practices of the genre. Far from simply offering pre-Christmas diversions for children, it conveys clear ideological messages.

The very title is revealing. The addition of the diminutive syllable -*chen* to the name of the child protagonist signifies the patronising attitude to children, the omission from the title of Peterchen's sister Anneliese who participates in all the action points towards a world dominated by male values. The third main character is not human at all, but an anthropomorphic June bug by the name of Sumsemann whose violin playing enables Peterchen and Anneliese to fly. The action is motivated by the quest to recover Sumsemann's missing sixth leg from the Moon Man. That this can only be achieved through the help of powerful allies demonstrates the children's dependence on adults and provides the author with a reason to send his three principals to various locations. At the Star Meadow they learn that each child has a star which darkens when the child misbehaves, and the Star Girls who are responsible for keeping them clean complain bitterly about inconsiderate children whose behaviour never allows them to have a rest. Pre-First World War militarism and sabre-rattling accompanies the Queen of the Night's coffee party when it is predicted that Peterchen will become an Artillery General because he successfully passed a test of courage involving thunder and lightning. When they reach the Christmas Meadow the children kneel at the cot of baby Jesus to comply with their religious obligations. Afterwards Father Christmas, completely ignoring the reality of industrial production,[6] shows them how toys grow on flower beds and vegetable patches. Finally, they are transported with the help of a big silver cannon to the top of Moon Mountain for their encounter with the Moon Man. More than anything in the play, this figure sums up the ideological position of *Peterchens Mondfahrt*. The description of the Moon Man as being a 'black, wild-looking giant', besides containing racist stereotyping, matches the archetypal bogeyman used by generations of adults to frighten children into submission. The Moon Man has been condemned to live on top of the dark inhospitable Moon Mountain because he once illegally cut down a birch (ripping off Sumsemann's leg which is still hanging on the tree). (In his discussion of *Peterchens Mondfahrt* Melchior Schedler highlights the disproportion between offence and punishment, with the sarcastic

6. Schedler, *Kindertheater*, p. 120.

aside that the crime must have been deeply upsetting to the play's author von Bassewitz who was a member of the landed gentry.[7]) The Moon Man is also the personification of the child's enemy *per se*. By directing all antagonism against this stock character it is easy to exclude even the slightest reference to the complexities of the repressive forces which operate within society. The effect of the Moon Man on Peterchen and Anneliese is so strong that they are glad when, at the end of the play, they return to the domain of their mother and discover that everything was just a dream. The message of *Peterchens Mondfahrt* is clearly that children should not leave the secure environment of the nursery where they learn to obey their elders and are protected from the outside world.

Deliberate opposition to this kind of ideology and attitude towards children had spawned the Reichskabarett's 'Theater für Kinder'. With *Stokkerlok und Millipilli* it launched a full-scale attack on the genre's bourgeois authoritarian stance by displaying a healthy scepticism towards the world of the grown-ups. Like *Peterchens Mondfahrt*, the play centres on a quest, in this case for the missing parts of a steam engine called Lokolieschen. These have been hidden by the engine's owner Kratzwurst because its driver Stokkerlok had allowed children to travel on it free of charge. The search necessitates visits to a variety of places in which the idiosyncrasies of the inhabitants have to be tackled. Both the setting and the dramaturgical device of self-contained, loosely connected scenes and one-dimensional characters place *Stokkerlok und Millipilli* firmly in the tradition of the *Weihnachtsmärchen*. They certainly made it easier for the older generation to digest its radical content; for Millipilli, the play's child protagonist, has abandoned the rhymed couplets of *Peterchens Mondfahrt*, and in her own, contemporary language asserts her independence from the adults. She takes the initiative to reassemble Lokolieschen and shows the adult engine driver Stokkerlok how to stand up to Kratzwurst and overcome obstacles. Her self-confidence anticipates one of the aims of the women's movement and relegates all the play's male characters to second place. When she meets the nephews of a general who, as future soldiers, are proud to act only on orders given to them, Millipilli rejects the male values of *Peterchens Mondfahrt* by telling the boys: 'Then you'll never become real men.'[8] Obedience for obedience's sake is

---

7. Ibid., p. 121.
8. 'Da werdet ihr ja nie richtige Männer!' *Theater Heute* 4 (1970), p. 42.

not acceptable. Rules and regulations are there to be questioned. Early in the play Millipilli establishes the authors' position by painting a sign 'It is forbidden to forbid'.[9] The authors' aim is clearly the emancipation of children by encouraging them to think independently. The first two places which Stokkerlok and Millipilli visit encapsulate the central issues of the early Grips plays which subsequently run through the entire work of the company: the importance of asking questions and the need to challenge established hierarchies. First they encounter a teacher who, frustrated by his pupils' inability to retain the facts which he tries to drum into them, has invented a machine which causes children to answer his questions like robots. Stokkerlok and Millipilli persuade him that a machine asking questions would be of much better use for learning. Next they meet an extremely fat man, barely able to move, who bosses a woman and two boys around and forces them to feed him constantly. His reasoning: 'I am the father of Wurstmax and Sülzkopp, and I am Torte's husband. That's why I can do what I like with them.'[10] Millipilli demonstrates the stupidity of such unquestioned paternal authority. In the next two scenes the notion of universal adult knowledge and the wisdom of strict obedience within a military context are challenged. The last stop is of particular interest to children: Stokkerlok and Millipilli convince two cleaning fanatics of the pleasures gained from being dirty. After thwarting one final attempt by Kratzwurst to prevent the completion of the engine, they take everybody on board and, singing songs from the show, drive several laps of honour. Unlike Peterchen and Anneliese, Stokkerlok and Millipilli do not have to be returned from a fantasy environment to a supposedly 'real' world, since the situations with which they have been confronted are real and of a kind to which a child can relate his own experiences. While young audiences took to *Stokkerlok und Millipilli* with enthusiasm, it was attacked from both sides of the political spectrum. Conservative critics discovered 'political and ideological filth' in the play[11], those advocating a faster and more radical departure from the

9. 'Es ist verboten, zu verbieten!' Ibid., p. 38.
10. 'He, ich bin doch der Vater von Wurstmax und Sülzkopp und der Mann von Torte, da kann ich doch mit denen machen, was ich will!' Ibid., p 39.
11. 'politisch-ideologischen Unrat', Wolfgang Kolneder, Volker Ludwig and Klaus Wagenbach, *Das Grips Theater—Geschichte und Geschichten, Erfahrungen und Gespräche aus einem Kinder- und Jugendtheater*, Berlin 1979, p. 12. This book is the most comprehensive collection of essays on Grips. It also contains an extensive bibliography.

Weihnachtsmärchen accused it of 'Kindertümelei'[12] (creating a world for children in a childish way). Both opinions can be explained by the fact that the play marks a point of change. The next play gives up the fairy-tale tradition altogether. *Maximilian Pfeiferling* (1969)[13] is set in a child's everyday environment, presents parents who make mistakes, and adds a further key-theme to the catalogue of Grips-subjects: the call for and necessity of solidarity. The early plays all emphasise the anti-authoritarian stance. They show arguments and conflicts of interests within the average family, restrictions imposed by adults through bans against the freedom to play (and the noise associated with it), the need for unity in order to achieve common objectives. The plays which evolved in the course of time are increasingly realistic and dialectically sophisticated. Starting with *Trummi kaputt* (1971)[14] they investigate the reasons for the attitudes of irritation and repression towards children and set them in social and work conditions. Parents (as well as traditional bogeymen such as caretakers and nosy neighbours who restrict children's freedom) are presented in a larger social context as victims of pressures exerted by those on whom they depend. *Mannomann!* (1972)[15] actually shows the father at his place of work and the arguments he has with the foreman who in turn is presented as being under pressure from the boss. The stock character of the one-dimensional arch-enemy, the convenient lightning conductor through whom the fairy-tale plays could 'solve' their problems, disappears. With *Doof bleibt doof* (1973),[16] a play about learning-problems at school, the Millipilli tradition of the exclusively positive and clever child who teaches adults lessons is abandoned; from now on the child characters have positive as well as negative traits. In *Ein Fest bei Papadakis* (1973)[17] the central conflict is between a German and a Greek father who argue over the right to put up their tents on a specific spot on a camping site. Mistrust, prejudices, antagonisms are shown as having their roots in social conditions.

Other significant developments helped to make Grips a permanent fixture of the German-speaking theatre scene. In 1971 the Reichskabarett company gave up political cabaret. Small subsidies

12. Schedler, *Kindertheater*, p. 120.
13. Munich and Frankfurt am Main 1971.
14. Munich and Frankfurt 1973.
15. Munich and Frankfurt 1973.
16. Starnberg 1974.
17. Starnberg 1974.

provided a rather shaky financial security for the children's theatre. In 1972 they adopted the name Grips, summing up the ability to use one's brains with wit and skill, the name was programmatic. The former actors, writers and musicians of the Reichskabarett took children and their intellectual faculties seriously. In 1974 Grips moved to a permanent home, a converted cinema at the Hansa Platz with an open stage, surrounded by the audience on three sides.

Outwardly Grips rejected the artificially created separate worlds for children and adults (which made the *Weihnachtsmärchen* so appealing to bourgeois audiences) by changing the designation of their plays from 'Theaterstücke für Kinder' (plays for children) to 'Theaterstücke für Menschen ab . . .' (plays for people from the age of . . .). They also gave up the traditional children's theatre practice of extracting bogus audience participation by talking to children and eliciting their reactions, and decided to play *for* children. The songs, which in the early plays had been fully integrated into the plot and advanced it in the fashion of a musical, were taken out of the action and appeared as tuneful summaries of the messages the authors wanted to get across. Though in certain productions characters and situations were deliberately overdrawn, the standard Grips style which evolved is best summed up as representational realist theatre. The actors do not ape children. They emphasise attitudes and movements typical for children and young people. The age difference between them and the characters they portray (which they never hide) helps to avoid naturalistic imitations. The resulting realism is related to that advocated by Brecht. Visually, this is reinforced through the use of selected real and essential props and furniture. The style of speech which emerged over the years is one of the most natural to be heard in any German-speaking theatre, particularly in the youth plays where the age gap between actors and characters portrayed is narrowed down. Concentrating on the typical, the realism of Grips does not generate contemplative critical detachment; rather the audience are encouraged to learn to recognise, in real life, uhe characters and situations represented on the stage. Stefan Fredrich, for example, was verbally attacked and even jostled by girls from the audience when he played a conceited macho in one of the youth plays. The familiar leads to recognition and reaction, the open endings of the plays which merely hint at possible solutions are designed to create awareness which in turn might result in action. To extend the effectiveness of the plays Grips early on began to sell scripts, programmes and background materials at cost price. The latter provide evidence for the statements made in the play and contain suggestions for further exploration of the issues raised. First introduced in 1973, these *Nachbereitungshefte* are central to the company's strategy to maintain close links with schools, to raise awareness and understanding of topical issues, and to foster emancipation.

Advocating the rejection of unquestioned authority and the collective decision-making in their plays, the Grips company applied what they were preaching to their own work. In 1971 they started to experiment with writing and producing plays collectively. For a time it seemed that they were realising a dream of the student movement which the American Germanist Jack Zipes summed up as follows:

The plays which they perform represent the products of real collective work with which they identify. This collective work has been difficult, and, as the history of the theatre reveals, it is not entirely 'collective' in the purest sense of the word. Yet, the historical struggle of the Grips people to develop collective theatre work is exemplary ...[18]

The difficulties in the collective work to which Zipes refers were at times so serious—particularly after these lines were written—that they repeatedly brought the company to breaking point. Eventually Grips returned to more traditional working methods which, under the influence of the collective experiments, resulted in a unique creative environment in which the specialisms of each individual contributor are respected, discussed, tested, and taken into account in the process from the conception of a play to its realisation on the stage. Decisions about the selection of plays and casting are taken collectively. Once the decision to tackle a particular issue has been reached (ready-made plays are the exception rather than the rule), research is undertaken by authors as well as actors, discussions with target groups, teachers and social workers take place. The writing of a play and its production go hand in hand, and actors contribute considerably to the final shape of the script. A play's ending may not be finalised until the day before opening night.

Because the plays are written for a specific audience which Grips has built up over the years (to a large extent from sections of the West Berlin community which normally do not go to the theatre), the company has developed an acute awareness of the needs and

18. Jack Zipes (ed. & trans.), *Political Plays for Children—The Grips Theater of Berlin*, St Louis, Miss. 1976, p. 18.

interests of this social group. This special relationship ensures that its repertoire is always in touch with the pulse of the time. The proximity to contemporary issues affecting young people is reinforced through young actors who, because of the nature of their roles and the reputation Grips performers have built for themselves as specialists in the portrayal of children and young people, rarely stay for more than half a dozen years (in most cases for shorter periods). The continuity and style of Grips is guaranteed through a nucleus of talents, some of whom have been with the company since the days of the Reichskabarett.[19] The significance of a permanent team becomes clearly apparent in connection with the *Jugendstücke* which Grips developed during the mid-1970s in response to the realisation that there were no plays for teenagers. The three indigenous youth plays of the Grips Theater—*Das hältste ja im Kopf nicht aus* (1975)[20], *Die schönste Zeit im Leben* (1978)[21] and *Alles Plastik* (1981)[22]—were created by the same team, the company's *Dramaturg* and stage director Wolfgang Kolneder, the authors Volker Ludwig and Detlef Michel, and the composer Birger Heymann.

In his detailed analysis of *Das hältste ja im Kopf nicht aus* and *Die schönste Zeit im Leben* Gerhard Fischer has demonstrated how the youth plays extend the realism of the earlier plays through the move away from clichés, stereotypes and linear plots and the introduction of 'multifaceted, fully individualised' characters with 'unmistakable identities' within complex plots, how the 'issues raised are shown to be interconnecting', how they 'affect the whole range of a person's life experience, and . . . appear as problems that can be solved only in the context of total situations'.[23] *Das hältste ja im Kopf nicht aus* was sparked off by the rising unemployment among pupils leaving school with no or just the lowest certificate of education. Like almost all Grips plays it is set in a working-class environment and shows how pupils destined for the dole develop political awareness and solidarity against the combined forces of school management and commercial exploitation of their labour during a period of work experience in a department store. Despite its open ending it does

19. They include the actors Dietrich Lehmann (who also directs) and Christian Veit who normally play adult roles, Thomas Ahrens (who so far is the only actor to have returned after a period of absence), the actor, director and author Jörg Friedrich, and author-director Reiner Lücker.
20. Munich 1977.
21. Munich 1979.
22. Munich 1982.
23. Gerhard Fischer, 'The Youth Plays of Grips', *Modern Drama* 13 (1981), p. 465.

contain one overtly optimistic element in the form of the protagonist's father who changes his conservative attitudes after a conversation with a progressive teacher. *Die schönste Zeit im Leben* is set in a
similar environment, but the solidarity among the young people
comes about without the presence of one clearly identifiable enemy.
Other concerns, such as alcoholism, drugs, self-deception, macho
attitudes, and youth crimes contribute to the complexities of a
real-life situation; and instead of one, the parents of two characters
are introduced. Since it is implied that both will solve their difficulties with their children, the characters of the parents are again
carriers of an overtly optimistic note. *Alles Plastik*—which was
written against the no-future feeling at the turn of the eighties—
extends realism and social complexities by setting the action in
working-class as well as middle-class environments. It provides a
more detailed look into the families of the two main characters
without creating any false optimism about reconciliation of or
understanding between the generations. It also has a protagonist
who in the end is still unable to understand his situation or to relate
to others. The solution which the play offers as a way of finding a
purpose in life—life in a community of squatters who are refur-
bishing a derelict house—is also shown as being problematic. The
close relationship between Grips and its time was vividly demonstrated when the enormously successful *Alles Plastik* disappeared
from the repertoire at the same time as the Berlin squatters were
losing their significance.

Changing times also had their effect on the one play which,
before *Linie 1*, the company did not specifically produce for children or young people. Because of the long run of Volker Ludwig's
Eine linke Geschichte (1980),[24] topical references had to be updated
regularly, and in May 1987 the fourth revised edition was published.
The play traces the biographies of three students, beginning with
their first encounter at Berlin's Free University in 1966, continuing
with their involvement in the student movement, and ending with
their settling down in the establishment. The play demonstrates the
extent to which Grips critically reviews its own development. It is
interspersed with original Reichskabarett sketches and chansons
from the years 1967 to 1970, and incorporates the performers of
these numbers as secondary character who, for example, make
sarcastic remarks about the 'never-ending stupid questions: whether

24. See *Theater Heute* 11 (1980), pp. 25–40.

we write all that stuff collectively, whether we donate the money to a political organisation, whether we haven't become part of the establishment a long time ago . . .'[25] Such critical reappraisals are not restricted to *Eine linke Geschichte* but form an intricate part of the company's work and development. When old plays are revived they are also revised in the light of the company's development and of changed social conditions.[26] In other cases changed circumstances or the desire to address a different age group have resulted in a new play on a subject tackled before: emancipation is central to both *Mannomann!* (1972) and *Mensch Mädchen!* (1975),[27] attitudes towards foreign workers to both *Ein Fest bei Papadakis* (1973) and *Voll auf der Rolle* (1984),[28] the deceptive world of advertising to both *Nashörner schießen nicht* (1974)[29] and its revised version *Der Spinner* (1983).[30] The way in which themes and subject-matter have developed over the years suggests that the company's work is advanced by constant checks and counterchecks of previous positions and practices, including experiments once discarded.

It is through the complex system of filters outlined above that *Linie 1* emerged during 1985–6. Volker Ludwig had always wanted to write a musical, and he had promised the musicians who performed the rock music for the youth plays that, after a lapse of almost five years, a play with a substantial amount of new music would be produced. Ludwig was under further pressure because Grips was losing money despite *Eine linke Geschichte* and the youth plays playing to sold-out houses. The general shift to the right which had been accelerated by the coming to power in Bonn of the Christian Democratic Union (CDU/CSU) in 1982 had a direct effect on Grips audiences. Since 1976 the theatre had had serious arguments with CDU politicians in Berlin. But, despite pressures on teachers in CDU-controlled districts not to take pupils to Grips productions, the disputes had increased rather than decreased audiences. Now, in the changing atmosphere, the demonstration of

25. 'Und immer dieselben blöden Fragen: Ob wir das im Kollektiv machen, ob wir die Einnahmen für 'ne politische Organisation spenden, . . . ob wir nicht längst etabliert sind . . .' Ibid., p. 32.
26. Over the years the following plays have been revived by Grips: *Maximilian Pfeiferling* (first production: 1969, revival 1972). *Trummi kaputt* (1971, 1975), *Mannomann!* (1972, 1978), *Ein Fest bei Papadakis* (1973, 1979), *Ruhe im Karton!* (1973, 1983) *Mensch Mädchen!* (1975, 1981), *Banana* (1976, 1979), *Max und Milli* (1978, 1987).
27. Munich and Frankfurt 1975.
28. Munich 1984.
29. Munich and Frankfurt 1977.
30. Berlin 1983.

defiance crumbled and turned into a feeling of general malaise. Teachers who once had supported Grips were getting older and tired, and were less prepared to take on the extra burden of arranging theatre trips. Parents thinking of their children's future were more concerned about examination successes than about theatre. For many of Grips' traditional working-class audiences the price of admission, though lower than a cinema ticket, was becoming an expense in the light of changing economic circumstances. The children of parents who had supported Grips since their own involvement in the student movement had outgrown the children's plays. Grips' experiments with non-realist plays had not met with the customary enthusiasm inside or outside the company. The plays for children under thirteen were losing money, and the theatre— which had always operated on a shoestring budget—was facing a financial crisis. (The revival of the political cabaret in 1983 under the name 'Institut für Lebensmut' did not pay off in the long run.) In the wake of the discovery of so-called 'conservative values' traditional fairy-tale plays and *Weihnachtsmärchen* were also beginning to experience a revival in certain quarters. Against these odds, in November 1985 Grips suddenly scored a hit with one of its most hilarious productions ever, *Jule, was ist los?*[31] for audiences from the age of five, showing the problems created for a young family by the arrival of a new baby. The success provided the security and peace of mind which was an essential prerequisite for the company's most ambitious and expensive production to date, that of *Linie 1*. The team which had been responsible for the youth plays was joined by a choreographer from the United States and a costume designer from Japan. Taking the lyrics of the musical numbers as point of departure, the work developed in the familiar way, with the eleven actors (who portray more than eighty characters) contributing their own experiences to the completion of the plot while rehearsals were in progress.

The musical's title refers to the underground line no. 1 which passes through West Berlin in an east-west direction. All the action takes place on the trains and platforms of that section of the line known as 'orient express', the connection between Zoo Station (the point of arrival for all those who come to West Berlin by train) and Schlesisches Tor (the centre of the Turkish immigrant community and, until recently, the squatters of the alternative scene). The plot

31. Berlin 1985.

relates the experiences of a girl from the backwaters of West Germany who has run away from home in order to look for her boy friend, a rock star, by whom she is expecting a baby. The musical opens with the Girl (she continually changes her name) coming down a flight of stairs. Having arrived early in the morning, she descends into the man-made artificially lit world of the underground. Her expectations of metropolitan thrills and adventures are instantly crushed as dossers, loafers, and unemployed youths molest her by begging for money. In the course of the day she encounters commuters hiding their indifference behind tabloids, pensioners graphically describing their ailments and getting upset about the irreverence of the young, foreigners isolated by German ignorance and hostility, tourists indulging in a slumming excursion into Kreuzberg. The skilful use of opposites creates a sense of realism rarely found in a musical. A glamorous lady who has made her fortune in real estate contrasts with an end-of-the-road junkie who upsets the passengers' routine by throwing herself in front of the train. A social democrat whose father was murdered during the Third Reich is set against unrelenting Nazi widows who convert their husbands' pensions into coats of Persian lamb and gâteaux with cream in Berlin's most expensive cafés. In the anonymity of the underground the Girl becomes a catalyst. In her presence façades crumble, hostilities break through, friendships are formed.

Structurally the roots of *Linie 1* reach back to the times of the Reichskabarett and to *Stokkerlok und Millipilli*. Through the character of the Girl, the simple linear plot links self-contained scenes and cabaret songs. The visits to the various locations are motivated by the Girl's search for her boy friend. Several of the characters whom she meets have ancestors in Grips's three youth plays: for example, the drug addict Lumpi in Silvia (*Die schönste Zeit im Leben*), the Punk in Goofy (*Alles Plastik*). Some have developed further, such as Hella, the theorising social worker who already rejected the *Leistungsdruck* (pressure to do well) in *Das hältste ja im Kopf nicht aus*, could have turned into the Folk Singer who, in *Linie 1* has dropped out of her social service job. The subjects of unemployment, drug addiction and running away from home were also addressed in the youth plays. But the issues have become more complex. Bambi, a likeable wheeler-dealer in the tradition of Erich Kästner's Hugo with the Horn (*Emil and the Detectives*) is also a drug dealer. The crushing effect of being made redundant is graphically presented by a man who has just been fired. Foreigners are no longer represented just by Greeks or Turks, but by Tamil refugees and harmless tourists who are attacked because they are not familiar with local customs. The most detailed and complex analysis, however, is reserved for the family.

Regarded as the smallest unit of West German society, the family is protected by a special law, and has come under regular scrutiny from the Grips Theater. In the youth plays the optimism with which problems were resolved in the children's plays, gradually gave way to a more pessimistic assessment of such possibilities. Julia, one of the characters in *Alles Plastik*, was unable to find reconciliation with her divorced parents and established her own family by moving into a *Wohngemeinschaft* (shared flat). In *Linie 1* all the youthful characters who refer to their parents have severed their links with them: the Girl has absconded, Maria's mother hates her daughter, the truant Bisi has been thrown out by her father. One of the men in the underground mentions that his son no longer wants to have anything to do with him. Aspects of married life are critically assessed through a variety of couples of all ages and from all walks of life. The Girl creates her own family from among the people whom she meets. Traditional forms of the family are presented in such a pessimistic light that the happy ending of the musical in which three couples are united can only be interpreted as an ironic statement. The Girl's new family seems to present a much better alternative.

It would take a separate chapter to delineate all the complexities and the multitude of perspectives through which *Linie 1*, with a very simple plot, portrays the present. The transient nature of the train journeys which, like the original, take the spectator above and below ground, allows the introduction of people from all walks of life. Through their positions and attitudes, prejudices and sympathies, the musical weaves a net of inter-relationships between young and old, affluent and desolate, Germans and non-Germans, political left and right, present and past, which develops into a blueprint of present-day society—a blueprint which is informed by the experiences and developments of the Grips people and their audiences.

The contradictions and complexities are summed up by those spectators who are exhilarated by the experience of an extremely entertaining musical which confronts them extensively with the subject of suicide, and who, after reading the script, declare the latter to be downright depressing. The Grips company faces similar problems. *Linie 1* is what the Hollywood tradepaper *Variety* would call a 'smash hit'. It is permanently sold out, but, because of Grips' pricing policies, does not make money. The Berlin Senate, now controlled by the CDU which for years tried to break the company, has officially given Grips the status of being one of the two theatres which best represent West Berlin. It also has guaranteed the financial support which the SPD governments in the past have failed to provide. Many, from inside and outside the company, have expressed concern over the threat to its integrity and artistic future which official recognition may pose. Given Grips' track record over the past eighteen years, such worries seem to be unjustified. Grips is the one group which has never succumbed to the general trend in West German theatre towards subjectivism, retreat into the private world of individual authors, or dominance of star directors. Providing unrivalled entertainment, Grips has never deviated from the principle of educating its audiences and raising their social awareness. For future historians its scripts and production recordings will be an invaluable index to the mood and key issues of our times.

8

A New Definition of 'Eingreifendes Theater'—Some Recent Productions in the Theatre of the GDR

Anthony Meech

THEATRE in the GDR is a serious business. This is not meant to imply that it takes itself too seriously, or overestimates its potential, nor that the theatre in the GDR lacks a sense of humour. What an English visitor will find in the theatre throughout Germany, both East and West, is a sense that the theatre as an institution is far too important to be left to the realm of the merely entertaining. In the GDR the theatre is a significant employer of labour and, playing as it does to almost capacity audiences six nights a week, a major medium for communication within society. This will probably come as something of a surprise to a visitor sated with a diet of British commercial theatre.

This attitude to the theatre as a fit place for the discussion of significant moral issues finds its roots, of course, in the German eighteenth century, and is the basis for consideration of the stage on both sides of the ideological divide. Another surprise for a visitor from England—one again shared by theatres in both East and West—is the level of financial subsidy, and the level of manpower, available to a theatre company in Germany, and the results of this on their production policies. To a visitor from England, then, there are many similarities between the theatres of the two Germanies. There are, however, also very significant differences. These differences, of repertoire, of approach and attitude in the East, which are of concern to *Intendanten*, directors and *Dramaturgen*[1] to a greater

---

1. There is no real English equivalent of the term *Intendant*, the general artistic and administrative director of a theatre. Similarly, the *Dramaturg* who selects and adapts plays for production is not often found in the English theatre.

or lesser extent throughout the country, could be seen quite coherently as the multifarious attempts of theatre practitioners in the GDR to come to terms with Brecht's prescription of an 'eingreifendes Theater'. It is in this concern that the theatre of the GDR differs fundamentally from that in the Federal Republic.

It would seem from conversations with theatre people in the GDR that the concept, or at least the term 'eingreifendes Theater' is carried like a talisman, to be produced whenever their policy is challenged or questioned. But what they mean by the concept, and how they try to embody it in their production policy differs very widely from place to place, and audience to audience. An examination of these variations might give us a clearer picture of the true state of the art in the GDR.

There have been a number of important changes in the conditions for theatre in the GDR over the past twenty years, most important of which, from our point of view, is undoubtedly the shift during the early seventies of the responsibility for censorship away from the centre to the *Intendanten* of the individual theatres. This change, and its immediate products, such as Plenzdorf's *Die neuen Leiden des jungen W.*, were seen initially as evidence of a new liberalisation on the part of the government, but a number of *Dramaturgen* have declared themselves less than happy with the new system, which they find more difficult to counter, as it is far less overt than the system it replaced. They also find it divisive. A director will now find himself arguing the case for a particular play against his *Intendant*, rather than the theatre fighting together for the production. Whereas an English director's access to texts may be very wide, and his choice of what will be put into production limited only by the censorship of the market place, the freedom even of an innovative and experimental *Intendant* in the GDR is limited above all by the publishing system for new work. The publishing house Henschel sends out, gratis, copies of new plays for theatres to consider for production. They will then produce scripts when theatres show an interest. This leads, of necessity, to the majority of the theatres in the country staging the same new plays in any season (as their access to new work is restricted to those plays issued by Henschel), in what gives a strong impression to an outsider of a centralised editorial policy on new writing for the stage. This is countered by practitioners in the GDR with complaints about the paucity of new writing by GDR playwrights. The evidence offered for this is their frequent recourse to plays by

111

foreign writers in particular areas of interest, above all to the socially critical works of the Russian playwright Alexander Gelman.

The model for a theatre company in the GDR is still universally that of the ensemble, derived from the Berliner Ensemble of Brecht and Weigel. Companies, even in small provincial towns, of fifty or so actors expect to stay together for extended periods, and to work with the same directors for a number of years. The GDR has yet to experience the mobility of actors which seems to be becoming commonplace in the Federal Republic. This type of employment allows for extensive, indeed exhaustive rehearsal periods, but also involves productions of sometimes great longevity. Theatres are expected to offer as many as twenty productions at any one time, which they rotate, usually on a one-night repertory system. Older productions lapse during a season, while new ones are added. As a system it offers a quite extraordinary level of continuity and variety of choice for an audience in even the smallest of theatres, while running the risk of staleness in playing. It involves actors throughout a season, militating against their transferring to other theatres, but also engenders some resentment in actors repeatedly cast in small roles in productions which may stay in a theatre's repertoire for a number of years.

In manpower terms, then, the GDR theatre can be seen to be richly endowed—partly, of course, a reflection of the government's policy of full employment. But some aspects of production, in particular on the technical side, are curiously out-of-step with this generous provision. A second reaction of a visiting English theatre practitioner (after his first of envy at the financial and human resources available), would probably be amazement at the rudimentary level of, above all, the lighting provision in most East German theatres. Even at the Komische Oper the rig does not allow much beyond basic states, and the soloists are highlighted by follow spots in the stage boxes. This inadequacy renders fanciful any ambitions in the direction of complex, subtle changes in states, except in theatres such as the recently, and very lavishly restored Semperoper in Dresden. Theatre is supremely the art of the possible, and it was a rare treat, if not a pleasure, at the Semperoper to watch a half-hour scene change between Acts one and two of the Siegfried Matthus opera *Die Weise von Liebe und Tod des Cornets Christoph Rilke*, controlled by an on-stage stage-manager.

Account must also be taken of the drain to the West of a

significant number of writers who feel that they can not achieve their aims within the theatre of the GDR. Their loss may well be something of a blow from the point of view of aesthetic experiment, but might well also be seen as inevitable on the principle of 'he who is not with us is against us'. Certainly the kind of experimentation found in the writing of some of those who have moved to the West would not be seen as relevant by those theatre people in the East active in the search for 'eingreifendes Theater'.

It is to these practitioners that we must now turn to investigate how they seek to provide a 'Jasagendes Theater', a positive theatre committed to the socialist system in the GDR. This does not mean that their theatre is a passive theatre of acquiescence in the system. Their criticism can be outspoken and directed against corruption, misguided or abused authority, or against romantic, muddle-headed views of revolution, but the basis from which they launch their attacks is one of fundamental support for the system. Their aim, via their theatre work, is to try to improve the system in which they believe, by producing theatre which is essentially relevant to the society which they seek to serve.

The first venue to be considered is the Mecklenburgisches Staats-theater in Schwerin. Schwerin is a small town, both in its population of 120,000 and its outlook. It has enjoyed something of a renaissance since its days as a residence town for the Dukes of Mecklenburg by way of an influx of new population serving light industries which have grown up around the town. Its theatre, housed normally in the century-old building opposite the castle, is remarkable for the twelve-year reign there of Christoph Schroth. He has developed an audience for his seasons of plays of one author, or one period, which he calls 'discoveries'. These collections, customarily staged together to make one long evening for an audience, are intended to give the audience a much broader appreciation of the author or period than is possible in a single play production. In *Antike* there were stagings of three tragedies following the Trojan War and its aftermath, Euripides' *Iphigenia in Aulis* and *The Trojan Women* and Aeschylus' *Agamemnon*. The evening was concluded by the Aristophanes comedy *The Acharnians*, with its view of a very different kind of peace. Such evenings (there have been Brecht-discoveries and this year Shakespeare-discoveries), educate a particular audience, which eats together in the intervals, for whom the plays by being grouped together gain an enhanced significance and relevance. 'Eingreifendes Theater' in a particular sense at

113

Schwerin is defined in terms of coming to an understanding of a number of classic plays of the world theatre repertoire around a central theme, and rendering them relevant anew by their reinterpretation together. Contemporary writing is by no means ignored, however, and the theatre has an enviable relationship with Volker Braun, whose plays feature frequently in their programme. The 'discoveries' idea seems to have worked with the Greeks, and in particular with Brecht, whose work is itself multi-faceted. A provincial theatre such as that at Schwerin, also has, however, to accommodate music-theatre and ballet. The company keeps in its repertoire a traditionally staged *Marriage of Figaro* as the Schwerin audience which enjoys a 'discoveries' evening of straight plays also expects traditionally staged opera and ballet and will not be content with modern music-theatre such as *Die Verurteilung des Lukullus*. As music-theatre and ballet are held to be less susceptible to change and interpretation, provincial theatres are inclined to give in to this demand; they would be happy to detach the ballet and the music-theatre from their work and see it performed elsewhere, but that is not an option in a provincial town. Somewhat envious eyes are cast at Dresden and Berlin.

It is perhaps a little unfair to criticise the Spring 1986 'discoveries', as the performances had to be staged for the most part in temporary accommodation in the Marstall while the main house was being renovated. Nonetheless it was hard to identify the linking theme in a range of productions comprising Volker Braun's *Schmitten*, Manfred Karge's *Jacke wie Hose*, Alexander Gelman's *Sinulja*, Dworezki's *Der Mann von draußen*, the music-theatre's offerings of *Die Verurteilung des Lukullus* and *Weiße Rose* (scenes for two singess), and a ballet workshop production entitled *Korrelationen*. Calling the season 'construction discoveries' does not provide the through-line which has become the hallmark of this theatre and its *Intendant*, indeed, its definition of 'eingreifendes Theater'.

The Staatsschauspiel at the Schauspielhaus in Dresden does have the advantage of not having to provide ballet and music-theatre, but in their theatre building they have inherited the worst of two worlds. At the end of the Second World War the theatre was rebuilt to the pre-First World War exterior design, rendering it singularly unwelcoming, while the interior was renovated in the early 1950s style—a particularly unattractive period in interior design. The company feel somewhat aggrieved that so much of the resources available have been diverted into the rebuilding and equipping of the Semperoper. It is indeed a considerable symbol of the Dresden people's faith in the theatre, even if the Schauspielhaus feels a poor relation by comparison. The Dresden Schauspielhaus is unique outside Berlin in not having to provide a varied diet of theatre, ballet and opera. The main auditorium seats 900, and there is also a 400-seater studio. Dr. Görne, the theatre's chief *Dramaturg* sees his audience as more heterogeneous than the audience at Schwerin, and a little more sophisticated. Christoph Schroth might produce *his* version of the complete *Faust*, but it would be an interpretation limited in its relevance and appeal to his audience in Schwerin; Dr. Görne feels that the productions in Dresden must appeal to a broader audience. The theatre offers a wide diet of the classics, Goethe, Schiller, Lessing, Molière, Chekhov, Gorki, Kleist and a season of Shakespeare, staged in an 'international' style, but it is also rediscovering or reinstating in the repertoire of the GDR theatre plays and authors discredited by their popularity during the Hitler period. In their 1984 programme they were staging Hebbel's *Die Nibelungen* against a certain amount of adverse feeling in the community. But the company feels strong enough to ride the criticism for the sake of extending the repertoire and reclaiming such lost classics.

But what of new writing? Dresden has nailed its flag firmly to the mast of quality, which takes precedence for them over the merely topical or 'relevant'. It is not that they do not want to stage the present flush of *Problemstücke*[2], but that they are unwilling to stage plays which they regard as poor pieces of theatre. There is nostalgia for the new writing of the 1960s and the adaptations of the 1970s, but a feeling that there is a dearth at present in GDR playwriting confronting the problems of the day. They will stage works by Volker Braun or Heiner Müller, both writers of international standing, but are not prepared to work with what they regard as sub-standard texts. For GDR writing on contemporary themes they substitute foreign plays, in particular those of the Soviet Union, where they perceive a longer tradition of socially critical playwriting. A play such as Gelman's *Wir die Endesunterzeichnenden* exposes the way in which officials within the party's decision-making machinery allow their corruption, their prejudice or their sheer indifference to affect their judgement. The play ends on a note

---

2. Plays focusing on controversial issues.

of despair that nothing can be done to change the situation. Very skilfully staged and sensitively acted, the play provoked a warm and sympathetic response from its audience, but not one that suggested a personal identification with the characters and their problems; although the sympathy was there, perhaps the problems were not seen to be near enough to the inhabitants of the city of Dresden, or perhaps they were insufficiently universalised in the play to provoke more than a general response.

The Dresden Schauspielhaus, then, is a theatre dedicated to quality of product, to interpretation of the plays of the classical repertoire to stand comparison with the productions of any 'national theatre'. In this it achieves the 'international' style, but the concept of 'eingreifendes Theater' for its audience rings somewhat hollow. It identifies the problems inherent in the search; those of the perhaps less than adequate literary quality of the recent *Problemstücke* from GDR playwrights, and the alternative which seems to be major adaptations of existing, or classic plays. It is not prepared to compromise on the literary quality of a text with a view to addressing contemporary problems, nor will it engage on an adaptation or reinterpretation on the level of a Christoph Schroth in the hope of rendering a classic text 'relevant' to today's audience.

A search for 'eingreifendes Theater' leads, naturally to Berlin— which functions as much more of a capital city, so far as theatre provision is concerned, for the GDR than can any city for the Federal Republic. Its numerous theatres have the chance of targeting specific audiences and offering specific products, as does the Maxim Gorki Theatre with its adherence to theatre of the revolutionary period. It is in the theatres of Berlin that the two strategies rejected in Dresden can be seen embraced in the director's hunt for contemporary relevance for theatre.

There has long been a view, somewhat carpingly reiterated by *Dramaturgen* at the Berliner Ensemble, that the Deutsches Theater regards itself as the 'national theatre' of the GDR, or at least behaves as though it did. In this role the theatre offered Johannes Becher's *Winterschlacht* dedicated to the eleventh party congress of the Socialist Unity Party (SED) held in Berlin at Easter 1986. It was fascinating for an outsider to watch the reception given to this classic of socialist theatre. GDR audiences tend to be at worst polite, but the audience for *Winterschlacht* was decidedly restive. A number of schoolchildren had frequently to be rebuked for talking during the performance, but they could hardly be blamed for that.

The production was lacklustre and frankly dull, doing little to enhance the reputation of Alexander Lang. This was in sharp contrast to the première of the *Vorspiel zur Winterschlacht* by Heiner Müller, which preceded the performance of *Winterschlacht* and was sensitively performed and well received by all sections of the audience.

If this production of *Winterschlacht* does not represent Lang's view of 'eingreifendes Theater' at the Deutsches Theater, what does? The answer would seem to be unconventional stagings of the classics in imaginative or unlikely couplings: *Herzog Theodor von Gothland* with Goethe's *Iphigenie auf Tauris*, and, staged in a single evening as a double bill, *Medea* and Goethe's *Stella*. These two plays were billed as a 'Trilogie der Leidenschaft' despite the fact that Strindberg's *Dance of Death* (to complete the trilogy) was not yet in the repertoire. The linking of *Medea* and *Stella* in the same evening was intended to produce a sharp contrast, and everything theatrically possible was done to heighten this contrast. 'Concept' productions are not new to Western European audiences, who would have felt quite at home with the lowering, claustrophobic atmosphere in Lang's *Medea*. Set in the orient of Marco Polo, the production was static and controlled. The actors were restrained by their costumes and the stylisation they had adopted for their movements. The strong, almost primary lighting and the troglodytic set added to the compelling sense of unreality, yet consistency and integrity in the world created within the production. As with all successful 'concept' productions, this *Medea* had to convince as a total package or fail. There was an obvious through-line, if at times this became apparent as the imposition of a director on the production and also at times rendered the play more opaque than it need have been. Throughout, however, there was a powerful stage picture dominated by the figure of Medea, central both to the interpretation and the staging, admirably played by Katja Paryla.

In marked contrast to the *Medea*, Lang played *Stella* as pure comedy bordering on farce. Against a fluid set of thin drapes Roman Kaminski, as Fernando, strode about frequently striking his head and threatening to faint away. This came as welcome light relief for an audience which had just experienced the intensity of *Medea*, but whether this narrow interpretation added anything to the audience's understanding of this infrequently performed piece must be open to question. Nonetheless, by the radical reappraisal of the classics, and the combining of them in a programme to subvert

117

the expectations of his audience, Alexander Lang is forging a new style of theatre evening.

Before leaving the Deutsches Theater it might be instructive to glance at one of the contemporary plays in their repertoire, *Die wahre Geschichte des Ah Q* by Christoph Hein. Himself a theatre employee, working as *Dramaturg* and assistant director at the Volksbühne in Berlin, Hein chooses the adaptation strategy to present a critique of naïve expectations of revolution. The story, taken from Lu Xun, is set in China in 1911, the time of the first anti-feudal revolutionary unrest in the country. Hein places the thinking revolutionary Wang in a dilapidated temple with the freebooter Ah Q. While awaiting the revolution, Wang tries to teach Ah Q the meaning of anarchy, as being the only true basis for revolution, but Ah Q is more interested in the physical attractions of the nun who brings them food. After bungling an attempt to seduce her, Ah Q goes to the city, and returns rich after 'liberating' money from an exploiter. While drinking and smoking the profits, they miss the revolution in the village. Later Ah Q rapes, and accidentally kills the nun, but is executed for a crime he could not have committed, as he was, at the time, drinking with the policeman who later has the task of executing him. The play has a depressing moral for those unwilling to become involved in the active further-ing of the revolution—it is the anarchists who are hanged first—but it also warns against the naïve confidence that the revolution will cure everything ('injustice and the roof', as Ah Q says). The only changes produced in the village by the revolution are the alteration of the name of 'Our Gracious Lord' to 'Our Revolutionary Lord' and the name of the convent to the 'Revolutionary Convent of the Immaculate Conception'. Hein takes the action away from specifics of period, frequently introducing anachronisms in both the lan-guage and the action, and successfully creates an environment with echoes of early Bond (of *The Narrow Road to the Deep North*). It is a sadder world than that of Brecht's Sezuan, but perhaps one that is more worldly wise. With its quick-fire banter, often reminiscent of Vladimir and Estragon, and its buffoon character of the policeman Maske, it is a play of considerable humanity and humour, but not without a moral. It was these features which contributed to its excellent reception when staged in West Germany and elsewhere, including England. The questions about personal responsibility to the revolutionary process are debated at length in the play. But Hein's characters, whose relationships have an absurd logic in their squalor, transcend this absurdity, this contrast of thought and action, and give the lie to the often held belief (by the English especially) that German discursive theatre need of necessity be tedious. However, with its flight into a far-off region and its concern with the theory of revolution in conflict with its practice, it can be seen to avoid, or at least not directly to address, the questions confronting its audience in the GDR in their everyday lives. Its direct relevance might, then, be seen to be a limited one.

For a consideration of such questions of the moment we must shift our attention to the Theater am Bertolt Brecht Platz and the Berliner Ensemble, which will bring us full circle in our search for 'eingreifendes Theater'—back to Brecht. There has been little mention of him so far. Thirty years after his death there is a marked desire in the theatre of the GDR to come out from under his shadow, and even more to escape the shadow of the received production of Brecht texts. *Dramaturgen* at other theatres admit to being tired of Brecht, or at least to being tired of the 'great plays'. There is some renewed interest in the early plays, but in general interest is centred elsewhere.

This cannot, however, be the case for the Berliner Ensemble, feeling as it does a responsibility to fill about half its programme with productions of Brecht texts. There is a requirement on them similar to that on the Royal Shakespeare Company in England to restage Shakespeare's plays. Unfortunately for the Ensemble, however, the much closer link with Brecht and the extant records of his production style and methods seem to impose considerable limitations. The Ensemble is happy to acknowledge its responsibility to produce the works of Brecht, but feels constricted in its attempts to render them 'eingreifend' by the demands of a largely tourist audience. These demands are amplified by the GDR government. The Berliner Ensemble is a powerful earner of very valuable hard currency, and is much in demand throughout the non-socialist world. It has even been suggested that there are members of the Ministry of Culture who could foresee an Ensemble permanently on tour in the West. Even this would be less of a strain artistically for the company if audiences abroad would accept productions by them of dramatists other than Brecht, and of productions of Brecht plays which do not simply ape the staging of Brecht himself, who has, after all, been dead for thirty years. A case in point was the recent visit of the Ensemble to Milan, where a production of *Die Dreigroschenoper* of which the company were 'frankly ashamed' for

119

its staleness and lack of invention was greeted with critical acclaim. The production brought by the Ensemble to the Edinburgh Festival which was best received was not the reinterpretation of Goethe's *Faust* but the production of *Leben des Galilei*, with Ekkehard Schall, which has been in the repertoire since 1978. There is, then, considerable pressure not to experiment with Brecht, or at least there are not the incentives there when such experimentation is undertaken. The Brecht fatigue mentioned in the provinces is also felt at the Ensemble, but only in this specific regard. It is very difficult for the Ensemble to justify biting the hand that brings it Westmarks.

Critics in the West have noted that Brecht did not engage in large-scale original playwriting after he was established with his own company in the then Theater am Schiffbauerdamm. He did however engage in a carefully documented production of Erwin Strittmatter's play *Katzgraben*. Brecht always saw one of the prime responsibilities of his ensemble, as well as the staging of his own plays to his satisfaction, to be the encouragement and promotion of new GDR writing. *Katzgraben* was intended as the first in this line. Following this lead, the Ensemble has premièred a considerable number of plays by GDR authors, not only those by established writers such as Volker Braun (with *Großer Frieden* in 1979 and *Simplex Deutsch* in 1980), but also those by less well established dramatists.

Two plays in this category would repay consideration. Different in the Ensemble's approach to their staging, they embody significant aspects of the Ensemble's 'non-Brecht' attempts at 'eingreifendes Theater'. The plays are *Außerhalb von Schuld* (1984) by Uwe Saeger, premièred at the Städtisches Theater Leipzig in 1984 and given its second production by the Ensemble in 1986, and *Jochen Schanotta* (1985) by Georg Seidel, premièred in February 1985 by the Ensemble.

A conventional production of *Außerhalb von Schuld* was shown on the Ensemble's rehearsal stage, a very basically equipped square auditorium set up in end-stage with raked seats on wooden rostra, and itself a recent innovation. The staging of the play was simple and naturalistic, its message direct. The play is set in a factory with a good reputation for productivity, where Proske, one of the workers has been killed in an accident. The action of the play comprises the investigation into this accident and its aftermath, including a suicide and a heart attack among the factory employees. Uwe Saeger makes no claims for the play as a work of great literary merit; it does however directly confront and expose a number of problems in contemporary GDR society and the workplace previously ignored. For instance a contributory factor to the accident was undoubtedly that Proske had been drinking, an admission of the until recently taboo subject of alcoholism at work. The factory was able to show commendable savings in its power consumption, but only by removing light bulbs to save electricity, and Proske fell in a badly lit area. The outstanding output from the factory was achieved through the innovations introduced by the works engineer; these, it emerges, consisted in removing safety guards so that production could move more quickly. As the investigation progresses, it emerges that indeed nobody in the works is free from guilt. Even the elderly worker whose main interest in the investigation is not to miss his bus, has been misappropriating copper piping. The strain of trying to resist a cover-up tells on Boldien, the 'honest man' union representative, who, having fought almost alone in the first half of the play, succumbs to a heart attack. In a lengthy scene at the start of the second half of the play, Boldien suggests that the young electrician Ziemann should take on the fight, only to be countered by Ziemann who says one is guilty by simply being in the world. Tension mounts as preparations are being made by the factory manager Albrecht for his speech to his staff, under the watchful eye of the party secretary Müller. Albrecht's bland speech is, however, interrupted, not by Ziemann, but by Thoms, whom we have seen disaffected in the first half of the play. The change which has taken place in the workforce becomes apparent when a number of the other workers take up Thoms's line, despite the attempts of Müller to stem their unseemly interjections. After the speech Müller feels that Albrecht handled the dissent well, and looks forward to a glass of cognac with him later that evening at the Sports festival. The experience has shaken Albrecht's confidence, however; nothing is now as simple as it appeared to him twenty years ago. He will not accept the jargon answer that it is simply 'a problem spiral of real-world socialism', and is left profoundly worried—less by the outburst than by the silence of the other workers.

Uwe Saeger presents no easy answers in this play. The nearest to any answer comes from Albrecht, when he says that the 'new man' must be the result of education, not compulsion, but the hope seems pious. Instead Saeger forcibly confronts his audience with a clearly argued, comprehensible play, conventional in form. Saeger has said that he does not want to cause any revolutions in the theatre, but that he would like his audience to sleep just a little less easily in their beds after seeing one of his plays. With the production of *Außerhalb von Schuld* at the Berliner Ensemble he achieves another of his aims, that of reaching not a theatre élite, but the man in the street. He does this with a dramatisation of problems of genuine and lively concern to him in his everyday life. In this the play can be seen to be truly interventionist, 'eingreifend'.

The production of *Jochen Schanotta* in the main auditorium is a somewhat different case. The character of Jochen has something in common with the Edgar Wibeau of Ulrich Plenzdorf's *Die neuen Leiden des jungen W.*; and we follow his career as a misfit, from throwing his school books out of the window to his eventual grinding down into an albeit unwilling member of society as he prepares to leave for his military service. The episodic scenes proceed chronologically through his despairing attempts to establish his independence. The play has some effective scenes and a certain amount of wry humour, but its structure is unimpressive. What was significant in theatrical terms about the production was the way in which the director Christoph Brück and his *Dramaturg* Jörg Mihan totally reorganised the original text to bring the scenes alive by imaginative juxtaposition, as well as by the additions they made to the performance—most notably in the introduction of the *Liedertheater Karls Enkel*. Their alienating musical commentary saved the play from becoming, or perhaps remaining, a self-indulgent apologia for Schanotta, raising it through wit to a lively critique of his character. His problems were not minimised by this, only relativised, and set in context. The imposed humour was sympathetic for all its implied criticism. This was apparent from the first, when a rickety box on pram wheels was brought on, into which the performers of *Karls Enkel* (after their musical procession through the auditorium) placed a Young Pioneer's outfit, followed by the blue shirt of the Free German Youth. The amusement of the audience was completed when this attempt at generating the acceptable GDR youth produced from the box a scruffy, jeans-clad, guitar-toting Jochen. This opening is in sharp contrast to the start of the play text, in which Jochen opines on conformity while playing chess with his friends. The rapport established with the audience was immediate, and was maintained by the integrity of the performance style found by the director. Of the many characters encountered by Jochen on his pseudo-picaresque journey through the GDR, the ageing *Wandervogel* couple (the man complete with

Lederhosen and crested stick) deserve specific mention for the skill of their 'thumb-nail' sketch characterisation. They can identify each year of their marriage by the extensions they have added to their family home. The man's suggestion that Jochen should take a job painting the white lines down the centre of the roads, if he wants an open-air life and a chance to travel, is met with the riposte that the country is so small, he would be back where he started in no time. It was a production full of wit and invention, and one exceptionally well received by its audience, many of whom were as young as the hero of the piece.

In conversation about the production Jörg Mihan was quick to point out that many of the ideas it contained might seem dated to someone from the West, but that the GDR had a great deal of catching up to do. He stressed the overwhelming need to encourage new writing (as Brecht himself had done), as long as the director and company were prepared to work on a script which might not be of the finest quality. He argued that any adaptation work on new writing was better done in rehearsal rather than in the study, making a strong case for the situation at the Ensemble, where six directors are serviced by three *Dramaturgen*, against the Deutsches Theater, where three directors are serviced by six *Dramaturgen*. His case was convincingly supported in practice by the success of the production of *Jochen Schanotta*.

This kind of work is, of course, only part of the overall responsibility of the Berliner Ensemble to the theatre of the GDR, but it does represent a truly engaged and innovative approach which is receiving positive support both from the members of the company and from their audiences. The GDR theatre is capable of staging productions in the 'international style' in which a visitor from the West can feel at home. The feeling one has as a foreign audience member for the two latter plays, however, is very much that of an interloper, an alien. These were performances in which there was a genuine symbiotic relationship between the stage and the audience; an audience quick to pick up the slightest nuance of GDR reference in the performance. It is this lively and active audience response by members of all ages, which will serve as evidence for the direct appeal of this type of theatre. This healthy symbiosis of stage and auditorium in productions of the current *Problemstücke* gives hope for the continuing efficacy of the theatre as a forum of debate on contemporary issues, and an answer in our search for a new definition of 'eingreifendes Theater'.

9

Back to the Future—Volker Braun and the German Theatrical Tradition

Julian Hilton

VOLKER BRAUN is a child of the ruins of post-war Germany, of the rise of the German Democratic Republic. He has had to contend with Stalinist politics, socialist realist aesthetics and the presence and then the ghost of Brecht. Like Brecht he is both poet and dramatist; his dramatic works to date were published by Henschel in 1983.[1] More recently he has ventured into prose fiction in his *Hinze-Kunze-Roman*[2] in which his dramatic interests are still clearly visible.

Like Günter Grass, Braun sees the artist as the unifier of Germany, using language and culture as a means of overcoming political sub-division.[3] He also sees the artist as a builder, a maker in a classical sense, a man of practice; as Bauch says in Braun's early play, *Die Kipper*: 'But everything that a man thinks comes out of what he has done! In the long run nothing holds together without us doing something and without something to be done.'[4] The role of the artist is analogous to that of the brigade-worker Bauch, to intervene in the development of socialism in a positive but critical

1. *Stücke: Mit einem Nachwort von Klaus Schumann*, Berlin 1983. All page references are to this edition. The collection does not include Braun's play, *Lenins Tod*, 1970. A useful bibliography is available in Jay Rosselini, *Volker Braun*, Munich, 1983, pp. 187–200.
2. Volker Braun, *Hinze-Kunze-Roman*, Halle/Leipzig, 1985.
3. Cf. for example, Günter Grass's novels *Das Treffen in Telgte*, Darmstadt 1979, p. 7, and *Headbirths or the Germans Are Dying Out*, London 1982, p. 124. See also my own introduction to the collection of modern German plays *Gambit 39/40: Special Double German Theatre Issue*, London 1982, p. 14.
4. 'Alles, was der Mensch denkt, kommt doch aus dem, was er gemacht hat! Auf die Dauer hält nichts zusammen, ohne dass wir was machen und ohne eine Aufgabe', p. 17.

spirit ('eingreifendes Theater'): 'We are standing right at the start. There will be a surplus of material goods, a surplus of thoughts and a surplus of feelings. There will no longer be any reason for not loving any fellow man. I say, the man of the new millenium will live as he pleases.'[5] This is the embodied *Prinzip Hoffnung*, the concrete utopia advocated by Ernst Bloch and so influential in both the GDR and the FRG. The only worry we might have about this vision is embedded in the phraseology: have we not heard about 'das neue Jahrtausend' from someone else?

The basis of this chapter is Braun's *Stücke*. The publication of that volume is not only a major theatrical achievement, but signals Braun's status within the GDR as a dramatist of the top rank, a status he will in time achieve elsewhere. His work satisfies both on first and subsequent encounters. The first impression is of someone who paints with a broad brush, whether in the more domestic atmosphere of East German factory life (which has the feel of a family rather than a public drama) or on the grand historical scale of *Grosser Frieden* or *Dmitri*. The stage bu·tles with life, incidents are packed in; the language is colloquial, dense, full of ironic humour and textual allusion. Braun's masters are Brecht, obviously, Shakespeare, Schiller and Büchner, also Beckett and Bunuel. He is eclectic without feeling fussy and highly energetic. Closer study reveals two things: the craftsmanship of a writer who builds his scripts with the precision of a well-made machine, and the ideological commitment of a man who has not lost faith in socialism despite all its failures. This affirmation of optimism in the future is perhaps the source of the energy, one might even say *energeia* since Braun's classical learning is never far from the surface.

Braun's writing to date may be considered in three groups: the first is the socialist realist plays, *Die Kipper, Hinze und Kunze* and *Tinka*, centring on problems such as industrialisation, personal and public attitudes in the workers' state and sexuality under socialism. The second group is experimental, bound by a common desire to explore new dramaturgical devices; these include *Schmitten, Guevara oder der Sonnenstaat* and *Simplex Deutsch*. The most demanding and mature writing is in *Grosser Frieden* and *Dmitri*, both, perhaps significantly, plays with a more traditional plot and

5. 'Wir stehn ganz am Anfang. Es wird ein Überfluss an materiellen Gütern dasein, ein Überfluss an Gedanken und ein Überfluss an Gefühlen. Es wird gar keinen Grund mehr geben, irgendeinen Menschen nicht zu lieben. Ich sage, der Mensch des neuen Jahrtausends wird leben wie es angenehm ist', p. 39.

both on world-historical themes.

One concern of Braun's aesthetic, perhaps appropriately for someone born in the great baroque city of Dresden, is a baroque sense of theme and variation, in which the theme is often, as in classical lyric, inherited from the German tradition (in which, as does Herder, Braun includes Shakespeare), from the history of socialist Germany, or from socialism as a whole. So Braun takes it on himself to complete Schiller's *Demetrius* in his play, *Dmitri*, as Peter Hacks had completed Goethe's *Das Jahrmarktfest zu Plundersweilern*.[6] The consequences of this preoccupation with tradition and with the wish to annex the German theatre to the cultural purposes of the East are considerable—an unequivocal bid for cultural dominance which has every prospect of success. In a culture which prizes theatre, as is the case on both sides of the inner-German border, the apparent acquiescence of the West in such dominance is striking.

The key to the issue perhaps lies with the complex problem of *Vergangenheitsbewältigung*, coping with the legacy of the past. It has been a remarkable achievement of the East, despite all the repressions of the past thirty years, to have emerged almost unscathed from the legacy of the Third Reich. Whatever the West fears in the GDR, it is not the renascence of right-wing fascism. The opposite is true of the West itself. The sins of the parents continue to be visited on the sons and daughters, and it is still impossible to observe the resurgence of nationalist sentiment in such areas as Bavaria without a tremor of concern that the whole cycle might be beginning again. What this means for dramatists is that while the West Germans have dealt almost obsessively with the need to explain, rebuke, apologise for the past, the East Germans have written unencumbered by the past, however much present concerns have weighed them down.

The rhetorical advantage of the East German aesthetic, poised between the classical Weimar tradition and the socialist present, is that it creates a potentially limitless task in semantic and aesthetic redefinition. Words, cultural constructs, social psychology, even narrative itself, all need re-examination. The founding of a new state has necessitated the generation of a new history, a new epos. As this epos is to become the new language of the new tribe it has to be written with care, refined within the all-consuming fire of socialist

6. Peter Hacks, *Das Jahrmarktsfest zu Plundersweilern*, Düsseldorf 1973.

ideology. As a result, what is unsaid is often as powerful as what is said, irony a way of life. Meaning itself becomes ambiguous since the reader, conversant with both the old and the new language is unsure which at any one time is operative, the same signifiers now signifying totally new things. Text functions as a mediating cipher, reflecting the current state of semantic dynamism. Not least for this reason is Braun fascinated by puns, especially sexual punning when it explores the relationship between physical and sexual effort. But the redefinition process does not confine itself to language. Even the human body changes, or rather, it must change, as Bauch, himself an embodied pun of Falstaffian complexion, says: 'We must get ourselves different eyes and different thoughts if we want to communicate with each other further.'⁷ It is the totality of such change which enables the GDR to distance itself so effectively from the fascist legacy, while the West still labours in its shadow. The cultural advantage is to annex to East German writing the German theatrical tradition, as expressed through the works of Goethe and Schiller. In the conscious return to the Weimar roots, Braun, like Peter Hacks and Heiner Müller, is laying claim to the mainstream of theatrical writing, while, ironically, filling a vacuum in post-war West German stage writing where Socialist Realism seems to have triumphed over the poetic tradition.

Four themes dominate the 1983 collection of plays: the crisis of unthinking and uncaring manifestations of socialism; the failure of the collective to accommodate individual aspiration; the necessity of personal and social change in pursuit of true socialism; and the need for an aesthetic redefinition of the present in positive socialist terms. These concerns have increasingly taken Braun's direct attention away from the present towards the past, which he approaches in much the same spirit as Brecht or Shakespeare, as a source of paradigmatic statements about the present. Hence perhaps Braun's admiration for the linguistic density of Shakespeare, an admiration he shares with Goethe, Schiller and Büchner. All four themes converge in the creation of a new aesthetic which in turn is predicated on a new state of mind. And in this new state of mind the true socialist state is to be born.

In *Die Kipper* (premières [East Germany] Leipzig, 1972; [West Germany] Wuppertal, 1973) Braun not only shows that he under-

---

7. 'Wir müssen uns andre Augen und andre Gedanken anschaffen, wenn wir uns weiter verständigen wolln', p. 21.

stands all too well the practical problems of socialism, he also flags
the underlying aesthetic concern of his work, the search for the
roots of the present in the past, back to the future. How, for
example, can the socialist utopia be equated with the stultifying
monotony of shifting mountains of sand? It cannot. 'The tip is no
place to develop men into anything that has no proper foundation in
this sort of place. Socialism, in such an environment, is not wholly
possible.[8] Yet within a few moments of this scene, Braun's fluent
conversancy with the German tradition is displayed in a long speech
by Marinka which is an undisguised variation on Marion's speech in
Büchner's *Dantons Tod*. Both women speak of sexual awakening,
one (Marion) in terms of spring, the other (Marinka) in terms of
summer. One brief example of Braun's technique must suffice here:

MARINKA. That was the summer. I still stood often in the garden and
everything was like in a fire that burned over the land, igniting the leaves
and the meadows, I grew sad and locked myself away for days on end.
But everything around me was still there, everything had passed over me,
I was a total stranger to myself.[9]

The sense of alienation and the correlation between psychology and
season is clearly derivative from Büchner:

MARION. Then the spring came, something was going on all around me
which I had no part of. I fell into a strange atmosphere that almost stifled
me, I gazed at my limbs, sometimes it seemed to me that I were double
and then melted again into one.[10]

Yet the speech is no mere variation on a famous theme. It signals a
deeper intertextual strategy for the whole play, a strategy of conscious development of the classic German theatrical tradition.

Bauch is similar in character and physical type to Büchner's
portrayal of Danton. This similarity suggests a specific historical
perspective to Braun's view of East Germany in the 1950s as a place

8. 'Die Kippe ist kein Ort, Menschen zu entwickeln zu irgendwas, das da gar
keine Basis hat. In dem Bereich ist der Sozialismus nicht ganz möglich', p. 18.
9. MARINKA: Das war der Sommer. Ich stand noch oft in dem Garten, es ging
alles hin, wie in einem Feuer, das über dem Land brannte und die Blätter und Wiesen
entzündete, ich wurde traurig, ich schloss mich tagelang ein. Aber es war noch alles
um mich, es war alles auf mich übergegangen, ich war mir ganz fremd (p. 25).
10. MARION: Da kam der Frühling, es ging überall etwas um mich vor, woran ich
keinen Theil hatte. Ich gerieth in eine eigne Atmosphäre, sie erstickte mich fast, ich
betrachtete meine Glieder, es war mir manchmal, als wäre ich doppelt und
verschmölze dann wieder in Eins. (Georg Büchner, *Dantons Tod*, in Georg Büchner,
Sämtliche Werke und Briefe, ed. Werner R. Lehmann, Hamburg 1979,
p. 22.)

akin to France in the 1790s. Not only buildings have to be rebuilt, but society as a whole, from the ground upwards. Bauch is a revolutionary of the body, a man whose body becomes a metaphor of work itself, as Shakespeare's Falstaff becomes an emblem of the body politic: 'I am the mine. The mine is what I am. As much as I want it to, it changes itself.'[11] This physicalisation of the revolutionary dynamic takes it out of the realm of metaphysics and into the realm of action: if a utopia is to be achieved it will be through work. Ideas have no force unless mediated through labour. Yet this work is not to be understood in a capitalist sense, as motivated by money. Money is earned, yes, but more important, work is satisfying, in the same way that sex is satisfying. Breaking a productivity record is as fulfilling as intense and sustained sexual pleasure. In work, as in sex, the body is celebrated.

Hinze und Kunze (première, Weimar, 1968 as *Hans Faust*, revised as *Hinze und Kunze*, Karl-Marx-Stadt, 1973, revised again 1977) is a play whose long gestation gives some hint of the struggles Braun has had to be allowed to say what he thinks. We begin at *Stunde Null*, the birth of a new state and a new ideology. The task is *Enttrümmerung*, whether the removal of the physical debris of war or the cultural debris of fascism. In both tasks the source of renewal is in collective socialism, in the work and in the speech of the working people. The work is dangerous in every sense; the ruins are unsafe, enemies still stalk the borders, and the common man, so recently fallen to fascism, will take much re-education. The setting is Chemnitz, the *locus classicus* of the rebuilt city, rebuilt so thoroughly it has a new name, Karl-Marx-Stadt, socialism in stone. The choice of location is not casual: the battle for cultural supremacy fought after 1945 is about both physical and cultural space, about both the walls of Chemnitz and also its nature. If the signified has changed so much, should not the signifier (Chemnitz) change as well? Hinze, a survivor of the war—or perhaps *the* survivor—announces the theme of rebuilding from the outset: 'See at last / What out of this desolate ruined bloody patch of ground will be.'[12] The language is deliberately biblical, apocalyptic, yet also colloquial. Then, like Brecht's Shen Te and Shui Ta, the two characters constitute in their selves and their own bodies the dialectic of

11. 'Ich bin der Tagebau. Der Tagebau ist, was ich bin. Soviel wie ich Lust hab, ändert er sich', p. 40.
12. 'Endlich sehn / Was aus diesem kahlen zertrümmerten blutigen Erdstrich wird', p. 63.

rebuilding, a dialectic which resolves itself in an endless set of choices, an endless conflict of individual wills with the common will. The new woman, Marlies, does not know which of the two she wants, her husband Hinze or his new double Kunze, so sleeps with both simultaneously.

The new worker, Molke, seeks to assert his power in demanding a return to the past: 'Wewantwhatwasbefore.' But in so demanding, he brings in tanks as the stage direction indicates: [*A chorus of voices. Noise. Engines revving*].[13] These are the very tanks that once liberated Berlin from the Nazis, but which have now returned to turn freedom on its head. That the battle for freedom is fought through language is encapsulated in one of the most theatrical and ironically witty exchanges in Braun's output:

KUNZE. Look. [*He writes on the tank* ꟼᴚƎƎ◗OW]
HINZE. And even if I stand on my head I can't read it. [*Hinze gets down from the tank, rubs out the writing and writes* FREEDOM]
KUNZE. [*Does a handstand*] Senseless word.[14]

The embattled relationship between signifiers and signifieds has taken on another, iconic, dimension here, the sign 'Freiheit' not only being defamiliarised by being written upside down, but doubly so by becoming part of an ironic icon, a tank bearing the word freedom on it (though no doubt NATO would see no irony in it); but writing the word upside down defamiliarises it in just the way Braun intends, making us ask anew what it is. What is it, then? A word? The phrase 'sinnloses Wort' is redolent of Hamlet's doubts about 'words mere words' and signals how in the new world of Hinze and Kunze even the relation between signifier and signified is uncertain. But the real irony of the situation, that tanks should reinforce freedom, is caught in the physical emblem, of Kunze standing upside down to read a word the right way up. This visual pun is reinforced by the idiomatic statement 'und wenn ich mich auf den Kopf stell / Ich kanns nicht lesen'. Indeed, he cannot and never will.

Yet all is not unwell. Hinze, like Bauch, expresses his identity with the whole working class through his body, in a speech that not

13. 'Wirwollnwasfrüherwar [. . .] *Sprechchor. Tumult. Dröhnende Motoren*', p. 92.
14. HINZE. Pass auf. [*Schreibt an den Panzer* ꟼᴚƎƗHƎIᴚꟻ]
KUNZE. Und wenn ich mich auf den Kopt stell Ich kanns nicht lesen. [*Hinze vom Panzer, wischt die Schrift aus, schreibt* FREIHEIT]
KUNZE. [*im Handstand*] Sinnloses Wort. (p. 94).

only demonstrates Braun's growing rhetorical skills but also illustrates his ability to compress remarkable energy into his language: 'One task tears a hundred more my way / I am knit in / With many who sustain me / At this pitch. O shovel / Digger Calculator—where am I bound.'[15] Just as words achieve meaning in interlocked networks, so people fulfil themselves in a knitted pattern of relationships which sustain and strengthen.

It is at this level that the individual and the class fuse (thereby solving the persistent dilemma of socialist playwrights of how to represent class concerns through the actions of individuals) and in their fusion they experience heightened sensibility of a kind familiar to Schiller. The problem, however, is that the optimistic vision has not turned into a practice that Hinze understands. On the one hand the new woman, Marlies, has taken socialist emancipation at its word, borne his child and gone off without him; on the other, the body that once stood him in such good stead has got tired, and the brain has begun to doubt: 'Work, work, tasks—was it t h a t! Why everything happens, the sweat runs down the spine, the arms spin on their hinges ten to the power ten brain cells labour—why! what w a s all that?' Hinze's doubts then lead to some rather unconvincing dialectical re-education, added after 1968:

KUNZE. How are you different from me—except that I don't just look to myself! Your affair. Did you think it was a walkover, the rough road from rubble to the future.
HINZE. I must begin at the beginning.
KUNZE. Yes. [*He holds out his hand. Hinze leaves his hands in his pockets. They leave together.*][16]

A hard road it is, suggestive perhaps of Canossa.

The exchange itself, however, suggests two other variations on themes familiar to Braun, the dialectical antagonism of Karl and Franz von Moor and the closing scene of Wedekind's *Frühlings*

---

15. 'Eine Arbeit reisst hundert zu mir / Ich bin verknüpft / Mit vielen, die mich halten, / Auf dieser Höhe. O Schaufel / Bagger Rechenmaschine—wohinauf gehts mit mir' (p. 89).
16. 'Arbeit, Arbeit, Aufgaben—war es das! Wofür alles geschieht, die Brühe läuft am Rücken, die Arme schleudern in den Angeln, zehn hoch zehn Hirnzellen arbeiten—wofür! was war das alles?'
    KUNZE. Was bist du anderes als ich!—nur dass ich nicht nur mich seh. Deine Sache. Dachtest du, es sei ein Spaziergang, die rauhe Strecke zwischen Schutt und Zukunft.
    HINZE. Ich muss von vorn beginnen.
    KUNZE. Ja. [*Streckt die Hand hin. Hinze hält die Hände in den Taschen. Zusammen ab*], p. 103.

Erwachen in which another Hinze/Kunze pair, Moritz and Melchior, arrive at a similar crossroads in their existence. Here Braun butts up against the constraints of the socialist realistic aesthetic with its demands of optimistic rather than pessimistic, or, dare one venture, realistic conclusions. The dramaturgical dynamic of *Hinze und Kunze* demands that the one displace the other, or at least that the one melt into the other in perhaps the absorption by Hinze of the ideological rectitude of Kunze. In fact this ending is not allowed.

A similar problem affects the ending of *Tinka* (première, Karl-Marx-Stadt, 1976, Mannheim, 1977) a play about a woman who trains to become an engineer in the interests of socialist self-improvement only to return to her factory to find that nothing has really changed. Men still look first at her body: 'that's the beautiful one who wasted her time studying', says one.[17] They degrade her with their lust and attempt to discredit her intelligence: 'You've been a student, but it hasn't taught you much.'[18] Here Braun pinpoints the classic dilemma of the Leninist intellectual, of being highly educated and yet not street-wise, indicating his recognition that the problem Tinka faces is not just one of sexist attitudes from men. She has educated herself out of their reach and finds herself torn between her sexual desire for a man and her recognition of his inferiority to her.

In a way, the sexual critique is a profounder indictment of the failure of the planned economy than jokes or satire about the economy itself since the state has clearly shown itself incapable of delivering changes of any attitudes, let alone those about collective ownership. So, implies Braun, if the state cannot change relations between men and women how will it ever change overall cultural positions? The result is a conclusion to the play that in ideological terms is highly sensitive. Tinka finally provokes the man who loves her, Brenner (an aptly Petrarchan name), into hitting her violently over the head with a beer bottle. As she sinks to the floor Brenner shouts: 'Now you've done. Now you've done. Now you've done.' [*Through the door comes music. Brenner falls on top of Tinka.*][19] The end is out of *Wozzeck* by *Othello*, an undisguised assault on two tenets of hard line socialist realism, for it is tragic in tone, about

---

17. 'Das ist die Schöne, die umsonst studiert hat', p. 139.
18. 'Du hast studiert, aber schlau bist du nicht geworden', p. 140.
19. 'Jetzt bist du still. Jetzt bist du still. Jetzt bist du still', *Aus der Tür Musik. Brenner fällt auf Tinka nieder*, p. 175.

the failures of two individuals, and it is sexual.

By printing the play in this form Braun indicates clearly enough his doubts about the achievements of socialism in the short term; but a footnote occludes this impression: 'The printed ending should only be played when other possible endings cannot be realised.'[20] The nature of the printed ending is aesthetically and politically so sensitive that without the compromises offered in the footnote, both of which imply more optimistic outcomes, the play would not be printed.

It would be too easy a target to poke fun here at socialist realism, since one of the profoundest misconceptions about the East in the West is that dissenting voices such as Braun's are by definition pro-western. If Braun is a dissident voice it is certainly not because he prizes the capitalist ethic, or indeed the capitalist aesthetic. Rather, he is critical of the failure of socialism to be socialist. This issue comes up in striking form in a speech provoked by the challenge Tinka's education poses to flagging, male chauvinist socialism:

LUDWIG. A clear-cut case. Whilst she was a student it was still OK; but an engineer, that's too much. That is emancipation: she's freeing herself from herself. Women are transforming themselves in the image of men, not making something of themselves, as if we were everything a person can be. Why do we live? To paper the world with our constructions? For taps and carburettors? We are more the heirs of Newton than of Marx.[21]

Like much of Braun's best writing, it captures very human confusions in a mixture of visionary clarity and prejudiced weakness. Ludwig recognises that it may be that the emancipation of women is the true future of feminism, but when he meets an emancipated woman his prejudice reasserts itself. Ludwig continues: 'Emancipation—should also mean eroticisation, otherwise women discover themselves but men and women don't discover each other.'[22] Therein lies the dilemma, for perhaps the Tinkas of the world will

20. 'Der notierte Schluß sollte nur gespielt werden, wenn andere mögliche Ausgänge nicht bewältigt werden', p. 175.
21. 'Ein klarer Fall. Als sie studierte, ging es noch; Ingenieur—das ist zuviel. Das ist die Emanzipierung: sie macht sich von sich selbst frei. Die Frauen baun sich nach dem Bild des Manns um, statt was aus sich zu machen. Als wenn wir alles wären, was der Mensch sein kann. Wozu leben wir? Um die Welt zu tapeziern mit Konstruktionen. Für Wasserhähne und Vergaser. Wir sind mehr die Erben Newtons als die von Marx', p. 144.
22. 'Emanzipierung—müsste auch Erotisierung sein, sonst kommt die Frau zu sich, aber Mann und Frau nicht', p. 144.

not only colonise the male domains of carburettors and taps, but also find social and sexual forms that essentially exclude men. In such a world Marx and Newton may not be dialectical opposites, but complementary equals, excluded both. The fear that underlies much of Braun's thinking is a fear of automation, whether in the political process by slavish adherence to an inflexible ideology, in the industrial process by computers, or in personal and sexual relations by stereotyping and prejudice. Here again his thinking is far from simple, since the subjection of the human body to the stultifying and robotic demands of shifting sand, as in *Die Kipper*, degrades it every bit as much as total automation. If there is a point to the whole plan of socialism it is to create a society free from prejudice, from sycophants, from subjugation, in which the individual is able to identify easily and openly with the state and in which the state enables the individual to be fully developed. But is the current state capable of such achievements? No. As Tinka puts it:

TINKA. Such a speedy society! Every condition, hard and circumscribed, sorts itself out and every practice thrusts its own theory aside and every direction runs towards another or let us say, learns from it—and can make no sense of itself. It's all go here, if you don't keep up, you're thrown to the wall. A rounded life. Rounded personalities. O what corners I have got. I—can't do anything.[23]

I hear Braun's own voice in this, signalling that he too has awkward corners, and it is these corners which characterise the more recent plays in the collection.

Signs of change are evident in the second group of plays mentioned above, those experimenting with the nature of theatrical form and convention. The first of these is *Schmitten* (première, Leizig, 1982), begun before *Tinka* but completed after it, in which Braun not only explores a wide range of theatrical aesthetics in the one piece, from realism to surrealism, but also displays a developing satiric edge. The *Neuer Werkleiter* is serving himself beer out of an automatic drinks machine in a scene much like the opening of Vaclav Havel's *Sorry*. Every few lines he drinks another beer, ending up so drunk that he embraces the machine. The fourth beer

---

23. 'Was für ne bewegliche Gesellschaft! Jeder Zustand, hart und abgezirkelt, gibt sich selber auf, und jede Praxis schlägt ihre Theorie weg, und jede Leitung läuft zur andern über, oder sagen wir: lernt von ihr—und wird nicht aus sich selbst schlau. Hier geht es rund. Läufst du nicht mit, fliegst du an den Rand. Das runde Leben. Runde Charaktere. O hab ich Ecken. Ich—kann nichts machen', p. 150.

seems to be the crucial one as it prompts the following associations: 'Man must master technology: Stalin. Cheers. / How did I just get on to Stalin. The machine / That thinks everything—that's called apparatus / Though in his tongue that means something else.'[24] Many themes converge here, the fear of automation, the relationship between man and machine, both technical and political, the competition between varying forms of discourse, here between Stalin's and the new manager's, and the underlying weakness of the individual who still prefers getting drunk to staying sober and whose socialism under the influence of alcohol is no more coherent than his attempts to make love to the drink dispenser. Typically for Braun, the whole issue is caught in a single pun: Apparat. What signified are we to attach to this signifier?

As the *Regisseur* comments in an earlier scene, there is much at stake in irony: 'For something to appear real, it cannot be real. Realism, that is what we mean by art, there's the point. First, it must be film, then it becomes life. Make-up.' To which the *Kaderleiterin* responds: 'Right. First the example, then the person. That's the right way round.'[25] The line must bring the house down. But of course Braun is flirting with danger by locating such explicit satire in the German present, so, like Hacks and Müller, he begins to explore his own 'corners' through the medium of geographical and historical distancing, an expedient that the master, Brecht, had discovered before.[26]

First the geographical distancing, in *Guevara oder Der Sonnenstaat* (1975). In this play the displaced hero of the Cuban revolution is at the centre of a very violent revolution, in which the depths of human action are plumbed. These are represented on stage by brutal and arbitrary killings of men and animals, acts of near cannibalism and other more minor atrocities. Inset into these scenes are clown routines. The language moves between colloquial prose and heightened iambics and in atmosphere the play is reminiscent of *Troilus and Cressida*, a play Braun much admires, or Grimmelshausen's

24. 'Der Mensch muss die Technik meistern: Stalin. Prost. / Wie komm ich jetzt auf Stalin? Die Maschine / Die alles denkt—das heisst dann Apparat / Das ist ein andres Ding mit seiner Sprache', p. 118. *Schmitten* has recently enjoyed a highly successful run in Schwerin, where the scene with the drinks dispenser was particularly well received.
25. 'Damit was echt wirkt, darf es nicht echt sein. Der Realismus, das ist nämlich Kunst, da liegt der Haken. Erst muss es Film sein, dann wird es Leben. Papier, dann Leben, Schminke.' 'Richtig. Erst das Beispiel, dann der Mensch, das ist die Folge', p. 110.
26. Cf. Walter Benjamin, *Versuche über Brecht*, Frankfurt 1966, pp. 26–27.

Courasche; characters are caught between the cynicism of Thersites and the flawed honour of Hector, in this case represented by the self-discrediting ideology of violence as embodied in Guevara. The one bright spot is represented by the woman Tania, who gives up her self to fight and yet is fighting for a self predicated on love. As she quotes back to Guevara: 'Love, you say, / The most important, you say, feeling, you say, / Of the revolutionary: because it changes / Himself. So your text, Guevara.'[27] The speech reads like a gloss on Tinka's behaviour, advancing in a more explicit form than before the concept of a 'female' socialist alternative. Against this is set male violence: 'The hour of violence / Namely is the hour of truth, when the mask / Tears and the state stands naked there and / Undisguised.'[28] The nakedness is itself significant since it once again points to the ultimate integration of private and public revolutions in an unembarrassed figurative and literal nakedness. In nakedness, socialism and prelapsarian Eden seem like une same ideal.

In *Simplex Deutsch* (1978–9), the textual debts are explicit: to Grimmelshausen, to Schiller and to Shakespeare. Following Brecht to Grimmelshausen, Braun saw in the character of Simplex a cipher of the naïve author, the camera-like viewer who merely reports uncensored what he sees, or at least appears to while lying through his teeth. The play works in the same way, as if Braun were trying his hand at reproducing everything of significance he could see in contemporary European theatre. The result is a mixture of very surefooted and very insecure writing, the latter being in the ascendant. There are weak skittish parodies of Beckett and Bunuel. Godot is brought onto a stage on which Vladimir and Estragon are now hippies, no longer concerned whether Godot will come or not. The scene shows more about Braun's unease about the challenge Godot constitutes to the socialist aesthetic than it does about his own talents, and the Bunuel parody is no more happy, despite its nice title, *Der diskrete Charme der Arbeiterklasse*. These relative failures to encompass the western absurd merely highlight Braun's remarkable gifts in the German historical tradition, and it is the two historical dramas which flank *Simplex* in the collected plays which mark his most significant writing for the stage.

Grosser Frieden (première, Berlin, 1979) gave Braun the most

27. 'Liebe, sagst du / Das wichtigste, sagst du, Gefühl, sagst du / Des Revolutionärs: weil es ihn selbst / Verändert. So dein Text, Guevara' (p. 199).
28. 'Die Stunde der Gewalt / Nämlich ist die der Wahrheit, weil die Maske / Zerreisst und der Staat steht nackt da und / Deutlich . . .', p. 203.

significant public recognition he had enjoyed to date, performance by the Berliner Ensemble. The play is recognisably Brechtian in that it has a similar setting and structure to Brecht's *Lehrstücke*, *The Caucasian Chalk Circle* and *The Good Person of Sezuan*, but in construction the play is more Aristotelian, more classical than either of the Brecht works, and while epic in scope the model structurally is Shakespearian rather than Brechtian. The world is the stage, and this fact is addressed in the stage direction, which calls for the state of the stage to represent the current state of social order. Thus the play starts with the stage as a series of sharply rising steps, each representing a distinct social level. After the great peasant revolution the stage is flattened, but by the end of the play it has become highly stepped again. This visual correlative, simple but effective, underpins a simple but powerful historical movement in the play, from one 'utopia', which is no such thing other than for the handful of aristocrats who enjoy it, through a period of battle and anarchy in which social values are inverted, to a point at which the new ruling aristocracy becomes as tyrannic as the one it had displaced. In one sense the play is a massive indictment of the ruling orthodoxy in Germany at the time and it is hard to escape the conclusion that Braun is condemning the party for becoming what it set out to depose. But Braun's optimism is such that these setbacks appear temporary; through education and self scrutiny improvements will be possible. One may not share his optimism in this respect, but on the other hand to refuse or refute it leaves us an even bleaker alternative than the one he confronts: which is that without re-education it is capitalism that eventually annexes any revolution, the merchants always in the end winning.

We may plot the progress of the revolutionary dialectic through three main phases; first, the exposition of the first Great Peace by the philosopher Wang; second, the recidivism of the leaders of the revolt at the very centre of the play; third, the return of Wang at the end to pass responsibility to the audience for the fate of socialism (a device borrowed from the last speech of Pandarus in *Troilus and Cressida*). The tone is set by Wang: 'HA, ALL MEN HAVE CONTACT WITH THE GODS AND HEAVEN. / SPEARS AND TANKS LIE SHATTERED, ARMS HANG LIMPLY, LAID TOGETHER IN GREETING ONLY, USED NO MORE TO WOUND EACH OTHER. IN LIKE SPIRIT MEN DO ONLY GOOD TO PLEASE THE LORD. / HA.' [*The Actor playing Wang grins, exits*][29] The scene is significant for two reasons.

JULIAN HILTON

In the smile alone, Wang undermines the whole of the heroic exposition of the utopian Great Peace. The result is that the audience is alerted to irony throughout, the possibility in other words that anything they see could be otherwise ('das Prinzip eingreifen') and that ultimately any historical process is susceptible of change. So when Wang hands the play back to the audience at the end it is only what they must by then expect. At the same time a fundamental theatrical issue is at stake. It is central to Benjamin's analysis of Brecht's theatre that Brecht uses *gestus*, because actions are less easily falsifiable than words in the pursuit of great socialist truths. What Wang's grin demonstrates, as Braun surely knew well before writing this play, is that actions are actually much more damagingly ambiguous than words, even revolutionary actions. Wang's grin is inscrutable, for we have no basis at this early stage in the play for telling why he is grinning: is he inscrutable and Chinese; is he sending up the nonsense we have just heard; is he smiling as the actor to remind us we are watching theatre? It could be any of these and others too.

The point at issue is that if Braun can throw off one of the main Brechtian rules he can also throw off others, which he duly does in returning to a more classical style of composition, with a plot through line and a necessary logic of scenic order. Indeed, this is the aesthetic message, that the history of the revolution proceeds all too predictably from one tyranny to another if there is a failure of political re-education. In other words, if the revolution fails it is our fault for not intervening in it to make it work. This, it seems to me, is what Brecht was trying to say but in fact rarely conveyed effectively to his audience, since he felt defensive about characterisation, and unsure of the wisdom of audience sympathy being engaged in pursuit of ideas. Braun, reading his Shakespeare, knows that the opposite is true, that Wang's grin, by winning our sympathy is the surest weapon the playwright has for rendering us open to his political message. Sympathy can be a prime weapon in the class struggle and the alienation effect can be its worst enemy.

Mediating between the simple sweep of revolutionary history and the detailed description of how the world enters and then leaves a

29. HA, ALLE HABEN KONTAKT ZU DEN GÖTTERN UND DEM HIMMEL. / SPIESSE LIEGEN ZERNICHTET, DIE ARME HÄNGEN LÄSSIG, NUR ZUM GRUß ZUSAMMENGELEGT UND NICHT MEHR BENUTZT, EINANDER ZU VERLETZEN, MIT GLEICHEM SINN TUT MAN NUR GUTES, UM DEN HERRSCHER ZU ERFREUEN. / HA. [*Darsteller des Wang grinst. Ab*], p. 222.

phase of great turbulence is a sense of dramatic and social ritual. The revolution threatens to descend into death and deceit, since with the collapse of the discredited aristocracy goes a collapse in all forms of social behaviour. The result is that the natural allies, the soldiers and the peasants, end up at war. Braun is increasingly clear that the desire to get rid of bad rules should not be equated with the desire to get rid of all rules. 'Ordnung muß sein'. In this respect he is more confident than Brecht, whose study of similar conditions in *Mother Courage* led him to an ultimately pessimistic conclusion about the capacity for improvement in history.

Gau Dsu, the peasant leader who becomes king puts the case for ritual:

DSU. Mr Wang, I must inform you who you are. We have witnessed here a ceremony more splendid than any other seen in Tschin. I must confess, I am moved. You say: rituals are a fraudulent system of inequality. No, do not speak, you will find it hard to contradict me. Yes, one must keep equality in mind, but acknowledge difference. Were one to let the people do and choose as they wished, setting them no limits, they would be totally confused in their minds and no longer capable of enjoying themselves. Ritual is no tactic, it is the holy truth of the classics. [*Wang sighs.*][30]

Wang's sigh is as eloquent as his grin, since even he cannot dispute that Gau Dsu is right about the need for mediating ritual, even if it is quite clear from the context that the particular one he has chosen is not to be taken positively by the audience.

The reason for Braun's interest in ritual has everything to do with his changing understanding of theatre, which is in itself a ritualising agent in social processes, mediating between life as it is and life as it could be, as Wang's own final speech indicates: 'Ladies and Gentlemen, you see I live and gladly. / [*Takes off his costume.*] The new age, from the old still sore / Is new enough when first we stand erect / Our troubles still persist but yet could fade / The grounds we hold in our own hands.'[31] Reaching back beyond the Weimar tradition,

---

30. 'Herr Wang, ich muß Euch sagen, wer Ihr seid. Wir haben hier eben eine Zeremonie erlebt, wie sie großartiger in Tschin noch nicht gesehen wurde. Ich muß sagen, ich bin gerührt. Ihr sagt: die Rituale seien ein verlogenes System der Ungleichheit. Nein, redet nicht, es wird Euch schwerfallen, mir zu entgegnen. Ja, man muß die Gleichheit im Auge behalten, aber die Verschiedenheit kennen. Denn ließe man das Volk handeln nach Lust und Laune, ohne ihm eine Grenze zu setzen, so würde es in seinem Sinn verwirrt und könnte sich überhaupt nicht mehr freuen. Das Ritual ist keine Taktik, es ist die heilige Wahrheit der Klassiker.' [*Wang stöhnt*], p. 261.
31. 'Damen und Herrn, Sie sehn ich lebe und gern. / [*Legt das Kostüm ab*] Die neuen Zeiten von den alten Wund / Sind neu genug erst wenn wir aufrecht stehn. /

Braun anchors his future for the theatre in its most aesthetically adventurous past, when theatre claimed to be the world. This claim as Braun recognises does not necessarily mean, as Benjamin feared it did, that theatre distracts from the revolutionary cause: quite the opposite. The equation of the world with the stage puts the world-stage at the very centre of socialist practice, as a place in which the world can literally be transformed. Theatre is the concrete utopia. Armed with this insight, Braun tackled Schiller's fragment *Demetrius* (première, Schwerin, 1984). He had perhaps three purposes in mind: first, the story is one of a prototypic revolution, a conflict of power blocks of aristocratic and democratic disposition, centred in this case on Russia and Poland. Second, to dare to complete a work by Schiller requires confidence of the kind that only a writer who feels his prentice days are served would have. It is, therefore, a claim for personal authority and membership of the tradition of German master playwrights. Third, crucially, it is an explicit example of the East German bid for the highground of theatrical culture. Claim Schiller by colonisation and you have annexed the most played of all German writers. The result in my view is a success, the implications of which cannot be overstated; for if Braun has succeeded the West will have its work cut out to keep up, especially now that it seems to have lost its own sense of direction, in theatre at least.

The victory is not an unequivocal one, for in winning Braun also seems to recognise that victory may be hollow, a prelude to absolutism and hence to corruption: as Lord Acton said, absolute power corrupts absolutely. This is the observation lurking behind the behaviour of Gau Dsu in *Grosser Frieden*, that no one is capable of wielding power, even in the name of the people, without sooner or later losing touch with the people. So *Dmitri* ends with a sobering statement from the Fourth Pole:

I'll never do your Demetrius. I don't want to be a Demetrius. I get enough politics in the factory and the paper. I'll never make that mistake and bring down consequences on my head with that sort of business. I've been punished enough. Let anyone who wants to scrap for the thing do so, it's not my bag. I'll stay a spectator, that's my right.[32]

Die Plage dauert und kann uns vergehn. / In unsern Händen halten wir den Grund', p. 268.
32. 'Ich mach ihnen ni den Demetrius. Ich will kein Demetrius sin. Ich hab genuch von Politik im Betrieb und der Zeitung. Den Fehler mach ich ni und zieh mir mit der Aktivität Konsequenzen aufs Haupt. Ich bin genuch gestraft. Soll sich um die

Perhaps it is not politicians who educate people, but people who educate politicians; what use is audience involvement (democracy?) if the audience do not want to be involved?

How does Braun reach this sobering conclusion, the conclusion that was to set him off on a train of thought that even the title of his subsequent play *Die Übergangsgesellschaft* flags, that the old forms and rhetoric of socialism are in crisis and that new ones are required if the revolution is to advance. The issue in *Demetrius* is power, and who has the right to exercise it. A stable boy is presented as the true heir to the Russian throne and, supported by the Poles, marches off to Moscow to claim his kingdom. He captures Moscow but then falls victim to a duplicity similar to his own and is killed. His body is ritually displayed in the streets for three days and so the episode ends. Braun commented in response to a question about his choice of time and place in *Grosser Frieden* that he was consciously seeking historical models to explain present events and the same strategy is explicit in *Dmitri*. Once Demetrius has taken Moscow we flash forward to 1918 and learn about the Revolution in an agit prop way, as if to make it clear that the purpose of such models is to teach us about the here and now.

But, and this is perhaps the mark of Braun's new maturity, nothing in his work can be taken at face value, either aesthetically or ideologically. For example, the beginning. We are in Poland and we are hearing about a Russian threat. How can a contemporary East German audience fail to be aware of the immediacy, or indeed the political riskiness of such a setting, still less when it hears this kind of speech: 'Here is not Moscow no fear of tyrants/ Ties here the free soul down, here may/ The truth walk abroad with head held high.'[33] I can almost hear the buzz in the auditorium as these opening lines, Schiller's of course, are delivered. Yet Braun gets away with it, for several reasons. The lines are Schiller's and one can hardly lay claim to the Schiller inheritance and then disavow bits of it. The threat from Russia is an aristocratic one, as we are reminded in the 1918 interlude to which I have referred. But the lines are also about a principle which unites theatre and politics, the principle of *Wand-*

Posten reißen wer will, ich spiel ni mit. Da bleibch Zuschauer, was mei Recht is', p. 353.

33. 'Hier ist nicht Moskau nicht Despotenfurcht/ Schnürt hier die freie Seele zu, hier darf / die Wahrheit wandeln mit erhabnem Haupt', p. 313. Cf. Friedrich Schiller, *Demetrius*, in *Werke in Drei Bänden*, Munich 1966, III, 651–707. The lines 'Hier darf / Die Wahrheit wandeln mit erhabnem Haupt' are spoken by Odowalsky, p. 661.

lung which is the effect to the cause *Eingreifen*. Intervene and you cause change. So the integration of theatrical and political reality occurs in the phrase 'hier darf die Wahrheit wandeln'. Theatrically, what Braun shows us is that the quality Keats identifies in Shakespeare, that of negative capability, is shared by Schiller. His *Demetrius* fragment, perhaps because it is a fragment, has the capacity to support very different meanings from those Schiller explicitly gave it, since European history has now added a whole new perspective on the play. All Braun has done in one sense is to write out those meanings into a full text.

But the concept of *Wandlung* is more fundamental. Braun's *Dmitri* has changed the meaning of *Demetrius*, just as each time an actor plays a role he changes it. Here again there are direct parallels between aesthetic and political realities. In *Dmitri*, an actor dresses up to represent a false Demetrius, a pretender to the throne. This pretender has, as Braun indicates, more claim to power than the true Demetrius, the true heir, because the false leader rules by consent of the people and not by lineage alone. Finally, the false ruler is treacherously killed, though his deposition leaves the onlookers in the play profoundly unmoved, their indifference to the whole action finally placing politics firmly outside the main sphere of popular concern. The people, just as Büchner so neatly presented them in *Leonce and Lena*[34], care first about their stomachs, as well they might:

FIRST. If I shake a little it's because I have nothing particular in my stomach, for general shortage on the earth.

THIRD. That's OK brother, we too have nothing general in our stomachs except very particular hunger. [*They wait.*][35]

This ability to capture a whole political position aphoristically and comically gives even the most ideologically trenchant scenes in *Dmitri* a lightness of touch that engages rather than repels its audience. Not only have we just heard a stark reminder of the real political agenda, *die Suppenfrage*, but we have also had a quick glimpse of the relationship between *Waiting for Godot* and socialism. Peasants are always waiting, and what they wait for never comes.

34. Georg Büchner, *Leonce und Lena*, III. 2. in Lehmann, I, 127.
35. ERSTER. Wenn ich ein wenig zittere, so weil ich nichts Besonderes im Magen habe aus allgemeinem Mangel auf der Erde.
    DRITTER. Macht nichts Bruder, wir haben auch nichts allgemeines im Magen als besonderen Hunger. [*Warten*] (p. 318).

Like Brecht, Braun is interested in parables, and the parable of the alternative Dmitris, the alternative rulers, has many similarities with the parable of the two mothers in *The Caucasian Chalk Circle*. Is the fit ruler the one who governs by consent or by right? Basmanow gives us the correct answer with his pronouncement that the false one has to become the real one in the interests of the freedom of the people: 'Yes, everything looks to you. You bring freedom. He [the true Demetrius] must disappear.'[36] But Braun is not content with this statement alone, which could in a socialist realist aesthetic be taken as the happy end, the people's choice winning power by acclamation. Next to Dmitri's assumption of power Braun interposes an agit prop scene in which we learn how the Bolsheviki took over Moscow from the Czar. Well and good. The faithful are being shown how the dynamic of history repeats itself. But not so, for right at the end of the interlude is this sharp stage direction: [*They freeze in their texts. Stage-hands carry the figures off.*][37] This wonderful moment not only ironises the historical parallel, it also reinforces beautifully the theatricality of the whole piece, so that the historical dynamic is shown as theatrical in nature.

This perception is crucial to the radical challenge Braun is laying down to Brechtian orthodoxy, because he is stating quite categorically that if there is negotiation to be done about development of social and political forms then the theatre is the place to conduct it. Theatre is at the centre of revolutionary action, for the very reason that theatre is about the right to change truth: 'hier darf die Wahrheit wandeln'. There is one further connection between politics and theatre in this, for just as the actor draws power from the audience and performs his role by consent of the audience, so the ruler draws power from the people and governs by their consent. This connection is made explicit by Dmitri: 'Señores, Lords, Messieurs, Lads and Efendis. Where do I get the right? I get the right from the living. From the people. The interests of the people are our politics. We protect the people and the people protect us. We have the people's mandate.'[38] This returns me to my starting point. I

36. 'Ja, alles blickt auf Euch. Ihr bringt die Freiheit. Er [der wahre Demetrius] muß verschwinden', p. 329.
37. [*Sie erstarren in ihrem Text. Bühnenarbeiter tragen die Figuren hinaus*], p. 331.
38. 'Señores, Lords, Messieurs, Kumpane und Efendis. Woher nehme ich das Recht? Ich nehme das Recht von den Lebenden. Vom Volk. Die Interessen des Volks sind unsere Politik. Wir schützen das Volk, und das Volk schützt uns. Wir haben den Auftrag des Volks', p. 342.

143

believe that East German writers see more clearly than their West German counterparts that a major battle is being conducted within the German speaking cultural area for power over language and hence for power over the people, a battle for possession of the German past in which the seeds of the future lie. If the theatre is a central place of negotiation about political power, control of the theatre is a prime political consideration.

The relative failure of West German theatre to address this problem has made the task of the East so much the easier, to the point where I sense that the East is now unassailably in control, a position only confirmed by the remarkable influence the East now exerts directly on the West through its exiles. If in the current climate of better relations between East and West the already active East to West traffic continues, it is only a matter of time before the contemporary German theatre repertoire means to all intents and purposes the achievements of the East, achievements to which Braun has already made one of the most significant contributions.

10

Homburg-Machine—Heiner Müller in the Shadow of Nuclear War

J. H. Reid

MY point of departure is the first of Müller's *Wolokolamsker Chaussee* plays, *Russische Eröffnung*, written as a prelude to a production of Johannes R. Becher's *Winterschlacht* at the Deutsches Theater in Berlin in 1985.[1] It takes as its material an incident from the war in Russia. Hitler's armies have advanced to 121 kilometres from Moscow; the Red Army lacks equipment, tanks and bombers; it is demoralised. The arrival of fugitives and deserters makes those who are waiting for the next onslaught of the Germans still more nervous. In order to find out who can be relied on their commander fires a machine-gun salvo into the river; the men think the Germans have arrived, panic breaks out, they leap from cover and run into the forest; gradually, as they realise that it is a false alarm, they return to their places. The captain of one platoon, however, has even shot himself in the hand to avoid further involvement. He is brought before the Commander, who gives orders for him to be executed in front of the assembled battalion. In the Commander's imagination, first the Captain unsuccessfully pleads for his life, then

---

1. The following abbreviations denote the editions used:
GP 1 = *Geschichten aus der Produktion*, vol. 1, Westberlin 1974
GP 2 = *Geschichten aus der Produktion*, vol. 2, Westberlin 1974
GT = *Germania Tod in Berlin*, Westberlin 1977
H = *Herzstück*, 2nd edn, Westberlin 1983
I = *Gesammelte Irrtümer, Interviews und Gespräche*, Frankfurt 1986
M = *Mauser*, Westberlin 1978
SF = *Shakespeare Factory I*, Westberlin 1985
TA = *Theater-Arbeit*, Westberlin 1975
U = *Die Umsiedlerin oder Das Leben auf dem Lande*, Westberlin 1975
A second *Wolokolamsker Chaussee* play was published in *Theater der Zeit* 41 (1986), no. 2, 60–1, and a third is planned—see *I*, p. 182.

he himself rescinds the sentence of execution; in reality, however, the order to fire is given, and the sound of the shots is one he will never forget.

Wolokolamsker Chaussee I is interesting on a number of counts. In the context of the GDR's literature, a few years ago the presentation of the Red Army as less than heroic would have been most provocative, although a number of recent works imply that the GDR is developing a new degree of self-assurance with regard to the Soviet Union.[2] So it is comic that, as Müller reports, one 'plucky spectator' at a première in Bochum demonstratively got up and said 'I'm off', when he heard the word 'Moscow'.[3]

Provocation was the keynote of Müller's early didactic plays such as *Der Lohndrücker* and *Die Umsiedlerin oder Das Leben auf dem Lande* in which he refused to accept the harmonising premises of the cultural establishment and accentuated, albeit from a socialist standpoint, the conflicts which developing socialism was producing. Conflict is the basis of Müller's theatre, both in the material he uses and in the tension he creates between audience and stage: 'I believe in conflict. Apart from that I believe in nothing. That's what I try to do in my works: to strengthen people's awareness of conflicts, confrontations and contradictions.'[4] In *Wolokolamsker Chaussee I* the conflict is between the desire to be humane and the necessity to win the war—in order to save Russia the Commander has to kill a Russian. There are Brechtian overtones in this theme.

Formally the play is interesting in that after the radically avant-garde plays of the later 1970s and early 1980s, plays such as *Hamletmaschine* and *Bildbeschreibung*, it represents a return to the didactic pattern of Müller's earlier years. It is 'narrative theatre', 'epic theatre' in the strict sense of the term. On the printed page it consists entirely of blank verse narration by the Commander. Müller leaves it to the individual director to split the text into various roles, insisting only that the part of the Commander be

2. Christa's Wolf's novel *Kindheitsmuster* (1977) includes an account of the terrorising of German women by drunken Soviet soldiers after the end of the war, and the third volume of Erwin Strittmatter's *Der Wundertäter* (1980) describes the rape and death of a young girl under similar circumstances. On Müller's own account his *Philoktet* was 'auch eine Auseinandersetzung mit Problemen und mit Fehlentwicklungen, die z.B. mit der Person Stalins zusammenhängen.' (Quoted by Ulrich Profitlich, 'Über den Umgang mit Heiner Müller's *Philoktet*', *Basis* 10 (1980), 145.)
3. 'Erinnerungen an Bochum', in *Theater 1986, Jahrbuch der Zeitschrift Theater Heute*, Zurich 1987, p. 108.
4. 'Ich glaube an Konflikt. Sonst glaube ich an nichts. Das versuche ich in meiner Arbeit zu tun: das Bewußtsein für Konflikte zu stärken, für Konfrontationen und Widersprüche.' *I*, p. 86.

taken by two actors, an older one looking back, a younger one contemporary with the incident (*SF*, p. 250). This narrative element can be traced back to the myth interpolations in *Zement* (see *I*, p. 18). It becomes dominant in *Verkommenes Ufer*, while *Bildbeschreibung* is, as the title implies, pure narrative description. In 1980 Müller spoke of structures in his plays which increasingly gave him difficulty with the distribution of roles: 'The things I say, I can and will no longer attach to characters. I'm delegating something to characters that I don't want to know. It's becoming more and more arbitrary who says and does what. I've no longer the slightest interest in Frederick the Great. It can equally be Otto X, whose part can be played by Frieda.'[5] According to Müller the Commander's memory is a 'collective memory . . . The characters are interchangeable'.[6] This radical scepticism with regard to individuality is one to which we shall return. Nevertheless, inasmuch as a 'story' can without difficulty be reconstructed from the text, *Wolokolamsker Chaussee I* is a more conventional play. *Bildbeschreibung*, said Müller, was the 'end of the line' in that particular phase of his writing, and he now found himself compelled to strike out in another direction (*I*, p. 184).

In 1977 he had written: 'I believe we must leave the didactic play now until the next earthquake takes place.' Brecht's most uncompromising didactic play *Die Maßnahme*, on which Müller had modelled such works as *Mauser*, still, he said, assumed the validity of Christian humanist values; today 'humanism occurs only as terrorism, the Molotov cocktail is the last middle-class cultural experience'.[7] By 1985 it seems, the 'next earthquake' had come. In what sense? In his postscript to *Wolokolamsker Chaussee I* Müller insisted that the execution of the captain should be presented realistically, 'so that a war can be imagined in which reprieve would be the realistic solution', and went on: 'In the shadow of nuclear war, the alternative to communism, it appears utopian.'[8] Nuclear

---

5. 'Die Sachen, die ich da sage, will und kann ich nicht mehr an Figuren festmachen. Ich delegiere etwas an Figuren, die ich gar nicht wissen will. Es wird immer beliebiger, wer was sagt oder spielt. Friedrich der Große interessiert mich überhaupt nicht mehr. Es kann auch Otto X sein, dessen Rolle von Frieda gespielt werden kann.' *I*, p. 60.
6. 'kollektive Erinnerung. . . . Die Figuren sind auswechselbar.' *I*, p. 188.
7. 'ich denke, daß wir uns vom LEHRSTÜCK bis zum nächsten Erdbeben verabschieden müssen. Die christliche Endzeit der MASSNAHME ist abgelaufen, die Geschichte hat den Prozeß auf die Straße vertagt, auch die gelernten Chöre singen nicht mehr, der Humanismus kommt nur noch als Terrorismus vor, der MolotowCocktail ist das letzte bürgerliche Bildungserlebnis.' *M*, p. 85.
8. 'damit ein Krieg gedacht werden kann, in dem die Begnadigung die realistische

war will be the alternative to communism—again there are echoes of Brecht: the antagonistic conflicts between humanity and self-fulfilment will be overcome only in a communist society. In an interview Müller justified his return to the didactic model by the current situation (*I*, p. 187). He referred to the arms race, the American SDI programme and the current debates on disarmament (*I*, p. 193); pacifism was a problem which always arose 'at the moment of greatest threat', and his play was a 'discourse on pacifism' (*I*, p. 184). It is not, however, a pacifist play—there is no question that the Commander had to act as he did, although we are equally left in no doubt of the permanent pain that his decision caused him.

Müller attended the conference on peace issues which brought together writers from East and West in East Berlin in 1981. He admitted that it was an important initiative, but he also insisted that 'peace' must not be regarded as something which merely reflected relations between the capitalist and socialist world, enabling capitalism to continue to exploit the Third World; it was a 'nightmare that the choice between socialism and barbarism is being replaced by the choice between apocalypse and barbarism'.[9] In this context his statement that the reprieve of the coward in *Wolokolamsker Chaussee I* would be 'utopian' in view of the shadow cast by nuclear war, represents a line opposed to that of the peace movement—compatriots such as Christa Wolf had actually proposed unilateral disarmament measures on the part of the Soviet Union.[10] Elsewhere he said: 'To be honest, I can't take this problem of the possibility of the collective suicide of humanity terribly seriously. After all it only generalises something that has always been the case for the individual, that some day he must die.'[11] The nuclear apocalypse is merely a symptom of the eternal fact of man's mortality. Müller has been preoccupied with death from earliest times; the suicide of his first

---

Lösung ist . . . Im Schatten des Atomkriegs, der Alternative zum Kommunismus, scheint sie utopisch.' *SF*, p. 250.

9. 'Alptraum, daß die Alternative Sozialismus oder Barbarei abgelöst wird durch die Alternative Untergang oder Barbarei', in *Berliner Begegnung zur Friedensförderung. Protokolle des Schriftstellertreffens am 13./14. Dezember 1981*, Darmstadt 1982, p. 107. See also *I*, pp. 123, and 158–61.

10. *Voraussetzungen einer Erzählung: Kassandra. Frankfurter Poetik-Vorlesungen*, Darmstadt 1983, p. 88.

11. 'Ich kann auch, ehrlich gesagt, dieses Problem um den möglichen kollektiven Selbstmord der Menschheit nicht so ganz ernst nehmen. Damit ist doch nur etwas allgemein geworden, was für den einzelnen immer schon gestimmt hat, nämlich daß er irgendwann einmal sterben muß.' *I*, p. 123f.

wife Inge is a motif to which he returns again and again. In 1982 he
described the 'formula for theatre' as 'simply birth and death. The
effect of theatre, its impact, is the fear of change, since the last
change is death.'[12] The motif is so central that Michael Schneider
goes so far as to speak of Müller's 'death wish'.[13] Genia Schulz
places it in the context of mythical elements which Müller sets
against the superficialities of conventional Marxism; elsewhere she
relates it to themes of the baroque theatre, not least to Shakespeare's
Hamlet.[14] Nevertheless, the specific theme of the apocalypse is an important
one. *Der Bau* already contains allusions to the 'third world war'
which the Berlin Wall has been built to prevent (*GP* 1, p. 99), and to
rain polluted by strontium (p. 93). Müller's later, more visionary
plays are set at the end of time itself. *Die Hamletmaschine* (1977)
begins with 'Hamlet' looking back at a time when he stood addressing the waves, 'behind me the ruins of Europe'.[15] The final part
of the triptychon *Verkommenes Ufer* 'presupposes . . . the catas-
trophes on which mankind is working. The landscape may be a dead
star on which a search party from another age or from another
region hears a voice and finds a dead body.'[16] *Bildbeschreibung*
'describes a landscape beyond death'.[17] *Der Auftrag* is in some ways
a more conventional play, with a reconstructable plot and psychologically definable characters. But the Kafkaesque episode of 'The
man in the lift' may be placed at the moment of the outbreak of
global war. When summoned to meet 'No. 1' to be given his
'mission' the speaker was in the basement, 'an extensive area with
empty concrete chambers and bomb shelter notices'.[18] The race
against time described here is a race against the end of the world; he
gets into 'wild speculations: the force of gravity is diminished, a

12. 'Die Formel für Theater ist einfach Geburt und Tod. Der Effekt von Theater,
seine Wirkung ist die Furcht vor Veränderung, denn die letzte Veränderung ist der
Tod.' *I*, p. 102; cf. also *TA* p. 126.
13. 'Heiner Müllers Endspiele. Vom aufhaltsamen Abstieg eines sozialistischen
Dramatikers', in Michael Schneider, *Den Kopf verkehrt aufgesetzt oder Die me-
lancholische Linke. Aspekte des Kulturzerfalls in den siebziger Jahren*, Darmstadt
1981, pp. 209–17.
14. Genia Schulz, *Heiner Müller*, Stuttgart 1980, pp. 13, 45f and elsewhere.
15. 'im Rücken die Ruinen von Europa', *M*, p. 89.
16. 'setzt . . . die Katastrophen voraus, an denen die Menschheit arbeitet. Die
Landschaft mag ein toter Stern sein, auf dem ein Suchtrupp aus einer andern Zeit
oder aus einem andern Raum eine Stimme hört und einen Toten findet.' *H*, p. 101.
17. 'beschreibt eine Landschaft jenseits des Todes', *SF*, p. 14.
18. 'einem ausgedehnten Areal mit leeren Betonkammern und Hinweisschildern
für den Bombenschutz', *H*, p. 57.

fault, a kind of stutter in the earth's rotation',[19] the times are 'out of joint', as in *Hamlet*, but possibly literally; the 'mission' was 'the last possible measure against apocalypse',[20] whose beginning he is now experiencing. He gets out of the lift and he finds himself in Peru; the world has not been destroyed—or is this another world? Technological Europe may well have been destroyed, here there is still 'hope', although in the European's eyes the landscape is one which has 'no other task than to await the disappearance of mankind'.[21] Three important impulses of Müller's thinking come together here: the Third World, the apocalypse and the revolution. The 'mission' of the main play was to bring the revolution to Jamaica; its failure is linked to an apocalyptic vision of a world beyond the end of the world—for Müller once more the only alternative to a third world war is communism.

In a letter to the Bulgarian director of a production of *Philoktet* in 1983 Müller again addressed the possibility of an imminent apocalypse:

> The complete make-or-break test to which human collectives are exposed in this our possibly . . . last century will be survived only if humanity becomes a collective. The communist principle NONE OR ALL finds its ultimate meaning against the background of the possible suicide of the species. But the first step towards the merging of the individual with this collective is that he is torn in pieces, death or caesarean section the alternatives faced by the NEW MAN. The theatre simulates this step, house of pleasure and chamber of horrors for the transformation.[22]

Here is the corollary: on the one side nuclear war as the alternative to communism, on the other 'NONE OR ALL', the alternative to communism is the destruction of the world. The individual must be destroyed in order to ensure the survival of the collective—this is the theme of *Wolokolamsker Chaussee I* but also of many other plays by Müller. Death is 'the last change' (*I*, p. 102), Müller's

19. 'wilde Spekulationen: die Schwerkraft läßt nach, eine Störung, eine Art Stottern der Erdrotation', *H*, p. 59.
20. 'die letzte mögliche Maßnahme gegen den Untergang', ibid.
21. 'die keine andre Arbeit hat als auf das Verschwinden des Menschen zu warten', *H*, p. 62.
22. 'Die totale Zerreißprobe, der die menschlichen Kollektive in unserm vielleicht . . . letzten Jahrhundert ausgesetzt sind, wird die Menschheit nur als ein Kollektiv überdauern. Der kommunistische Grundsatz KEINER ODER ALLE erfährt auf dem Hintergrund des möglichen Selbstmords der Gattung seinen endgültigen Sinn. Aber der erste Schritt zur Aufhebung des Individuums in diesem Kollektiv ist seine Zerreißung, Tod oder Kaiserschnitt die Alternative des NEUEN MENSCHEN. Das Theater simuliert den Schritt, Lusthaus und Schreckenskammer der Verwandlung.' *H*, p. 103.

theatre simulates the destruction of the individual in order that the collective may emerge as the only hope for the survival of the human race. One way in which his plays take account of this anti-individualist insight is their lack of dramatic roles in the received sense—the 'interchangeability' of the characters of *Wolokolamsker Chaussee I*, for example.

The letter goes on to relate the bow of Philoctetes to the machine gun and by extension to nuclear weapons:

The final product of humanism, the emancipation of man from nature, is, provisionally, the neutron bomb. . . . The spiral of history ruins the centres by grinding its way through the margins. This form of movement, which for any one generation eludes understanding, leads to scepticism about progress, a scepticism which is existential so long as humanity has not redeveloped an awareness of itself as a species, which alone makes universal history possible and whose loss was the price which had to be paid for the exodus from the animal kingdom. The way back is cowboys-and-Indians romanticism, the modern attempt to bend the course of the spiral into a circle aims at the destruction of the planet.[23]

In these terms nuclear weapons, the means of destroying the planet, belong to the dialectics of the Enlightenment: man's rationality, the 'emancipation of man from nature', has led to the possibility of destroying nature itself. Unless he evolves a collective consciousness he will perish.

The relation between the Enlightenment and the current predicament of humanity is one to which Müller has addressed himself on a number of occasions. *Quartett* is set in a 'Salon before the French Revolution/Bunker after the third world war'.[24] Müller jokingly suggested this was an expression of historical optimism—there would be a life after the third world war (*I*, p. 107). More seriously, however, he is implying the relation between the eighteenth century, the age of the Enlightenment, and the future apocalypse. Choderlos de Laclos, on whose *Les Liaisons dangereuses Quartett* is

23. 'das vorläufige Endprodukt des Humanismus, als der Emanzipation des Menschen vom Naturzusammenhang, ist die Neutronenbombe . . . Die Spirale der Geschichte ruiniert die Zentren, indem sie sich durch die Randzonen mahlt. In dieser Gangart, die sich aus dem Blickpunkt einer Generation der Sinngebung entzieht, liegt der Zweifel am Fortschritt begründet. Er ist existentiell, solange die Menschheit Gattungsbewußtsein, dessen Voraussetzung die Möglichkeit von Universalgeschichte, nicht neu entwickelt hat. Sein Verlust war der Preis, der für den Auszug aus der Tierwelt gezahlt werden mußte. Der Weg zurück ist Indianerromantik, der moderne Versuch, den Gang der Spirale in eine Kreisbahn abzubiegen, zielt auf die Zerstörung des Planeten.' *H*, p. 110.
24. 'Salon vor der Französischen Revolution / Bunker nach dem dritten Weltkrieg', *H*, p. 71.

based, stands in the tradition of the rationality of the Marquis de
Sade; in Müller's version Merteuil asks rhetorically, 'Can it be less
than a mortal sin not to do that which it is given to us to think?' and
comments: 'The thought that does not become deed poisons the
soul.'[25] The eighteenth-century characters use their reason to devise
more and more torments for one another, more and more subtle
ways of seducing innocent young girls. So too new and ever more
terrible ways of destroying humanity are thinkable and must therefore be realised. *Quartett* is the third and last of a series of plays set
in the eighteenth century. It was preceded by *Leben Gundlings
Friedrich von Preußen Lessings Schlaf Traum Schrei* and *Der Auftrag.* In *Leben Gundlings,* according to Wolfgang Emmerich,
Müller appears as a radical critic of the Enlightenment. For Emmerich the central scene of the play is that set in a Prussian
madhouse, with its straitjacket, its anti-masturbation device, and the
professor who wishes to turn man into a machine, an allusion to the
eighteenth-century philosopher La Mettrie. Müller, says Emmerich,
'evidently does not believe in the *dialectics* of the Enlightenment . . .
rather he presents enlightenment itself, at least its Prussian version,
as repressive from the outset, anti-emancipatory, instrumental,
normalising, doing violence to (human) nature.'[26] This play too
ends apocalyptically, in a 'car-cemetery' in the United States of
America, the technological heir to the Enlightenment, whose 'last
president' turns out to be a robot, the realisation of La Mettrie's
'l'homme machine'. Müller's critique of the Enlightenment is, it
seems to me, more dialectical than Emmerich gives him credit for.
There is no return—'the way back is cowboys-and-Indians romanticism' (*H*, p. 110); but the robot president is itself executed by the
machine, the electric chair. This vision of the 'death of the machine
on the electric chair'[27] is followed by further visions which include
'HUMAN BEINGS OF NEW FLESH'.[28] The machine will even-

---

25. 'Kann es weniger als eine Todsünde sein, was uns zu denken gegeben ist nicht
auch zu tun . . . Der Gedanke der nicht Tat wird vergiftet die Seele.' *H*, pp. 79f.
26. 'glaubt offenbar nicht an eine *Dialektik* der Aufklärung . . . sondern setzt
Aufklärung selbst, jedenfalls ihre preußische Version, als von vornherein repressiv,
antiemanzipatorisch, instrumentell, (menschliche) Natur abrichtend, vergewal-
tigend.' Wolfgang Emmerich, 'Der Alp der Geschichte. "Preußen" in Heiner Müllers
"Leben Gundlings Friedrich von Preußen Lessings Schlaf Traum Schrei"', in *Deutsche Misere einst und jetzt. Die deutsche Misere als Thema der Gegenwartsliteratur.
Das Preußensyndrom in der Literatur der DDR,* ed. Paul Gerhard Klussmann and
Heinrich Mohr, Bonn 1982, p. 143.
27. 'Tod der Maschine auf dem Elektrischen Stuhl', *H*, p. 36.
28. 'MENSCHEN AUS NEUEM FLEISCH', ibid.

tually 'execute' itself, opening up the possibility of new utopian forms of life. The nuclear apocalypse would for Müller be just such a possibility, and there is a degree of coquettishness in his aestheticising of this motif (see *I*, pp. 176–81): nevertheless, in this sense he is not so pessimistic as is usually claimed.

To return to *Wolokolamsker Chaussee I*: Müller also described his play as a 'variation on HOMBURG'.[29] It contains a number of parallels to Heinrich von Kleist's early-nineteenth-century play *Prinz Friedrich von Homburg*. The Commander is the Elector: he tests his men by firing into the river, just as the Elector tests Homburg at the beginning of Kleist's play by giving his sleepwalking nephew the impression that he is to receive the victor's laurels from the hand of Natalie—this 'joke' leads to Homburg's absentmindedness on the following morning when he is to receive instructions on the conduct of the battle and thus indirectly to his disobeying orders and being sentenced to death. As in Kleist's play others plead with the Commander for the life of the Captain. The Commander replies (the blank verse in the original underlines the parallel): 'My command will be obeyed / And if 'twas wrong 'tis me that they shall shoot.'[30] Similarly the Elector gives Homburg the opportunity to decide whether the decision to execute him is unjust: 'If he can find the judgement is unjust / The order I'll rescind: he can go free.'[31] True, Homburg wins a battle, the Captain runs away and mutilates himself to avoid any action. But in both cases there is the motif of sheer physical terror—in Homburg's case when he sees his grave waiting for him. The Captain is to be executed 'because he could not keep control of himself'[32]—the same was true of Homburg, whose impetuosity had frustrated his uncle's strategy on more than one occasion in the past. And there is the 'dream scene' at the close of both plays. Homburg accepts his fate, extolling the 'sacred law of War' which he admits he infringed. Although he does not know it he is then pardoned by his uncle, who goes through the show of an execution in a scene which parallels the sleepwalking scene of the beginning: Homburg receives the laurels and the hand of Natalie, and the play ends with the chorus: 'Down with all the

---

29. 'Eine Variante auf HOMBURG', *I*, p. 185.
30. 'Mein Befehl wird ausgeführt / Und war es Unrecht soll man mich erschießen', *SF*, p. 247.
31. 'Wenn er den Spruch für ungerecht kann halten, / Kassier ich die Artikel: er ist frei.', IV. 1.
32. 'Weil er sich selber nicht befehlen konnte', *SF*, p. 247.

foes of Brandenburg!'[33] In *Wolokolamsker Chaussee I* the Commander dreams that after a testing sixty minutes he pardons the Captain amid gales of relieved laughter (*SF*, p. 248). Here, however, the dream remains a dream. Fehrbellin was, after all, a victory; the Red Army is still waiting for victories. That is one historical difference between the two situations. Müller suggested that the 'happy end' in *Homburg* was possible 'because it stays in the family, in the ruling class';[34] but the Captain and the Commander in *Wolokolamsker Chaussee I* are likewise of the 'ruling class', the post-revolutionary Soviet people. It is not the least of Müller's provocations that a variation on a play which has traditionally been viewed as glorifying Prussian-Brandenburgian militarism should be placed in the setting of the Soviet Union. The 'Prussianism' of the play implies a connection to *Leben Gundlings*. Kleist's idealism, the confidence that it is possible to reconcile the demands of individuality with those of the State, is rejected. Today's individuals are wholly subject to the 'machine'. But the Soviet setting suggests that Müller does not regard this completely negatively.

Wolokolamsker Chaussee I was not Müller's first play to imply the *Homburg* pattern. The execution motif is one to which he returns again and again. He must have retained a lasting memory of the executions of deserters and 'defeatists' in the closing months of the second world war, evoked, for example, in the opening image of *Traktor*: 'Some hung on lamp posts, tongues hanging out / On their bellies the sign I am a coward.'[35] In its first scene a German soldier is hanged for suggesting that it is unwise to plant mines in a field of potatoes, as they may need the potatoes when the war is over. *Germania Tod in Berlin* does not use the motif, but the Rotbuch edition contains a montage of photographs, including one of the newspaper report of the decision to execute Gary Gilmore in the United States. *Der Auftrag* is based on the story 'Das Licht auf dem Galgen' by Anna Seghers; it opens with the information that Sasportas has been hanged in Port Royal.

The scene 'Petty bourgeois wedding' from *Die Schlacht* is, perhaps surprisingly, relevant here. Hitler has committed suicide and the husband declares that they must follow his example. When the daughter is reluctant to die, he ties her to a chair, shoots her, then

---

33. 'In Staub mit allen Feinden Brandenburgs!' V II.
34. 'da es in der Familie bleibt, in der herrschenden Schicht', *I*, p. 185.
35. 'Einige hingen an Lichtmasten, Zunge heraus/ Vor dem Bauch das Schild Ich bin ein Feigling', *GP* 2, p. 9.

his wife, but cannot pluck up the courage to kill himself, not even when Hitler steps out of the portrait on the wall. Bourgeois ideology is unmasked: 'The best thing in life is to die for one's country' justifies the execution of daughter and wife; 'The strong man is most powerful on his own' justifies his own survival.[36] The scene is partly slapstick, however—one is reminded of Mel Brooks' film *Blazing Saddles*. When the husband first presses the trigger to shoot his daughter nothing happens—he has forgotten to load the gun. The audience collapses into relieved laughter, only to be still more horrified when the man loads and shoots. Here is one hint at the close of *Homburg*, foreshadowing that of *Wolokolamsker Chaussee I*: the utopia of a reprieve does not occur.

More obviously related to *Homburg* are the two didactic plays on the role of inhumanity in the service of humanity, *Der Horatier* and *Mauser*. In the former the Horatian, victorious over the Curatian, is enraged to find his sister lamenting the death of her fiancé, and kills her. His impetuosity causes him, like Homburg, to lose control, first by unnecessarily killing his opponent, who had already surrendered, then by killing his sister. For winning the duel the 'victor' is crowned with laurels; for 'going too far' he is then beheaded. Again there is no reprieve, although interestingly Müller originally intended his play to have an open ending, with the audience as judge.[37] *Mauser* is foreshadowed in the early prose piece 'The peasants stood . . .' (*GT*, p. 13). The three peasants to be executed are 'enemies of the revolution', their hands, like the hands of the officer who gives the order to fire, are 'worn from work'—as in *Wolokolamsker Chaussee I* the contradiction is that of killing members of the working classes in the name of the working classes. In *Mauser A* is to be executed for losing control in the course of his duty: day after day he has to execute the enemies of the revolution; eventually he 'loses consciousness', like Homburg, and tramples one of his victims into the ground. He too is condemned to death, but before he is executed he has to agree that his sentence is correct; like Homburg he endures the agony, but eventually accepts his fate. Unlike Homburg, *A* is not reprieved; the play ends, paralleling Kleist's 'Down with all the foes of Brandenburg' with the chorus : 'DEATH TO THE ENEMIES OF THE REVOLUTION'.[38] *A*

36. 'Das Schönste im Leben ist der Heldentod . . . Der Starke ist am mächtigsten allein', *U*, p. 11. The first quotation is from Horace, the second from Schiller's *Wilhelm Tell*.
37. Quoted by Schulz, *Heiner Müller*, p. 98.
38. 'TOD DEN FEINDEN DER REVOLUTION', *M*, p. 68.

defends himself to the Chorus with the words: 'I am a man. Man is
not a machine. / Killing and killing, remaining the same after each
death, / I could not do. Give me the sleep of the machine.'[39] He has
been required to behave like a machine in the service of the Revolution: his 'sleep', unlike that of the machine, contains dreams. The
contradiction here is that to create a humane world the individual
must first be dehumanised. Dehumanisation in the cause of progress
is, as we have seen, a theme of Leben Gundlings: 'man, alas is not a
machine' laments the Prussian professor.[40] 'I want to be a machine',
declares the Hamlet actor near the end of Hamletmaschine.[41] In
Quartett Merteuil describes her body as 'this machine' (H, p.
71)—sex, human relationships have become entirely mechanical,
governed by the mind. It is not the least of Müller's provocations
that he does not reject this mechanisation of life out of hand. Schulz
attributes his abandoning the original plan of leaving open the
ending of Der Horatier to his pessimism over the suppression of
democratic socialism in Czechoslovakia in 1968; in fact the words
she quotes suggest that Müller's concerns were less political than
scientific: 'At the end of 1968 the freedom of choice no longer
seemed to me to be a given; the question of the individual's
divisibility (reassemble-ability), by way of biochemistry, genetics,
medicine, seems to be a practical question . . .'[42] Marxism, 'scientific socialism', is, after all, the heir to the Enlightenment, revolutionary communism the heir to Marxism.

Executions are a leitmotiv of Zement. The play begins with a
quotation from Mauser, 'Sleep of the machines', here referring to
the factory machines which are still idle after the 1917 revolution. A
central scene involves Makar, whom the revolutionary tribunal had
condemned to death by firing squad: he had spared the life of a
woman traitor in return for sexual favours and has to be shot
because the reaction claims that the revolutionaries rape women.
The scene is a moving one: Makar is only nineteen; he too momen-
tarily lost control; he makes no effort to have himself reprieved and
in due course we hear the fatal shot. On three other occasions,
however, a reprieve of some kind takes place. The engineer Kleist
(nomen est omen?) had earlier betrayed four communists to White

39. 'Ich bin ein Mensch. Der Mensch ist keine Maschine. / Töten und töten, der
gleiche nach jedem Tod / Konnte ich nicht. Gebt mir den Schlaf der Maschine.' M,
p. 66.
40. 'der Mensch, leider, ist keine Maschine', H, p. 26.
41. 'Ich will eine Maschine sein', M, p. 96.
42. Schulz, Heiner Müller, p. 98.

Russians but is now working for the revolutionaries. Tschumalow cannot forgive him; twice he is about to kill him, but each time the characters 'freeze', a narrative passage intervenes and Kleist's life is then spared. Dascha, one of the revolutionaries, is captured by the White Guards and is about to be hanged; the officer offers to spare her if she will sleep with him (like Makar); eventually he frees her, only to be shot himself by members of the Red Army. And the last scene, set after the final victory of the Revolution, introduces a young officer of the White Guards, who accuses himself of having murdered revolutionaries and begs to be shot. But he is not shot; the former enemies are asked to place their services at the disposal of the Soviet Republic, and the ending, as in *Homburg*, is one of reconciliation.

Finally, there is, once again, *Leben Gundlings*. As a play about Prussia it invites the comparison; Kleist himself appears at one point (*H*, p. 33). At least two scenes have a direct bearing on the Homburg theme. The first is the execution of Katte, one of the historical episodes which inspired Kleist's play. The young Frederick, later to become Frederick II of Prussia, fled the tyrannical army régime with his friend Katte, only to be captured and court-martialled by his father. In Müller's version Frederick enters blindfolded, assuming that he is to be executed; suddenly the blindfold is removed and Katte is shot instead. There is no question of purification here, nor of Katte's willingness to die, it is a purely gratuitous killing, and the soldiers even joke about it. Homburg's 'execution' too was a joke, but he was not killed. Müller once directed *Homburg* in tandem with Brecht's *Fatzer*, commenting: 'The PRINCE OF HOM-BURG can be read as a play about a taming, the taming of an outsider, who is made to conform by this coarse joke with the pretended execution.'[43] In *Leben Gundlings* this is precisely what happens to Frederick, who now loses all his individuality and sensitivity and is almost literally 'extinguished' — as Katte falls dead his father callously remarks, 'That was Katte', to which Frederick replies, 'Sire, that was me'.[44] In the following scene we see him some years later behaving like his father, driving his soldiers back into battle. And the next scene but one repeats the Katte episode with Frederick now in the role of his father. A Saxon lady comes to him

43. 'Man kann den PRINZEN VON HOMBURG lesen als ein Stück über eine Zähmung, die Zähmung eines Außenseiters, der angepaßt wird mit diesem groben Scherz der gespielten Hinrichtung.' *I*, p. 53.
44. 'Das war Katte ... Sire, das war ich.' *H*, p. 16.

157

to plead for the life of her husband, who is to be shot for desertion. Varying the Elector's offer in Kleist's play, Frederick promises a reprieve and the destruction of his own myth, that of the uncompromising monarch, if that is what she wishes. She shakes her head—she cannot wish away the myth of Frederick the Great. And her husband is promptly shot before her eyes. Finally, a third execution occurs, as we have seen, at the end of the play, when the 'last president of the United States', a robot, is destroyed on the electric chair.

Müller is not the only dramatist to use the *Homburg* motif, although few have done so as consistently. From the reprieve of Macheath at the close of *Die Dreigroschenoper* through the deaths of Swiss Cheese and Eilif in *Mutter Courage* to the hanging of Azdak, frustrated at the last moment, in *Der kaukasische Kreidekreis*, Brecht again must have been a model for Müller. *Die Maßnahme*, on the execution by his comrades of a man who endangered the revolution by his impetuous actions, was the inspiration for *Mauser* and provides the closest parallel to Kleist's play, something which, so far as I am aware, has been noted only by one of the earliest reviewers of Brecht's play.[45]

Müller's obsession with the motif has a number of grounds. One element is evidently parody, the questioning of the literary heritage. He once declared, tongue in cheek no doubt, 'My chief interest in writing plays is to destroy things.'[46] Hamlet was for thirty years 'an obsession'; he attempted to destroy him with *Die Hamletmaschine*. What I have called Müller's 'Homburg-machine' is part of a satire on the Prussian tradition. Unlike Emmerich, however, I do not find Müller's attitude unambiguous—in 1982 he actually accused the GDR of having suppressed the positive aspects of Prussian history (*I*, p. 79), and in view of the official rehabilitation of Prussia which has been taking place in the GDR since the end of the 1970s he is not too far out of step with his compatriots. What distinguishes

---

45. A. E., 'Brecht und Eisler: "Die Maßnahme"', in *Berliner Tageblatt*, 15 Dec. 1930, reprinted in *Bertolt Brecht, Die Maßnahme. Kritische Ausgabe mit einer Spielanleitung*, ed. Reiner Steinweg, Frankfurt 1972, pp. 334–6. When in 1951 Brecht was rehearsing Becher's *Winterschlacht*, the play to which *Wolokolamsker Chaussee I* was the prelude, he referred to Homburg's 'Todesfurcht' as a parallel to one of the scenes there (*Gesammelte Werke*, ch. 16, Frankfurt 1967, p. 893.) Emmerich, 'Der Alp der Geschichte' mentions Rainer Kirsch's essay 'Implikationen aus "Prinz von Homburg"' and Brecht's poem 'Über Kleists Stück "Der Prinz von Homburg"', pp. 132–3.
46. 'Mein Hauptinteresse beim Stückeschreiben ist es, Dinge zu zerstören.' *I*, p. 102.

Müller's treatment of Prussia from that of other writers and critics is his uncompromising and provocative insistence on the unity of the progressive and dehumanising elements. Another motif is the theme of death, one of Müller's central preoccupations, as we have seen. Execution is a way of dying which confronts the victim with the reality of his mortality in a very direct way. Moreover its ritualistic aspects make it peculiarly theatrical, and this, I suspect, is one reason for its fascination for Müller, who has stressed on many occasions his opposition to 'illusionism' in the theatre.[47] His plays frequently draw attention to their own theatricality by their use of theatrical metaphors and by introducing a play within a play. In *Hamletmaschine* the 'Hamlet actor' is not Hamlet but an actor playing Hamlet; in *Der Auftrag* the revolutionaries put on masks—'very important' for Müller (*I*, p. 151)—before going about their business, and later they perform the 'Theatre of the Revolution' (*H*, pp. 53–61). It is not surprising to learn that Müller has translated 'All the world's a stage . . .' from *As you like it*. In *Quartett* Valmont suggests that the tedium of pre-revolutionary society can only be overcome by the spectacle of a war: 'A good antidote to the boredom of devastation. Life quickens when dying becomes a spectacle . . .'[48] But the notion of a 'spectacle' reflects back on the 'spectacle' *Quartett* and on the same motif in *Homburg*, where the prince takes part unwittingly in a 'play' for the benefit of his uncle and the court. Similarly in *Wolokolamsker Chaussee I* when the Commander fires his salvo into the river the men behave like 'puppets on a wire'; he 'stared at the spectacle . . . on my stage', where he had 'played the role of the Germans . . . and with great success the flight was my applause'.[49] By thematising theatricality in this way Müller is evoking a distanced, critical attitude in his audience.

There is one final point. Death demonstrates 'the irreversibility of time'.[50] But execution, after the *Homburg* pattern, always implies the possibility of a reprieve. This is the 'utopian' aspect of Müller's plays. In *Leben Gundlings* at the end of a 'patriotic puppet play' the stage is transformed into a 'ghost ship on which dead sailors nail

---

47. *TA*, p. 125; 'Erinnerungen an Bochum', p. 108.
48. 'Ein gutes Gift gegen die Langeweile der Verwüstung. Das Leben wird schneller, wenn das Sterben zum Schauspiel wird . . .' *H*, p. 76.
49. 'Puppen am Draht . . . / . . . Ich / . . . starrte auf das Schauspiel / Die Hand am Lauf der Waffe mit der ich / Auf meiner Bühne . . . / Den deutschen Part gegeben hatte und / Mit viel Erfolg die Flucht war der Applaus.' *SF*, p. 245.
50. 'die Unumkehrbarkeit der Zeit', *GT*, p. 32.

their captain to the mast. The film runs backwards, forwards again, backwards again. And so on, down through the centuries.'[51] This might be viewed as historical pessimism, a Nietzschean 'eternal recurrence'. But a film can be stopped; what a man has made man can also unmake. In *Wolokolamsker Chaussee I*, too, the dream of reprieve is a 'film', but one which 'breaks' (*SF*, p. 248). For Müller theatre is a 'process'; he refuses to do the audience's work for it by presenting solutions or 'positive heroes' (*TA*, pp. 121–3; cf. *I*, p. 39). His 'optimism' consists in his hope that his audience will find alternatives, imagining, for example, 'a war in which a reprieve would be the realistic solution' (*SF*, p. 250).

51. 'Geisterschiff, auf dem tote Matrosen den Kapitän an den Mast nageln. Der Film läuft rückwärts, wieder vorwärts, wieder rückwärts. Usw. durch die Jahrhunderte.' *H*, p. 17.

11

The Excitement of
Boredom—Thomas Bernhard

Rüdiger Görner

'SOMETIMES boredom was unobtrusive and sometimes nauseating and when I could no longer stand it', Sartre wrote in his auto-biographical essay *Les Mots*, 'I would succumb to the deadliest temptation. Orpheus lost Eurydice through impatience; I often lost myself through impatience.'[1] There can be no doubt that ennui has become one of the most debilitating and chronic afflictions of our age. Moreover, the diagnosis is now almost as commonplace as is the syndrome. All needs seem to be satiated, all unknown terrain has been explored, all taboos have been broken. The disillusionment is complete. Only inveterate humanists like the psychoanalyst Bruno Bettelheim will still speak out publicly against the *ennui général* and maintain that human life is not pointless.[2] Such claims, however, have become curiously dated. By the same token, the recognition that ennui is one of the most pervasive phenomena of post-industrialist society is no longer merely the prerogative of the cynic. Sartre's statement is not just meant as a verdict, it marks the moralist's position and holds out the hope that ennui might become productive if it were to lead to self-analysis, that it is not necessarily a depraved form of self-love as another Frenchman, André Glucks-mann, suggested.[3] The question of what sustains the individual, given the overwhelming sense of pointlessness, is one of the main concerns in Thomas Bernhard's dramatic works. This is not a mere coincidence but an integral part of Bernhard's artistic message. His play *Am Ziel* focuses on a dramatist who feels quite unable to create

1. Jean-Paul Sartre, *Words*, trans. Irene Clephane, Harmondsworth 1986, p. 152.
2. In *The Listener*, 24 April 1987. See also Viktor E. Frankl, *Der Mensch vor der Frage nach dem Sinn*, Munich 1980, pp. 180–86.
3. *Frankfurter Allgemeine Zeitung*, 27 March 1987.

a truly dramatic situation—in the classical sense of the word. If there is any tension, it is only in the accounts of how the characters try to extract themselves from the tedium of their lives. Not surprisingly, Bernhard's young dramatist makes his debut with a piece entitled 'Save yourself if you can'.

Bernhard's own first play, *Ein Fest für Boris*, set the tone for a whole sequence of dramatic sketches, all of them characterised by a feeling of futility so irredeemable that it borders on the grotesque. The protagonist in *Ein Fest für Boris* is the embodiment of this mood. She is disabled but her handicap seems only to have increased her resoluteness and her thirst for power. Despite her indefatigable will, this monstrous female, like most of Bernhard's dramatis personae, is subject to fits of excessive boredom: 'Everything', she says, 'is just a daily grind, day after day, a repeating of repetitions.'[4]

In his *Ethics* Aristotle argued that living to a set pattern was one of the preconditions for a virtuous life. Nothing could be further removed from Bernhard's position. For the latter-day characters in Bernhard's plays, reduced and exhausted as they are, the habitual is sheer hell. Their lives are made up of a series of 'blue Mondays', days of repentance one might say, for blue used to be the colour of repentance in medieval times. But what is it that they repent? Nothing less, it seems, than their own presence, reprehensible to themselves, in this world of unrelieved boredom. They know that the curse which prescribes the endless repetition of the same can only be broken if they turn around to take a last look at Eurydice, at the burning Gomorrah or, as Sartre would have put it, at their own madness.[5]

In Bernhard's scenarios we encounter people weighed down by depression. Their virtual immobility has nothing to do with a calm or composed state of mind, rather it is marked by acute inhibition and extreme fretfulness. Most of his characters suffer from mental and/or physical defects. They are hypochondriacs, dissatisfied and eccentric individuals, failures who have lost all sense of direction. Their only true possessions are their anxieties and their madness and perhaps their hatred of those equally as pathetic as they are themselves, with whom they share their lives.

Nietzsche's counterpoint to his own vitalistic aspirations, the idea of 'eternal recurrence of the same', is unfolded into a complete

---

4. 'Alles ist jeden Tag tagtäglich / eine Wiederholung von Wiederholungen', Bernhard, *Die Stücke 1969–1981*, Frankfurt 1983 (henceforward *DS*), p. 12.
5. *Words*, p. 152.

pathology of autistic behaviour in Bernhard's plays. One of Bernhard's characters, Moritz Meister, summarises this connection as follows: 'Nietzsche Stieglitz and back again you understand . . .'.[6] And back again—from one artificial world into another equally artificial one. In *Ein Fest für Boris* the possibilities of coming to terms with such limitations are reduced to a single idea, a veritable *idée fixe*. The crippled and ostracised characters who make up the cast of this play 'constantly wonder what kind of /suicide/ would be the most bearable one'.[7] Whatever reaches these people from the outside is immediately transformed into a litany of repetitions. Thus, in *Ein Fest für Boris*, 'The Song of the Wagtail' is meant to bring hope to the crippled outcasts, but they receive only its somewhat sombre refrain which becomes the signature tune of their meaningless lives. 'In the dark, in the dark/it has ceased to fly.'[8] In this world steeped in *taedium vitae* the word 'change' is unknown. Everything is dominated by an irreconcilable hatred, a hatred which absorbs all energies. Whether Thomas Bernhard shares his characters' by now almost proverbial hatred is a moot point. It is clear, however, that he seems to try and free himself from his pent-up resentments through incessant writing and it remains to be seen whether his literary excesses will prove more therapeutic than his characters' monomaniacal pursuits.

In Camus's *Etat de Siège* Diego exclaims at one point 'I prefer hatred to your smile. I despise you'[9]—a statement which could be adopted to describe Bernhard's fraught relationship with his native Austria. Apart from his preoccupation with the monstrosity that is human life, it is primarily Austria and the Austrian past which compel Bernhard to write; his relationship with his native country is clearly determined by a double bind. The emotional pressure generated by this constellation is, however, balanced by an extraordinary degree of formal control. Bernhard's cascades of words are by no means the result of random verbal proliferation. The method of composition is that of 'a musician in words', to use Busoni's characterisation of Rilke. The dramaturgic principle behind Bernhard's scenes—in both senses of the word—is a kind of serialism in words which, almost by definition, tends towards an eternal mono-

---

6. 'Nietzsche Stieglitz und wieder zurück verstehen Sie . . .!, *DS*, p. 281.
7. 'Wir denken fortwährend darüber nach auf welche Weise / der Selbstmord / für uns am erträglichsten ist', *DS*, p. 67.
8. 'Im Finstern im Finstern / sie fliegt schon lang nicht mehr', *DS*, p. 68.
9. Paris 1948, p. 29.

logue. Bernhard likes to structure these monologues by inserting the phrases 'on the one hand . . . on the other hand . . .'. Unlike Kierkegaard's famous existentialist challenge *Either* . . . *Or*, the pseudo-alternatives thus introduced do not oblige the characters to make up their minds, but provide a mechanism which allows them to encircle their pet hatreds again and again.

It goes without saying that Bernhard rejects the amorphous Austrian myth which is propagated, with differing degrees of intensity, by writers such as Schnitzler, Hofmannsthal, Stefan Zweig and Joseph Roth. Bernhard's resentment centres on what he sees as an unreflected, opportunistic glorification of a defunct past which gave rise to one of the most despicable collective aberrations of this century. Compared with Bernhard's relentless onslaughts, Hofmannsthal's critique of language looks positively tame and timid and even Schnitzler's discoveries in the field of social psychology seem no more than an innocuous divertissement.

There is no indication in Bernhard's work that he is interested in a sophisticated critique of language of the kind developed by other contemporary playwrights such as Botho Strauss or Peter Handke. The destructive diatribes into which Bernhard's characters almost habitually launch themselves assault the audience and in this they are reminiscent of the earliest position adopted by Handke in his play *Publikumsbeschimpfung*. These recurrent verbal assaults are rehearsals for a rebellion that can never really be unleashed because its champions are emotionally attached to the objects of their hatred.

Nor are Bernhard's plays based on plots in the accepted sense of the term. When the curtain rises we are presented with a situation which became petrified and irredeemable a long time ago. It is clear from the outset that nothing will give any more. The characters, perfectionists of despair, will keep on going through their motions. They no longer even entertain the hope that they might be liberated by a sudden turn of events or at least a *coup de théâtre*. Bernhard provides scarcely any stage directions. The settings are bare: last resorts, much like the minimal environments of zoos in which animals eke out the remainder of their lives.

Despite these singularly unattractive facets of Bernhard's dramatic works, they have acquired an absolutely devoted following. In their complete faithfulness Bernhard enthusiasts almost resemble the congregation at Bayreuth. Yet there is a difference. Wagner's music has frequently been described as an addictive drug. Bernhard's tirades, however, could be said to be infused with poison. Amazingly, though, the audience gobbles up the unwholesome meal, knowing that it is virtually indigestible. At the end, when paralysis has set in all round, Bernhard himself occasionally appears upon the stage where, having subjected the audience to his venom throughout the evening, he takes a deep bow in front of those whom he so unremittingly despises. Hatred has become an ornament, part of a complex game of double standards which culminates, appropriately, in a gesture of utter malice, a sort of silent monologue on the theme of contempt.

But let us return to what the plays actually do articulate. No matter who is holding forth in Bernhard's plays, the speeches invariably revolve round certain grandiloquent terms which seem to act as stabilisers in a linguistic realm threatened by centrifugal forces. 'Life', 'fear', 'death', 'art', 'science', 'the state', 'the world', 'nature', 'everything' and 'nothing'—these wholesale concepts are invoked in Bernhard's rhetorical effusions but are never differentiated or tested against any concrete reality. As hypostatised notions they are the cornerstones in monologues employed as a means to power by those who are both ignorant and impotent. This is what Bernhard's plays demonstrate in a unique way. Monologue stands for arrogance or presumption and, ultimately, for tyranny.

Hardly any writer since Thomas Mann has dedicated himself so exclusively to the subject of art as has Thomas Bernhard. What is the place of art or its message in this agonising pandemonium which we call life? Can it provide a measure of diversion or relief in this tiresome gamut of repetitions? These are questions which Bernhard and his characters ask obsessively and to which—quite naturally, as Bernhard would say—there can be no answer. On the one hand, Bernhard presents art as the object of repetitive exercises which wear everything down. An instance of this is the farce *Die Macht der Gewohnheit* in which a number of oddly assorted musicians try—in vain—to produce a passable rendering of Schubert's *Forellenquintett*. On the other hand repetition is seen as the object of art, for example when one of the characters in *Die Berühmten* mocks the eternal recurrence of the same by imitating the voices of animals.

Inscribed in Bernhard's plays is, therefore, not only a pathology of the eternal recurrence of the same but also a pathology of the arts which is revealed through a visit backstage. In *Der Ignorant und der Wahnsinnige*, one of the central figures is the 'Queen of the Night',

165

a world famous soprano who has sacrificed her personal life and become one with the role she has sung so many times. Through constant practice she has completely mastered her art, at the price of her own humanity—she has turned into an art machine. Her outlook is jaded. 'We know all operas/all plays/we have read everything/we know all the most beautiful places/and secretly we hate the audience.'[10] It is the selfsame feeling of ennui at the endless recurrence of both natural and artificial phenomena that not only inspires Bernhard's writing but has, in fact, become its substance. The repetitive pattern so completely dominates Bernhard's style that there is no appreciable difference between his prose and his dramatic language. And whatever the theme, it is subjected to the same stylistic treatment. Bernhard's readers know after the first few words that they are reading Bernhard. It almost seems as though, out of a deep-seated fear of anonymity, Bernhard feels compelled to assert his identity by cultivating his extremely mannered and unmistakable style.

Although Bernhard does put the patience of his audience to the test by presenting it with his unending variations on the theme of pointlessness, this does not mean that he is incapable of inventing profoundly moving scenes. His short piece *Minetti* comes to mind, a play at the centre of which there is a clapped-out actor in his late seventies who is reduced to day-dreaming about the great roles of the dramatic repertoire. He still entertains the hope that the artistic director of the Flensburg Theatre, not exactly the focal point of West Germany's cultural life, will engage him to play King Lear. But it is obvious that nothing will come of such dreams. Minetti is finished. Only the ability to survive on the absolute minimum fulfilment of his wishes keeps him going. That and a substantial dose of hatred which he vents by denouncing his own origins: 'The place where one is born is one's murderer.'[11]

Claus Peymann once remarked that in each of Bernhard's plays the bourgeoisie is made to perform a *danse macabre*. At the same time Peymann referred to the almost 'classical' aspects in Bernhard's works for the stage. The terminal decline of the bourgeoisie and the desire for self-sacrifice which the classical line of development suggests, complement and permeate each other in bizarre ara-

---

10. 'Wir kennen alle Opern / alle Schauspiele / wir haben alles gelesen / und wir kennen die schönsten Gegenden auf der Welt / und insgeheim hassen wir das Publikum', *DS*, p. 116.
11. 'Der Geburtsort ist der Mörder des Menschen', *DS*, p. 581.

besques. Peymann argues that the more complex and idiosyncratic Bernhard's plays are, the more they demand a realistic and literal production, a meticulously straight transposition of 'the text'.[12] Peymann, however, ignored his own prescriptions when he produced *Die Jagdgesellschaft*. Where Bernhard wanted to see trees in the hunting lodge, Peymann put them outside and, in consequence, distorted the meaning of the play at that particular point. Bernhard knew what he was alluding to. After all, there is only one scene in the history of European drama where trees form part of an interior setting representing the unity of inside and outside world: the hunting lodge in *Die Jagdgesellschaft* is intended as a reference to Hunding's abode in *Die Walküre*. Bernhard, who is given to quoting his own chapter and verse, repeating, almost compulsively apodictic statements from earlier works, also likes to quote the great names and works of the past. Quotations of this sort reveal the artistic heritage as a sham. Travesty remains the only possible answer. Yet the comic elements which arise from the destruction of exalted precedents provide no more of an answer than did the aborted tragedies. Bernhard's point and counterpoint never lead to any kind of resolution. The contradictions are patently irreconcilable.

A central paradigm of this is perhaps that of health and sickness. In Bernhard's plays, those who are able-bodied and enjoy seemingly everlasting health, generally display fascist or crypto-fascist traits. On the other hand, moral and intellectual superiority is predicated upon physical handicaps. 'My paralysis is possibly/the cause of my genius', speculates the eponymous hero in *Der Weltverbesserer*,[13] and in *Vor dem Ruhestand* Rudolf tells his sister who is paralysed but intellectually far superior to him: 'Only your crippled state/gave you the chance to survive.'[14] Misfortune in Bernhard's plays is compounded because 'healthiness' is a state no less chronic and incurable than most severe forms of paralysis.

Pathological deformations wherever one turns. It is this state of affairs that informs Bernhard's highly charged, extremist diction of which Ingeborg Bachmann said: 'Bernhard's words are full of pathos, if we still know what this term originally meant, full of

12. Claus Peymann, 'Mündliches Statement zum Thema: Thomas Bernhard auf der Bühne'. In *Literarisches Kolloquium Linz 1984: Thomas Bernhard*, ed. A. Pittertschatscher and J. Laichinger, Linz 1985, p. 191.
13. 'Möglicherweise ist meine Lähmung / die Urheberin meines Genies', *DS*, p. 912.
14. 'nur mit deiner Verkrüppelung / hattest du eine Überlebenschance', *DS*, p. 739.

sorrow and suffering.'[15] True, there is a great deal of authentic pathos in Bernhard's language but also much eccentric ranting. His characters quite literally talk everything to pieces. The objective correlative of these exercises in dissolution is the debris of culture. Herr von Wegener, the ultra-conservative journalist in *Über allen Gipfeln ist Ruh*, serves up the following hotch-potch: 'This reminds me of Kierkegaard / Enten Eller / Either Or / even this giant up there in the North / what we have in him is our Liszt as philosopher / as aesthetic and ethical thinker living in desperation / I am convinced it was your husband's attachment to Kierkegaard / that made him into the extraordinary man / he is today / And at one point in the Germania novel he actually speaks / of My inner Copenhagen.'[16]

Bernhard's characters continue to function as language machines even though they have long since died an inner death. Their words, generated by the resounding emptiness inside them, are as redundant as their atrophied lives. For the audience the point of fascination lies in the question as to how long these wretched creatures will be able to endure themselves, let alone others. In *Der Präsident* the president's wife seems to have reached the end of her tether. Outraged by her husband's favourite pastime, she exclaims: 'He is reading Metternich / nothing but Metternich / Metternich / Metternich.'[17] Clearly, it is repetitiveness that renders everything absurd and that is the cause of the stalemate the characters have reached. Bernhard's plays are, essentially, about stalemates. There is no room for manoeuvre. The pattern is broken only occasionally when the characters discover something 'new' that will preoccupy them for a while, distract them from their pedantic rituals. In *Der Präsident* the temporary relief is provided by a game called 'being afraid of anarchists'. At last there is something to talk about. Paranoia as a new lease of life. Not that this leads anywhere. The excitement subsides, doleful silence sets in.

There is also a different kind of silence in Bernhard's plays, the

---

15. Ingeborg Bachmann, *Thomas Bernhard*. In *Werke*, vol. IV ed. C. Koschel, I. Weidenbaum and C. Münster, Munich and Zürich 1978, p. 364. ('Sie sind voll Pathos, wenn man noch weiß, was dieses Wort wirklich bedeutet, sie sind voll Leiden, und die Erträglichkeit und Unerträglichkeit hängen damit aufs Engste zusammen.')

16. 'Dazu fällt mir Kierkegaard ein / Enten Eller / Entweder Oder / selbst ein derartig im Norden Ringender / hier haben wir Liszt als Philosophen / Ästhetiker und Ethiker und Verzweiflungsmenschen / Ich glaube die Kierkegaardbeziehung Ihres Mannes / hat ihn zu dem Außerordentlichen gemacht / der er heute ist / An irgendeiner Stelle im Germaniaroman steht ja auch / Mein Kopenhagen des Geistes.' *DS*, p. 868.

17. *DS*, p. 383.

silence of those who at one point in their lives appear to have encountered something like 'meaning', who got to know themselves and others (a horrifying experience, according to Nietzsche). Clara's silences, in *Vor dem Ruhestand*, are a means of revenge. By simply not saying anything, Clara makes the rules of a game which implies incestuous feelings between Rudolf and Vera, her brother and sister. The emotions escalate because of Clara's persistent silence and eventually lead to Rudolf's death. Vera's reaction: 'You are to be blamed / you and your silence / you and your endless silence.'[18]

Whether Clara really is guilty remains an unresolved point. She is guilty in one sense because through her relentless silence she literally extinguished her brother; and in another because she failed to inform the authorities that Rudolf was a committed fascist. The two forms of guilt cancel and compound each other, a prototypical Bernhard paradox. This is as close as Bernhard ever gets to making concrete allegations. The crimes of his protagonists are anonymous. Of course those who were (and are) fascists are despicable. But those who resisted passively and claim some kind of moral superiority are not any less despicable for all that. They are all in the same family. Philosophically, the vigour of Bernhard's pessimism owes much to Schopenhauer; in terms of dramaturgic dispositions it is influenced by the recognition that the most debilitating influence on our lives is the family bond, as the play *Ritter, Dene, Voss* with its echoes of Chekhov demonstrates. In Bernhard, the dream of love between brothers and sisters, which bourgeois culture both relegated and secretly entertained, has finally come to an end. We are all united now—not by our love but by the pathetic beastliness which Bernhard identifies as being the hallmark of the human condition in our age.

When boredom regularly turns into hatred and hatred into boredom the main purpose of the exercise seems to be an exposition of the *élan négatif*. Paradoxically, the idea of negativity in Bernhard's plays is often introduced by characters who say 'yes' to everything. Yet they only appear to represent what has been termed by Marcuse 'affirmative culture'; in fact they only say 'yes' because they have lost all interest in a critical investigation of the conditions of their lives.

Those who take a critical stance do so compulsively and to the

---

18. 'Du bist schuld / mit deinem Schweigen / du mit deinem ewigen Schweigen', *DS*, p. 792.

point of self-caricature. Bernhard's *Weltverbesserer* represents this particular type of character deformation. We are given to understand that he has elaborated a complex scheme for wide-ranging and general improvements but we do not learn anything about its actual content. The constant references to 'factual logic' and the manifest desire to undermine the conventional suggests that the *Traktat zur Verbesserung der Welt* is a cross between the *Tractatus-logico-philosophicus* and the *Steppenwolf*.

Many of Bernhard's characters dream of a self-liberating revolt, of subversion and anarchy; but they are too weak to translate their dreams into practice. The 'mother' in Bernhard's scenic eschatology *Am Ziel* is an example of this. She tries to break free from her personal prison by talking ceaselessly; she talks until she comes to feel a certain strength that might enable her to change her life. Even so she needs additional support from someone else. The prop in her case happens to be a young writer who describes himself as an anarchist. But he too is capable only of *talking* about anarchism and ultimately the curious pair's options are limited to the destruction of their own mirror images.

Nietzsche once characterised the theatrical world of his time by saying that it reflected both the utter boredom that governed society and its frantic search for distraction.[19] Bernhard's stage characters do not even know the difference between ennui and *divertissement* any more. Pain and pleasure have merged, forming an erratic bloc that serves as pedestal for negativity. Despite this pronounced tendency towards petrification Bernhard's plays undeniably generate an element of excitement, chiefly because the author contrives to construct a kind of *machina ex deo*, that is to say he creates a sense of mechanical repetition which might, or so the spectator is made to believe, eventually wear itself out and be replaced by something yet to come. However, this messianic 'something' never materialises. Prophecy, for Bernhard, has lost its enigma and turned into the enunciation of platitudes like 'Death completes / life'.[20]

Bernhard's at once elliptic and rambling style poses special problems for his interpreters. Vast generalisations of deliberate imprecision obscure rather than reveal meaning. The characters' monologues have, for the most part, a cyclic structure, but the circles never become hermeneutic. Nor does it help to take the temporal and

19. *Werke*, vol I, Munich, Vienna, Berlin 1978, p. 410.
20. 'Der Tod komplettiert / das Leben', *DS*, p. 377.

spatial structures in Bernhard's plays as points of reference since both space and time are of minor importance in his stage works.[21] Bernhard shows people who might be anywhere, at any time, going through their motions; there is no sense of teleology, no indication of where we are at. All calendars have been suspended, the roads are no longer passable. Condemned to remaining at home with nothing to relate to but their own company Bernhard's characters lose all sense of proportion, of nearness and distance. It is indicative of this state that outsize conjectures and myopic observations are virtually interchangeable. Reasoning under these circumstances becomes a kind of dunces' game, a form of banishing the fear of darkness and any attempt to create order is reduced to the counting of steps and similar rituals of regularity and security.

It is for these reasons that interpreters of the roles Bernhard has written often find it difficult to provide more than approximations of uncertainties. They inherit the disorientation of the characters and in order to find their way about they have to look for hints other than those given by the traditional meaning of words. They have to sense the various degrees of imbalance between how much is said and what is said. Moreover the varying rhythms have to be considered as well as the ever-changing relationships between the mass of spoken words and the sudden silences that break into the 'dialogue'. A passage from *Die Jagdgesellschaft* illustrates this point.

WRITER. [*pouring a glass of sherry for himself, another one for the Generalin and returning to the window*]
Two hours of Lermontov
and then another two hours of Lermontov
GENERALIN. Or two hours of Majakowski
and then another two hours of Majakowski
WRITER. Or Pushkin
All of a sudden I remembered that aphorism
It is stillness puts things right
But I did not come back
Nothing but that phrase It is
Stillness puts things right
after a pause[22]

---

21. This is in contrast to his prose. In *Beton* and in *Wittgenstein's Neffe*, for instance, space is of great importance.
22. SCHRIFTSTELLER. [*schenkt sich ein Glas Sherry ein, auch der Generalin, und er geht wieder zum Fenster zurück*] Zwei Stunden Lermontow / und dann wieder zwei Stunden Lermontow

Both Writer and Generalin follow, to begin with, the same rhythmical pattern indicating the identity of their mood and view. When this pattern breaks up (after 'Or Pushkin') there appears to be a sort of prospect of change, but it remains unrealised since the aphoristic fragment which comes to the Writer's mind itself produces a different pattern, both in terms of rhythm and of thought. The sudden silence which then sets in renounces the idea expressed in the wistful phrase though this scarcely makes an appreciable difference in the oblique exchanges between the two characters.

An endless comedy of words, reminiscent perhaps of Arthur Schnitzler and his verbal relativism as expressed in his *Komödie der Worte*. The lines of tradition connecting Austrian playwrights are fairly pronounced and it is therefore not surprising that in Schnitzler's *Stunde des Erkennens* we come across the following passage:

ORMIN. We do not wish to take the words
    too seriously, do we.
KLARA. Take them as seriously or
    literally as you like.[23]

This extract would be an apposite motto for most of Bernhard's plays, except that Bernhard, in contrast to Schnitzler, has stripped his particular brand of verbal relativism of any residual human feeling and hope. Schnitzler had always reserved for himself the right to sketch into his dialogues faint glimmers of hope, even in plays like *Der einsame Weg* where he introduces people who are very tired of life and surrounded by a deep sense of melancholy.

Despite (or because of) his relativistic use of language, Bernhard frequently employs the vocabulary of ontology but, as would be expected, with parodistic inflections. The linguistic relics of Existentialism are presented as alien, erratic verbal blocs that will not fit into any rhythmic scheme. We hear of 'the becoming of the being' and of 'the being of the becoming' and realise what it is that attracts Bernhard to these resoundingly vacuous concepts. They allow him to demonstrate how the language of (Heidegger's) existentialism,

---

GENERALIN. Oder zwei Stunden Majakowski / und dann wieder zwei Stunden Majakowski
SCHRIFTSTELLER. Oder Puschkin / Auf einmal fiel mir der Aphorismus ein / Die Ruhe macht es wider gut / Aber ich kam nicht wider / nur immer Die Ruhe macht es wieder gut / *nach einer Pause*', DS, p. 177.
23. *Das dramatische Werk*, vol VII, Frankfurt 1979, p. 21.
ORMIN. Wir wollen die Wörte nicht gar zu schwer und wichtig nehmen.
KLARA. Nehmen Sie aut so wichtig und / wörtlich als Sie wollen.

which serves as a paradigm for all corrupted language, spins out of control, generates more and more words and almost buries the questions of life which gave rise to philosophical investigation in the first place. Much of Bernhard's indefatigable hatred stems from his awareness that he has to work with a totally spoiled language; at the same time there is, as with any other writer, the sheer love of expressing himself. This love-hate relationship with language results in a form of rhetorical invective which, in contrast to Dürrenmatt or Ionesco, avoids all metaphors. Metaphors throughout Bernhard's plays are replaced by obdurate repetition, a device which refers the audience to the one and only truth of the 'eternal recurrence of the same'. The objective correlative of this is the experience of boredom documented in literature since the early nineteenth century. Büchner's Lenz believes boredom to be the cause of all human actions, emotions and thoughts: 'Most of us pray out of boredom, others fall in love out of boredom, some are virtuous and some are evil—only I am nothing, nothing—I do not even feel like doing away with myself; it really is too boring!'[24] Any of Bernhard's stage characters could have said that too. Each of them is his own organ-grinder whose mind is gnawed by his repetitive tune. All fantasies and dreams have been abandoned; the great myths are defunct. Bernhard does not try to revive them. If he alludes to them at all—as for instance in *Die Jagdgesellschaft* where he evokes memories of the myth of nature—the attempt reminds one of a coroner's inquest. The indictment inherent in this is that the very nature of life has changed, that life no longer lives but has become a simulation of something we have long since lost and gambled away.

24. *Lenz*, trans. Michael Hamburger, Chicago 1972, p. 56.

12

The Art of Transformation—Herbert Achternbusch's Theatrical Mission

W. G. Sebald

HERBERT ACHTERNBUSCH's literary output clearly defies any notion of an orderly body of work.[1] One text grows out of another, or alternatively, into another, and no sooner has a thing been more or less knocked into shape and put up for publication than it is already being cannibalised all over again for the next project. Disorder is turned into a system and encouraged by an editorial policy that is both abstruse and impenetrable. The chaos has been compounded over the last few years by Achternbusch's presentation of his collected works, an enterprise which has resulted in further rearrangements of his kaleidoscopically mobile texts. The motivating force behind the continuous process of de- and reconstruction is doubtless the author's compulsion to reclaim and to hoard everything that he considers his own. A primitive collector's instinct seems to lead him to reassemble, continually, his stray bits and pieces, to sweep his fragmentary production, time and again, into one big pile as if this was the only way of making quite sure that it is still all there.

This perpetual process of disruption and reconstitution has somehow generated half a dozen plays for the theatre—a surprising turn of events since Achternbusch loathes the theatre as an institution as much as he loathes most other institutions. According to a state-

---

1. Jörg Drews, 'Alexanderschlachtbeschreibung', in *Herbert Achternbusch*, ed. Jörg Drews, Frankfurt 1982, pp. 15f.

ment he made in 1981, he has been to the theatre five or six times in his life and each time was bored to death. It is a complete mystery to him why people bother to go to the theatre and why they are prepared to put up with the most pointless proceedings for hours on end. His sole intention in writing plays is simply to provide himself with an income in his old age. He therefore quite consciously conceives his dramatic works in such a way that they will not be understood until some point in the future.[2] It is small wonder, then, that the heavily subsidised and quasi-nationalised theatres of the Federal Republic are not entirely sure what to make of Achternbusch's dramaturgic innovations. After his latest exploit, the play *Linz* which was first performed in Munich in 1987 and which purports to present the undead agents and victims 'des alpenländischen Faschismus', the question whether Achternbusch is a prophet or an impostor is once again wide open. By all accounts the production was a complete débâcle, but this may not be the final word.

Achternbusch certainly has no great theatrical talent in any traditional sense. One could, however, argue that his dramatic texts are the logical extension of his other works, taking these all in all to be the product of—as it often seems to me—a sort of compulsion to speak rather than to write. Individual figures in their monologues are constantly being foregrounded to such an extent that they *need* to step out of the prose and up onto the stage. Thus parts of the plays *Susn* and *Gust*, first performed in 1980, are already to be found in the novel *Die Alexanderschlacht* of 1971. The dramaturgic ruthlessness with which Achternbusch transfers his narrative characters from semi-relief to three dimensions is by no means an exception among contemporary playwrights. However, his theatrical excursions do demonstrate more forcefully than most other contemporary plays that a 'small organon', a canon of rules governing playwrighting of the sort Brecht still thought feasible is no longer adequate to deal with our traumatised consciousness.

Achternbusch's view of himself is conditioned by a feeling of panic at not being allowed to stay in one place for any length of time, not even in his own skin. The illegitimate son of a carefree dental technician and a naïve country belle from Lower Bavarian peasant stock Achternbusch was born in Munich in 1938, a child of pre-war euphoria. His mother, incapable or unwilling to look after

2. For these statements see ibid., p. 122, 'Theater-Theater nicht'.

him, deposits the boy with his grandmother in Mietraching, a place at the back of beyond where he grows up left for the most time to his own devices, an experience which, by a process of literary recollection, gives rise to the *enfant sauvage* complex so central to Achternbusch's imagination. The primitive quality of Lower Bavarian life—to us almost exotic—in the closing stages of the war and the immediate post-war period, which Achternbusch never tires of evoking and mythologising, is, despite its more horrific aspects, the site of Achternbusch's strongest emotional investment, his home territory. But he is not allowed to stay here either. The young and untutored man—this is Achternbusch's image of himself despite the fact that he did complete his schooling—is forced out of his 'natural' barbarity and arrives in Munich where he has to contend with the forces of an alien civilisation. This second experience of separation corresponds almost exactly to the anthropological paradigm of the movement of our earliest ancestors from the forests out onto the treeless plains, a parallel which is all the more significant in view of the severe threats to our natural habitat that have occurred during Achternbusch's life time.

Rudolf Bilz has described the phase in the prehistory of mankind in which, as a result of the exile from the trees, the state of naïve thinking was left behind as an emotional catastrophe of unimaginable proportions, as a first irredeemable loss of nature.[3] An increasingly disturbing lack of meaning has ever since been counterbalanced by a largely compensatory production of artefacts and other symbols of meaning, be they technical/purposeful or fanciful/mythopoeic. It is by means of such real or imaginary items that our species, ever more frantically, seeks to establish conditions of relative harmony, knowing all too well that there is now no turning back. The intensity with which Achternbusch in the circumstances of his own life has relived the phylogenetic catastrophe of expulsion in an abbreviated form, also explains why he cannot afford the time which is necessary for any kind of refinement. Hardly settled, he faces the possibility of being driven out again. He sees himself as the last of the Mohicans wandering a benighted Southern Germany reduced to dust and ashes.

Provincial Lower Bavaria, largely spared by the spread of machines in the 1950s, has since been overrun. Achternbusch writes in the introduction to *Plattling*:

---

3. *Studien über Angst und Schmerz*, Frankfurt 1971, pp. 276f.

This used to be Bavaria. Now the world rules here. Like the Congo or Canada, even Bavaria has been conquered by the world and is governed by the world. Bavaria is a colony of the world. Even this bit of earth has become the world. The more the world rules, the more the earth is destroyed and we who live in this bit of earth are destroyed too. The world destroys us, you could say. The world is technology, whatever the political control.[4]

Memories of the Bavarian forest, of a nature supremely indifferent and unaffected by our antics as it seemed to be only a short while ago, are now out of step with the reality referred to in Achternbusch's statements about the technological colonisation of Bavaria. The discrepancy is decisive, for the more difficult it becomes to see a significant connection—particularly in the context of a single life—between the discordant semantic and operational fields of that which once was, is now and is still to come, the more difficult it is to dislodge the fear that we are moving further and further in the wrong direction and soon will no longer be able to find the traces of our own experience. Achternbusch's positively atavistic fear of separation is an expression of this. His answer is to invest all the fragments of his past that he can still get hold of with an excess of symbolic meaning—like totem pieces, they must testify to his desire not to lose anything, not even ephemera like the incomparable images that Kuschwarda City, the last of the Mohicans alias Achternbusch, saw as a child on the low ceiling of his room, or the morning light on the heads of lettuce in the garden at the foot of the sheer rock face, or the big wooden butt full of dark water.[5]

In particular, Achternbusch seems to feel called upon to remember his ancestors and relations, the accounts of whose incredible lives form a good part of his dramatic output. A great uncle and an aunt, Gust and Ella, the eponymous protagonists of two plays, are central figures of the clan threatened with extinction of which Achternbusch, the red-skin, is a descendant. Gust, now aged eighty-three, tells his life story on a stage consisting of a large apiary. Trees and foliage and a rock face form the background and

4. 'Früher ist hier Bayern gewesen. Jetzt herrscht hier die Welt. Auch Bayern ist wie der Kongo oder Kanada von der Welt unterworfen, wird von der Welt regiert. Bayern ist eine Kolonie der Welt. Auch dieses Stück Erde ist Welt geworden. Je mehr die Welt regiert, desto mehr wird die Erde vernichtet, werden wir, die dieses Stück Erde bewohnen, vernichtet. Die Welt vernichtet uns, das kann man sagen. Die Welt ist Technik, egal in welcher politischen Hand.' *Plattling*, in *Die Olympiasiegerin*, Frankfurt 1982, p. 11.
5. See *Kuschwarda City*, in *Es ist ein leichtes beim Gehen den Boden zu berühen*, Frankfurt 1980, p. 192.

there is a view of the glowing sky—reminiscences of the Danube School, and of Altdorfer who painted 'Die Alexanderschlacht'.[6] Here Gust relates *sa vie de travaille* in a badly mangled language, lurching precariously between Lower Bavarian and attempts at a sort of standard German. Meanwhile in the background his second wife Lies is lying on a curved sofa moaning and gasping her way to death throughout the two hours which the play takes to run its course. The text—difficult to read and even more difficult to act— was the theatrical event of 1985 in Achternbusch's own production at the Munich Residenztheater with Sepp Bierbichler in the role of Gust. Not without some justification, Achternbusch's demonstration of what can be achieved on the stage has been compared to Beckett's own productions of *Endgame* and *Krapp's Last Tape*.[7] The darkness separating the characters was illuminated by the same indifference and the same compassion, the nearness of death becoming an incitement to recollection, the most commonplace gestures a reminder of the futility and grandeur of the effort. Gust relates the details of his semi-nomadic existence between the Bavarian Forest and the plain of Gäuboden, the accidents, which time and time again nearly cost him his life—as when the back wheel of a threshing machine completely crushed his leg, or when he got caught in the baler and a spike went right through his hand and he yanked it out with the little strength he had left before the blade sliced off his hand and fingers. For six weeks afterwards he was ill with tetanus, got sicker and sicker, couldn't even close an eye for a single moment or move an inch for that matter, though he could hear everything, better, sharper, than ever before in his life.[8] In the Munich production Gust's tale became an exemplary account of suffering and torment, of one damn thing after another. At the end of it all Gust breaks into the great complaint, characteristic of all myths, about the onrush of old-age and the brevity of life. 'I always thought I'd never reach eighteen, it took an eternity before I got to be eighteen. God it didn't half drag! And now all at once I'm eighty-three . . .'[9] This reflection on the disproportion in the pas-

6. This picture, in the *Alte Pinakothek* in Munich, is a central reference point in Achternbusch's work.
7. Peter von Becker, 'Die Stadt, das Land und der Tod', *Theater Heute*, 1985, 7, pp. 22f.
8. Paraphrase from *Gust*, in *Die Atlantikschwimmer. Schriften 1973–1979*, Frankfurt 1986, pp. 430f.
9. 'Ich habe mir allweil denkt ich werd nie 18 Jahr, hat das lang dauert, bis ich 18 Jahr alt worn bin. Mei war das was Langsames! Und jetzt bin ich auf einmal 83 . . .', ibid. p. 455.

sage of time is his only comment on his imminent demise. Lies has already passed away, then with the words 'I must go now or the pain of leavetaking will get me' Gust turns away, about to meet his own death.

The emotional indifference verging on the heroic displayed by Gust in his struggle right to the end has its counterpart or equivalent in the paralysis of poor Ella, who right from the start of her particular endgame sits motionless, a dead soul in front of the television, while her son, taking her place in an apron and a wig made of chicken's feathers on his head, describes the sort of life she has had. From the word go a creature deprived of all rights, Ella wanders from one man to another, from place to place, from cheap lodgings to night shelter, ending up by way of miscarriages and suicide attempts in a mental home where she remains until, after twelve years, she is sufficiently broken to hold down a menial job in a sanatorium for TB patients. Unlike Gust, Ella is no longer capable of telling her own story, but she must have told it once or perhaps over and over again, otherwise the son, Josef would not have been able to take her part in that strange changing of roles through which—an echo of Hitchcock's psychodrama—he preserves his mother in a state of mummification. The stages of her life of suffering through which Josef takes the observers of this horror story, are a catalogue of punishments wiich are as dreadful as they are unjustified. Every attempt to escape from the system designed for the correction of the individual is met by an increase in the severity of treatment, for example by what Ella/Josef calls 'Speispritzen' ('injections to make you throw up'). 'For three days I just threw up, blood and everything . . . you're not really there any more. Yes, that was the punishment. It was nothing but a punishment. Punishment, pure punishment that was.'[10] The story lived through by Ella/Josef until it is ended by a sugar cube soaked in cyanide, is in fact so remorseless that the only adequate parallel would seem to be the trials of Job and his complaint that one life alone is too short for so much misery and his wish that no one had ever set eyes on him, that he had been taken straight from his mother's womb to the grave. Looking back Ella/Josef comes to the devastatingly unpathetic conclusion: 'I haven't had a decent mo-

10. 'Da hab ich 3 Tage gespien und Blut und alles ist raus. . . Da bist du gar nicht mehr da. Ja das war die Strafe. Das war reine Strafe. Reine Strafe war das.' *Ella*, in *Die Atlantikschwimmer*, p. 335.
11. 'Überhaupt in meinem ganzen Leben habe ich keine gute Stunde noch nicht erlebt', ibid. p. 343.

ment all my life.'[11] This bare statement is reminiscent of the verdict, blasphemous is its irony, with which Voltaire's Jacob sums up the one hundred and thirty years of his life, saying that he has experienced 'pas un jour heureux dans ce court pèlerinage'.[12]

In *Crowds and Power* Elias Canetti describes how the bushmen can feel the distant approach of people whom they can neither hear nor see. A bushmen tells his children to keep a lookout for their grandfather: 'Look ye around, for your grandfather seems to be coming. This is why I feel the place of his body's old wound.'[13] It is, Canetti continues: 'the kind of scar that hurts from time to time and the old man has often been heard speaking of it. It is what might be called his distinctive mark. When the son thinks of his father he thinks of his old wound.'[14] Achternbusch's relationship to his mutilated ancestors is based on a parallel effort at empathy. The magic return of the ancestors is achieved by the assimilation of their suffering in the person of a descendant. This kind of physical recall thus has to make use of transformation, an art largely lost from sight in our civilisation and whose only but declining sphere of influence is the work of the artist, one of the last reserves of primitive thinking. The remarkable thing about Achternbusch's literary method is that he appears unable to think in any other way than the primitive and the identificatory. His language never transcends the object of reflection. For that reason Achternbusch's plays have no dramatic discourse, hardly ever do we find passages that could be described as dialogue. Any attempt in that direction turns out to be almost imbecilic. The art of transformation is not based on several points of view but is generated by what might be termed autistic monologue.

The bushmen get a feeling in their feet when the springbok are near. 'We have a sensation in our face on account of the blackness of the stripe of the face of the springbok.' This black stripe runs down the middle of the forehead and finishes at the tip of the nose. The bushman feels it on his own face.[14] In Achternbusch's writing we continually find attempts at ecstatic transformation similar to those described by Canetti. And it is just this aspect of his work that reveals its theatrical tendency. As Achternbusch's most inspired scenes illustrate, it has remarkable dramatic possibilities. When Josef puts on his headdress of chicken's feathers to play the difficult

12. *Dictionnaire Philosophique*, under 'Joseph'.
13. Quoted from the translation by Carol Stewart, London 1962, pp. 337 and 338.
14. Ibid., p. 387.

role of his mother Ella, whom we see at the same time spending the last days of her life with a lot of white Hebrideans in a hen-house (perhaps signifying that she has already joined her ancestors), it is a tremendous theatrical moment of transformation. As a result of this metamorphosis a ritual of repetition is set in motion in which—as in Lévi-Strauss' description of the mourning rites of so-called primitive peoples—a human being who is still alive personifies a distant forebear in order to ensure the transubstantiation of the deceased into an ancestor.[15] In such complex two-way processes one is dealing with a communal activity of the living and the dead, a dissolution of the opposition between diachronic and synchronic, reversible and irreversible chronology. Lévi-Strauss has drawn attention to the crucial difference between mourning rites and historical rites. Historical rites bring the past into the present—a process that still dominates German dramatic literature as it always has done. Mourning rites on the other hand take the present into the past. The difference is one of memory as against remembrance. And the physical realisation of remembrance upon the stage is at the heart of any truly theatrical event. That such events can still be brought about is demonstrated by the difficult mourning processes of plays such as *Ella* and *Gust* which are devoted to the extinct lives of the lost and the wasted.

From another point of view transformation into a dead ancestor can also represent an escape from one's own existence. The position of the survivor is always precarious, especially if, like Achternbusch, he considers himself to be the last of a long line of victims that have gone on ahead of him. Taking on the shape of the ancestors also represents a magic ritual of self-protection. There are countless myths and tales about the changing of form as a means of escaping one's pursuers. Achternbusch's unstable identities reflect this strategy. The psychopathological equivalent of this art of transformation is, as Canetti has shown, a type of derangement generally referred to as mania.[16] With every metamorphosis one starts a new life; it is incredibly easy, in this state of mind, to open up escape routes via flights of the imagination. If long passages of Achternbusch's texts in fact show signs of manic production, these escapes with the help of transformation nevertheless eventually reach their inevitable conclusion at such times when the individual

15. Claude Lévi-Strauss, *Das wilde Denken*, Frankfurt 1973, p. 273.
16. Trans. cit., p. 347.

sees the futility of the whole thing and that there is nothing for it but to pretend to be ill or dead. The play *Der Frosch* is a parable of this. The eponymous hero, Achternbusch's *alter ego*, has reached the end of all transformations. Up till now he has always managed to escape his pursuers, but now he crouches in the darkness, paralysed and no longer aware of who he is. His frog's skin is much too thin and much too sensitive. For some days it has been night-time and death is near at hand. As in Kafka's parable of the beetle, here too metamorphosis into a non-human form no longer provides protection from the inhumanity of the human beings who continue to walk or cycle past the garden as though everything were just right with the world. Unlike the frog, they are oblivious to the fact that time is speeding up—the church clock strikes the hour every few minutes. They also fail to notice that, as the frog is most painfully aware, the green and beautiful Bavarian countryside is already drying out, invaded by the first signs of the desert into which the characters of this strange local farce will eventually be driven.[17]

In the images of the desert and devastation, leitmotifs of Achternbusch's plays, the mourning process shifts from the disasters of the past to those of the future. One of the conditioning factors behind his depression is the ancient fear of a cosmic catastrophe which, in our age, has become so tangible that it needs to be systematically repressed. The Klamath myth of the bird's-nest robber, as described by Lévi-Strauss,[18] at the end of which Kmukamch daubs the heavens with resin in order to see everything go up in flames, could go straight into the tableau of a world hell-bent on destruction presented by Achternbusch on the stage. Of course the pursuit of happiness is still on,[19] and the beer-drinkers still get merry on the steep hillside below the holy mountain of Andechs.[20] In reality, however, we are already feeling neck-pains, the first sign of panic, all over our bodies, and the sacred mountain is—as Achternbusch's stage direction indicates—torn open to reveal nothing but bare rocks and skeletons. The brass band plays 'Abide with me' while people's chatter is drowned by the roar of jet fighters.[20] Such a scenario predicts a time when Kuschwarda City, the Bavarian-

---

17. *Der Frosch*, in *Das Haus am Nil*, Frankfurt 1981, p. 41 and passim.
18. *Mythologica* IV, Frankfurt 1975, p. 36.
19. 'sitzma angeschnallt in unserer Glücksfabrik'. *Kuschwarda City*, in *Es ist ein leichtes*, p. 187.
20. *Der Frosch*, third scene. Kloster Andechs, a monastery outside Munich, is famous for the beer which is brewed there. The place is firmly linked in Achternbusch's fantasies with excessive drinking and a kind of lethal stupor.

Indian hero of the play of the same name, crouches on the branch of a tree in a burnt-out forest, a bird without feathers in a tree without leaves. He has a red streak going down from his hair-line to the end of his nose, and he allows his imagination to soar. He sees a catastrophe of mammoth proportions that even causes the sun to darken in Cairo 3000 kilometres away, and in Khartoum it makes polished brass grow dim. In Cologne the ash is 20 centimetres thick, there is not one survivor between Mainz, Wiesbaden and Hanau and where Frankfurt once stood there is now a hole in the earth one kilometre deep. In Deggendorf people jump into the boiling water of the Danube and he, Kuschwarda, is the only one not to have met his death because, as a result of some crime or other, he was imprisoned like a raccoon in a pit protected by a roof made of branches.[21] Like so many of Achternbusch's tales, this episode could have been derived from the body of Indian myth that Lévi-Strauss refers to.

These are fantasies about the end that awaits us and tragedy turns into madness as a last consolation. Time won't wait, is the melancholy verdict. Spring, summer, autumn, and winter could be the titles of the stages in the life of a woman which form the play *Susn*. As the curtain goes up on the last scene we are already almost on the other side. Susn is sitting in the sand before a fire that has gone out and filling her pipe. Alongside her the author of the play, with nothing for a costume but an old pair of long underpants and a gun and that red streak from his hair-line down to the end of his nose.[22] The closing scene is not so much of a life than of life in general, a parable of the yawning gap between the character of man and a natural environment that for so long protected him—like the proverbial shelter of branches.

According to an Australian myth,[23] the primeval ancestor of the opossum gives birth first of all to the opossums and then his human sons. And the number of sons increases; every night more human sons come into the world, fifty in a single night. They are all sent out hunting the opossums that they feed on. But the totem father does not produce any more opossums; they came into being all at once right at the beginning. In the end they are all eaten up, the father and his sons together have consumed them all—an exact model of the over-hunting and extermination of that which keeps us

21. *Kuschwarda City*, in *Es ist ein leichtes*, pp. 173f.
22. *Susn*, in ibid., p. 34.
23. Canetti, trans. cit., 357.

alive. To get at the truth, however, we don't need to go back to the prehistoric antipodes. Even in Plattling, as Achternbusch's play of the same name shows us, everything is covered with concrete. Plattling, in Lower Bavaria, a place at the back of beyond, is now one big motorway intersection. In the middle of it, half madman and half angel, the play shows us the prophet Herbert, a palm-branch in his hand, looking to see whether there is a possibility of salvaging anything. But it doesn't look too good. From a trailer which has 'pigs' written on it and which is destined for the abattoir is to be heard the frightful shrieking of a multitude of voices—the choir of the damned. Roles, as myth shows us, can be reversed. The survival chances of humans are in the end equal to the survival chances of the pigs or the opossum. The dreadful communal shrieking from the cattle truck on the Plattling motorway turn-off is an analogy—and Achternbusch's phraseology suggests as much—for the shrieking of a humanity condemned to death. This scene too exemplifies the process of transformation. Thomas Bernhard's recent observation—that the pig is now more human than the human being who in the last hundred years has become more and more like a pig[24]—is an ethical verdict that cannot be easily dismissed, at least in as much as the fate of the pigs in the death factory is in fact our own. The common denominator between Auschwitz and the animal concentration camps is the extreme exploitation of nature. At issue in both cases is the maintenance of one species at the expense of another. We are pigs, in both senses of the word. We are flesh of their flesh and we consume nature, not only the natural environment around us, but also our own nature and therefore in the end ourselves. The mutation of mankind is under way—what Achternbusch calls 'brain regularisation'. It is all just a question of morality. As Silvia Bovenschen points out in her brilliant essay 'Bestial Speculations',[25] Walt Disney's Donald and his nephews Tick, Trick and Track, those paragons of adaptability, have no qualms on Christmas Day, about eating a duck for their dinner.

24. *Die Auslöschung*, Frankfurt 1987, p. 480.
25. *Neue Rundschau*, 94/ I, 1983, p. 27.

Notes on Playwrights and Directors

NOTE: Publication dates refer, where possible, to the first (or the most readily available) publication in book form. Given in brackets are the place and year of first performance (or performances—double premières are not uncommon in Germany). For comprehensive biographical information and primary and secondary bibliographies see H. L. Arnold (ed.), *Kritisches Lexikon zur deutschsprachigen Gegenwartsliteratur*, 6 vols, Munich 1987, which is regularly updated.

Herbert Achternbusch was born in Munich in 1938 and grew up in his grandmother's house in Mietraching in the Bavarian Forest. He studied at the Nuremberg and Munich Academies of Art. His first publications date from the mid-1960s though his literary breakthrough came only in the early 1970s. Achternbusch's first play, *Ella*, had its première at the Staatstheater Stuttgart in 1978. Since then he has written a number of works for the stage. These are not, normally, published separately as they tend to form part of wider writing projects comprising all manner of literary and paraliterary expression. Achternbusch's works for the stage comprise:
Ella, in *Die Atlantikschwimmer*, Frankfurt 1978. (Württ. Staatstheater Stuttgart 1978).
Susn, in *Es ist ein leichtes . . .*, Frankfurt 1980. (Schauspielhaus Bochum 1980).
Gust, ibid. (Comédie de Caen 1984).
Kuschwarda City, ibid. (Schauspielhaus Bochum 1980).
Plattling, in *Die Olympiasiegerin*, Frankfurt 1982. (Schauspiel Frankfurt 1982).
Der Frosch, in *Theater Heute*, 1982, 5. (Schauspielhaus Bochum 1982).
Mein Herbert, in *Revolten*, Frankfurt 1982. (Vereinigte Bühnen Graz 1983).
Sintflut, in *Wellen*, Frankfurt 1983. (Schauspielhaus Bochum 1984).
Linz, in *Ambacher Exil*, Cologne 1987. (Residenztheater Munich 1987).

Thomas Bernhard was born in 1931 in Heerlen, Holland, the son of Austrian parents. He was brought up by his grandparents who lived in

185

Vienna and, subsequently, in Upper Bavaria. From 1943 to 1947 Bernhard attended a boarding school in Salzburg. In 1947 he decided to leave school and work as an assistant in a grocer's shop. A serious tubercular infection of the lungs, diagnosed in 1949, brought with it protracted periods of hospitalisation in Salzburg and in the nearby sanatorium at Grafenhof. From 1952 to 1957 Bernhard read Music and Drama at the Salzburg Mozarteum. He has been a full-time writer since 1957 and lives in Ohlsdorf in Upper Austria. His principal works for the theatre are:

Ein Fest für Boris, Frankfurt 1970. (Deutsches Schauspielhaus Hamburg 1970).

Der Ignorant und der Wahnsinnige, Frankfurt 1972. (Salzburger Festspiele 1972).

Die Jagdgesellschaft, Frankfurt 1974. (Burgtheater Vienna 1974).

Die Macht der Gewohnheit, Frankfurt 1975. (Salzburger Festspiele 1974).

Der Präsident, Frankfurt 1975. (Akademietheater Vienna 1975).

Die Berühmten, Frankfurt 1976. (Theater an der Wien, Vienna 1976).

Minetti, Frankfurt 1977. (Württ. Staatstheater Stuttgart 1976).

Immanuel Kant, Frankfurt 1978. (Württ. Staatstheater Stuttgart 1978).

Vor dem Ruhestand, Frankfurt 1979. (Württ. Staatstheater Stuttgart 1979).

Der Weltverbesserer, Frankfurt 1979. (Schauspielhaus Bochum 1980).

Am Ziel, Frankfurt 1981. (Salzburger Festspiele 1981).

Über allen Gipfeln ist Ruh, Frankfurt 1981. (Schloßtheater Ludwigsburg 1982).

Der Schein trügt, Frankfurt 1983. (Schauspielhaus Bochum 1984).

Der Theatermacher, Frankfurt 1984. (Salzburger Festspiele 1984).

Ritter, Dene, Voss, Frankfurt 1984. (Schauspielhaus Bochum 1984).

Einfach kompliziert, Frankfurt 1986.

Volker Braun was born in Dresden in 1939. From 1957 to 1960 he had various jobs in the printing and mining industries. From 1960 to 1964 he read philosophy at the University of Leipzig. In 1965/66 Braun was dramaturgic adviser with the Berliner Ensemble and since 1972 he has been associated with the Deutsches Theater, Berlin. Braun's main works for the stage, all printed in *Stücke*, Berlin (East) 1983, are:

Die Kipper (Städtische Bühnen Leipzig 1972).

Hinze und Kunze (New version: Städtische Bühnen Karl-Marx-Stadt 1973).

Schmitten (Kellertheater der Oper Leipzig 1982).

Guevara oder der Sonnenstaat (Nationaltheater Mannheim 1977).

Großer Frieden (Berliner Ensemble, Berlin (East) 1979).

Simplex Deutsch (Probenbühne des Berliner Ensembles 1980).

Dmitri (Badisches Staatstheater Karlsruhe 1982).

Tankred Dorst was born in 1925 in Sonneberg/Thuringia. He was called up into the army in 1942, and was held as a prisoner of war by the British and the Americans from the end of the war until 1947. In the early 1950s he studied German, art history and drama in Munich and was involved in puppet theatre. Dorst started writing plays in the late 1950s and he came to prominence as a playwright in the late 1960s. His most important stage works are:

Toller, Frankfurt 1968. (Württ. Staatstheater Stuttgart 1968).
Kleiner Mann, was nun?, Frankfurt 1972. (Schauspielhaus Bochum 1972).
Eiszeit, Frankfurt 1973. (Schauspielhaus Bochum 1973).
Auf dem Chimborazo, Frankfurt 1974. (Schloßparktheater Berlin (West) 1975).
Die Villa, Frankfurt 1980. (Düsseldorfer Schauspielhaus; Staatstheater Stuttgart 1980).
Merlin oder Das wüste Land, Frankfurt 1981. (Düsseldorfer Schauspielhaus 1982).
Heinrich oder Die Schmerzen der Phantasie, Frankfurt 1985. (Düsseldorfer Schauspielhaus 1985).
Ich, Feuerbach, Frankfurt 1986. (Residenztheater Munich 1986).

Franz Xaver Kroetz was born in Munich in 1946. He trained as an actor and moved between casual, unskilled jobs and fitful engagements in regional and fringe theatres until he was awarded a six-month playwright's grant by the publishing house Suhrkamp. Kroetz was a member of the German Communist Party (DKP) from 1972 to 1980. Since the late 1970s he has been increasingly active in directing and acting his own and others' plays. Kroetz's principal plays are:

Wildwechsel, in *Gesammelte Stücke*, Frankfurt 1975. (Dortmunder Schauspielhaus 1971).
Heimarbeit, ibid. (Kammerspiele Munich 1971).
Hartnäckig, ibid. (Kammerspiele Munich 1971).
Männersache, ibid. (Landestheater Darmstadt 1972).
Michis Blut, ibid. (proT Munich 1971).
Stallerhof, ibid. (Deutsches Schauspielhaus Hamburg 1972).
Lieber Fritz, ibid. (Staatstheater Darmstadt 1975).
Wunschkonzert, ibid. (Württ. Staatstheater Stuttgart 1973).
Oberösterreich, ibid. (Städtische Bühnen Heidelberg 1972).
Sterntaler, in *Weitere Aussichten ... Ein Lesebuch*, Cologne 1976. (Staatstheater Braunschweig 1977).
Das Nest, ibid. (Modernes Theater Munich 1975).
Agnes Bernauer, ibid. (Leipziger Theater 1977).
Mensch Meier, in *Mensch Meier / Der stramme Max / Wer durchs Laub geht*, Frankfurt 1979. (Schauspielhaus Düsseldorf 1978).

Der stramme Max, ibid. (Ruhrfestspiele Recklinghausen 1980).
Wer durchs Laub geht, ibid. (Marburger Schauspiel 1981).
Nicht Fisch, nicht Fleisch, in *Nicht Fisch, nicht Fleisch, Verfassungsfeinde, Jumbo Track*, Frankfurt 1981. (Schauspielhaus Düsseldorf 1981).
Furcht und Hoffnung der BRD, Frankfurt 1984. (Schauspielhaus Bochum 1984).
Der Weihnachtstod, in *Düsseldorfer Debatte* (1984), 4, pp. 24-44.
Bauern sterben, Frankfurt 1986. (Kammerspiele Munich 1985).
Der Nusser, in *Theater Heute* 1986, 5, pp. 42-50. (Residenztheater Munich 1986).
There is now also a new edition of Kroetz's collected plays: *Stücke*, 3 vols, Frankfurt 1987.

Volker Ludwig, pseudonym for Eckardt Hachfeld, was born in 1937 in Ludwigshafen. His father, Eckardt Hachfeld, was a writer and author of cabaret texts. Ludwig studied German literature and art history in Munich and Berlin. He began writing cabaret sketches and songs in 1959. From 1965 to 1971 he was director and main author of the Reichskabarett in West Berlin. He initiated the Theater für Kinder im Reichskabarett which, in 1972, became the Grips Theater. The most important Grips plays, written by Ludwig on his own or in collaboration with (an)other author(s), are available in a series published jointly by the Ellermann Verlag and the Verlag der Autoren. All first performances by the Grips Theater.
Vol. 1. *Maximilian Pfeiferling, Mugnog-Kinder, Balle, Malle, Hupe und Artur*, Munich 1971.
Vol. 2. *Mannomann!, Trummi kaputt*, Munich 1973.
Vol. 3. *Stokkerlok und Millipilli, Ruhe im Karton, Mensch Mädchen!*, Munich 1975.
Vol. 5. *Kannst du zaubern, Opa?* Munich 1976.
Vol. 6. *Vatermutterkind, Die Ruckzuckmaschine, Nashörner schießen nicht*, Munich 1977.
The following Grips plays have been published separately in the series *Materialien* by the Weismann Verlag:
Doof bleibt doof, Ein Fest bei Papadakis, Starnberg 1974.
Banana, Munich 1974.
Wasser im Eimer, Munich 1978.
Die schönste Zeit im Leben, Munich 1979.
Alles Plastik, Munich 1982.
A number of Grips plays are not available in these series but have been published elsewhere:
Das hältste ja im Kopf nicht aus in: *Spektakulum*, vol. XXV, Frankfurt 1976.
Eine linke Geschichte in: *Theater Heute*, 1980, 11 pp. 25-40.

Linie 1, Grips edition, Berlin (West) 1986.
Two Grips plays which do not have Volker Ludwig as (co)author are:
Leonie Ossowski, *Voll auf der Rolle*, Munich 1984.
Jörg Friedrich, *Jule, was ist los?*, Grips edition, Berlin (West) 1985.

Heiner Müller was born in 1929 in Eppendorf, Saxony. He experienced the closing months of the Second World War in action, was taken prisoner by the Americans, but chose to return to what was then the Soviet Zone of Occupation, later to become the German Democratic Republic, where he has lived ever since, although he has travelled widely in the West. He began to write soon after the war, almost exclusively for the theatre. His involvement with the theatre has always been a direct one: from 1958 to 1960 he was on the staff of the Maxim Gorki theatre in Berlin, from 1970 to 1976 he worked with the Berliner Ensemble and since 1976 he has been associated with the Berlin Volksbühne, but he has also directed plays elsewhere, including the Federal Republic, and has collaborated with the American Robert Wilson (*The Civil Wars*). He has experimented with a wide range of theatrical forms: socialist realist 'production plays', didactic plays after Brecht, adaptations of Greek classics and of Shakespeare, and avant-garde plays reminiscent of Beckett and Artaud. His relations with the GDR's ruling communist party have frequently been strained: in 1961 he was expelled from the Writers Union over the comedy *Die Bauern*, in 1965 he was publicly attacked for his play *Der Bau*, and many of his plays have not been performed, or indeed published, in his own country at all. The last named work did not receive its first GDR performance until 1980. Müller's principal plays and their dates of publication are:

Der Lohndrücker, in *Geschichten aus der Produktion I*, Berlin (West) 1974. (Städtisches Theater Leipzig 1958).
Die Korrektur, ibid.
Der Bau, ibid. (Volksbühne Berlin (East) 1980).
Traktor, in *Geschichten aus der Produktion II*, Berlin (West) 1974. (Volksbühne Berlin (East) 1975).
Zement, ibid. (Berliner Ensemble, Berlin (East) 1973).
Die Umsiedlerin, Berlin (West) 1975. (Studentenbühne der Hochschule für Ökonomie, Berlin (East) 1961).
Die Schlacht, ibid. (Volksbühne Berlin (East) 1975).
Die Bauern, ibid. (Volksbühne Berlin (East) 1976).
Weiberkomödie, in *Theater-Arbeit*, Berlin (West) 1975. (Magdeburg 1971).
Germania Tod in Berlin, Berlin (West) 1977. (Kammerspiele Munich 1978).
Mauser, Berlin (West) 1978. (Austin Theatre Group, Austin Texas 1975).
Philoktet, ibid. (Residenztheater Munich 1968).

Der Horatier, ibid. (Schillertheater Berlin (West) 1973).
Die Hamletmaschine, ibid. (Théâtre Gérard Philipe, Saint Denis 1979).
Leben Gundlings Friedrich von Preußen Lessings Schlaf Traum Schrei, in
Herzstück, Berlin (West) 1983. (Schauspiel Frankfurt 1979).
Der Auftrag, ibid. (Volksbühne Berlin (East) 1980).
Quartett, ibid. (Schauspielhaus Bochum 1982).
Verkommenes Ufer Medeamaterial Landschaft mit Argonauten, ibid.
(Schauspielhaus Bochum 1983).
Macbeth in *Shakespeare Factory I*, Berlin (West) 1985. (Brandenburg
1972).
Bildbeschreibung, ibid. (Steirischer Herbst, Graz 1985).
Wolokolamsker Chaussee I, ibid. (Deutsches Theater Berlin (East) 1985).
Wolokolamsker Chaussee II, *Theater der Zeit* 41 (1986), Nr. 2, pp. 60-1.

Friederike Roth was born in Sindelfingen/Swabia in 1948. She studied
philosophy and linguistics at the University of Stuttgart. From 1976 to
1979 she taught at the Fochhochschule Esslingen/Neckar. Since 1979 she
has been working as dramaturgic adviser for South German Radio in
Stuttgart. Her plays to date are:
Klavierspiele, Frankfurt 1980. (Deutsches Schauspielhaus Hamburg
1981).
Ritt auf die Wartburg, Frankfurt 1981. (Württ. Staatstheater Stuttgart
1982).
Krötenbrunnen, Frankfurt 1984. (Kammerspiele Cologne 1984).
Die einzige Geschichte, Frankfurt 1985. (Schauspielhaus Bremen 1985).
Das Ganze ein Stück, Frankfurt 1986. (Bremer Theater 1986).

Peter Stein was born in Munich in 1937. He first came to prominence with
his production of *Saved* by Edward Bond at the Munich Kammerspiele
in 1967. In 1970 he was appointed director of the Schaubühne am
Halleschen Ufer in Berlin, the home of the ensemble which under his
aegis was to win for itself a place in the history of the German stage no
less important than those associated with the names of Max Reinhardt,
Erwin Piscator and Bert Brecht. In 1981 the company moved into a new
theatre, the completely reconstructed Mendelsohn building on the Leh-
niner Platz. In 1985 Stein resigned as director of the Schaubühne Company, with an arrangement to return for regular 'guest' productions.

Botho Strauss was born in Naumburg/Saale in 1944. He read German
literature, theatre history and sociology at the universities of Cologne
and Munich. From 1967 to 1970 he was on the staff of the influential
magazine *Theater Heute*. From 1970 to 1975 he was dramaturgic adviser
at the Schaubühne am Halleschen Ufer in Berlin. Botho Strauss lives in
West Berlin. His works for the stage comprise:

Trilogie des Wiedersehens, Munich 1976. (Deutsches Schauspielhaus Hamburg 1977).

Groß und Klein, Munich 1978. (Schaubühne am Halleschen Ufer, Berlin (West) 1978).

Die Hypochonder, Munich 1979. (Deutsches Schauspielhaus Hamburg 1972).

Bekannte Gesichter, gemischte Gefühle, Munich 1979. (Württ. Staatstheater Stuttgart 1975).

Kalldewey Farce, Munich 1981. (Deutsches Schauspielhaus Hamburg 1982).

Der Park, Munich 1983. (Städtische Bühnen, Freiburg 1984).

Die Fremdenführerin, 1986. (Schaubühne am Lehninerplatz, Berlin (West) 1985).

Notes on Contributors

David Bradby, MA Oxon, PhD Glasgow, has taught at the Universities of Glasgow, Ibadan and Caen. He is at present reader in French theatre studies and the director of the drama degree course at the University of Kent at Canterbury. He has directed plays by Molière, Havel, Adamov, Beckett and Vinaver at the University's Gulbenkian Theatre. Recent publications include: *Modern French Drama 1940-1980* (Cambridge University Press, 1984) and (together with Rachel Anderson) *Renard the Fox* (Oxford University Press, 1986).

Horst Claus studied drama at the Universities of Graz, Hamburg and Kansas (MA, PhD) and film at the Polytechnic of Central London (MA). He has worked as producer and literary adviser at, among others, the Thalia-Theater in Hamburg and has taught drama and film at the Universities of Kansas and Bristol and at the College of St Matthias (Bristol). He is currently principal lecturer in the deparment of modern languages at Bristol Polytechnic.

Steve Giles is lecturer in German at Nottingham University. He read modern languages at Christ's College Cambridge and subsequently researched into modern drama and social theory at the University of East Anglia, Norwich. Dr Giles is the author of *The Problem of Action in Modern European Drama*, Stuttgart 1981, and of several articles on modern literature and critical theory. He is currently preparing a book on Marxism and culture in the early years of the Weimar Republic.

Rüdiger Görner, MA Tübingen, BA London, teaches cultural history and politics at the University of Surrey. He is also a poet and has published widely in important journals and newspapers such as *Neue Rundschau*, *Neue Zürcher Zeitung*, *Frankfurter Allgemeine Zeitung* and *Universitas*. Among his recent publications and editions are: *Logos Musicae*, Wiesbaden 1982; *Das Tagebuch*, Munich and Zurich 1986 and *Rilke–Wege der Forschung*, Darmstadt 1987.

Julian Hilton, MA, PhD Oxon, studied English and comparative literature at Oxford, Munich, Grenoble and Salamanca. He is Professor of Theatre

Studies at the University of East Anglia, Norwich. Himself a playwright, Julian Hilton has translated Volker Braun's *Die Übergangsgesellschaft* for the stage as the official translation. He has also published widely on German theatre. His recent publications include *Georg Büchner*, London 1982 and *Gambit 39/40: Special German Theatre Issue*, London 1982.

Moray McGowan, DPhil Hamburg, studied German, English, philosophy and politics at the University of Newcastle-upon-Tyne. He has taught at the Universities of Siegen, Kassel, Lancaster and Hull. Since 1981 he has been lecturer in German studies at the University of Strathclyde. His research interests are in German literature and society since 1918, especially 1918–1933 and post-1968. Recent publications include articles for *Text und Kritik* and the *Kritisches Lexikon zur deutschsprachigen Gegenwartsliteratur* as well as a book on *Marie-Luise Fleisser*, Munich 1987. Dr McGowan also writes reviews and features for *Theater Heute* and the BBC German Service.

Anthony Mathews studied German literature at the University of Newcastle. From 1969 he taught in West Africa, England, Germany, Morocco and Jersey. In 1985 he completed an MA course in comparative literature at the University of East Anglia, Norwich, where he is at present preparing a PhD thesis on the interpretation and reception of Kafka's *Der Prozeß*.

Anthony Meech, MA, read German and drama at Manchester and Bristol. He is currently lecturer in drama at the University of Hull. His publications include numerous translations of plays from German, including, recently, *Leonce und Lena* and *Die Wahre Geschichte des Ah Q*. Anthony Meech has also published several articles in *Theatre Quarterly*.

J. H. Reid, MA, PhD Glasgow, is reader in German at the University of Nottingham. Among his publications are two books on Heinrich Böll and a volume on the twentieth-century German novel (with E. Boa) as well as numerous articles on twentieth-century German fiction. He is at present working on a book on recent East German literature.

Lucinda Rennison graduated from the University of Durham in 1983. Since then she has lived and worked in West Berlin as a free-lance journalist. She is also writing a doctoral dissertation on problems of historical understanding in the dramatic work of Rolf Hochhuth.

Irmela Schneider studied German literature and theology and was awarded her DPhil in 1974 and DHabil in 1980. She currently teaches at the Technische Universität Berlin and is associated with the research project on media aesthetics at the University of Siegen. Dr Schneider's main publications are: *Kritische Rezeption – 'Die Blechtrommel' als Modell*, Frankfurt 1975; *Der verwandelte Text – Wege zu einer Theorie der Literatur-Verfilmung*, Tübingen 1981; Dr Schneider has edited *Die Rolle des Autors – Analysen und Gespräche*, Stuttgart 1981 and *Radio-Kultur in der Weimarer Republik*, Tübingen 1984.

W. G. Sebald read German literature at the Universities of Freiburg, Fribourg (Lic. ès. Lettres 1966), Manchester (MA 1968) and East Anglia (PhD 1974). In 1986 he was awarded the degree of DHabil by the University of Hamburg. He is Professor of German literature at the University of East Anglia. His publications include *Carl Sternheim*, Stuttgart 1968; *Der Mythus der Zerstörung im Werk Alfred Döblins*, Stuttgart 1980; *Die Beschreibung des Unglücks*, Salzburg 1985, as well as numerous articles on nineteenth- and twentieth-century German literature.

Sybille Wirsing completed a humanities degree in 1962 and then began work as a journalist in Berlin. She is regarded as one of the leading German theatre critics and in 1985 was awarded the prestigious Johann-Heinrich-Merck Prize for her journalistic work.

Select Bibliography

For information about journal articles, reviews etc. see H. L. Arnold (ed.), *Kritisches Lexikon zur deutschen Gegenwartsliteratur*, 6 vols, Munich 1987.

Arnold, H. L. (ed.), *Positionen des Dramas*, Munich 1977.
—, *Heiner Müller*, Munich 1982.
—, *Franz Xaver Kroetz*, Munich 1978.
—, *Thomas Bernhard*, Munich 1982.
—, *Botho Strauss*, Munich 1984.

Calandra, D., *New German Dramatists*, London 1983.
Carl, R. P., *Franz Xaver Kroetz*, Munich 1978.

Gamper, H., *Thomas Bernhard*, Munich 1977.

Iden, P., *Die Schaubühne am Halleschen Ufer*, Munich 1979.
—, *Theater als Widerspruch*, Munich 1984.
Innes, C., *Modern German Drama*, Cambridge 1979.
Ismayer, W., *Das politische Theater in Westdeutschland*, Königstein 1984.

Meyerhofer, N., *Thomas Bernhard*, Berlin 1985.

Pikulik, L., Kurzenberger, H. and Guntermann, G. (eds), *Deutsche Gegenwartsdramatik*, 2 vols, Göttingen 1986.

Rühle, G., *Theater in unserer Zeit*, Frankfurt 1978.

Schulz, G., *Heiner Müller*, Stuttgart 1980.
Silbermann, M., *Heiner Müller*, Amsterdam 1980.

Wieghaus, G., *Heiner Müller*, Munich 1981.

Index

Achternbusch, Herbert VIII, 3, 8, 174ff
Aeschylus 113
Anouilh, Jean 1
Aragon, Louis 33
Aristophanes 113
Aristotle 162
Auerbach, Erich 72

Barthes, Roland 32
Baumgart, Reinhardt 34
Becher, Johannes R. 116, 145
Beckett, Samuel 69, 83, 125, 136
Benjamin, Walter 138
Berliner Ensemble 12, 116, 119ff
Berliner Schaubühne 3ff, 4, 5, 20, 21, 28, 35, 46
Bernhard, Thomas VII, 3, 8, 85, 161ff, 184
Bernstein, Basil 81
Bettelheim, Bruno 161
Bierbichler, Sepp 178
Bilz, Rudolf 176
Blin, Roger 18, 23
Bloch, Ernst 125
Boito, Arigo 27
Bond, Edward 11, 82, 118
Bondy, Luc 35, 46
Braun, Volker VII, 114f, 120, 124ff
Brecht, Bertolt 2, 7, 13, 21, 28f, 31, 77, 111ff, 124, 128, 129, 135ff, 143, 157f, 175
Bremer Bühne 3
Brück, Christoph 122
Büchner, Georg 7, 125, 127f, 142, 173
Bunuel, Luis 125, 136

Calderón, Pedro de la Barca 37
Camus, Albert 1, 163
Canetti, Elias 180ff
Chekhov, Anton 67, 115, 169
Clever, Edith 2, 37
Coenen, Günther VIII

de Laclos, Choderlos 151
de Sade, Donatien 152
Deutsches Theater, Berlin 116
Diderot, Denis 72
Dittbrenner, Nina 3
Dorst, Tankred 5, 64ff

Eisenstein, Sergei 74
Euripides 113
Everding, August 12

Fanti, Lucio 78, 30
Fassbinder, Rainer Werner 2, 9, 10, 78
Fehling, Jürgen 11f, 15
Fleisser, Marie-Luise 2
Freie Volksbühne 3, 10

Ganz, Bruno 2, 46
Gelman, Alexander 112, 114f
Genet, Jean 18f
Giraudoux, Jean 16
Glucksmann, André 161
Godden, Janet VIII
Goebbels, Joseph 11
Goethe, Johann Wolfgang V, 3, 13, 16, 46f, 79, 115f, 126f
Goldschmidt, Miriam 23
Gorki, Maxim 19, 115
Grass, Günter 74, 124
Grimmelshausen 135f
Grips Theater 6f, 38, 98ff
Grüber, Klaus Michael VII, 2, 3, 5
Gründgens, Gustav 3

Hacks, Peter 126f, 135
Handke, Peter 164
Hauptmann, Gerhard 72
Havel, Vaclav 134
Hebbel, Friedrich 3, 115
Hein, Christoph 118
Heyme, Hansgünther 10
Hitchcock, Alfred 3, 179
Hochhuth, Rolf 2, 9, 11

Hoffmann, E. T. A. 41, 44f
Hofmannsthal, Hugo V. 164
Horváth, Ödön V. 2, 81
Hübner, Kurt 3, 4, 10

Ibsen, Henrik 67

Jelinek, Elfriede 6

Kafka, Franz 182
Kaminski, Roman 117
Kammerspiele, Munich 12, 77
Karge, Manfred 114
Karsunke, Yaak 10
Kästner, Erich 107
Kipphardt, Heinar 2, 3
Kleist, Heinrich von 3, 7, 115, 153ff
Komische Oper, Berlin 112
Krauel, Martina 24
Kroetz, Franz Xaver VII, 2, 3, 5, 11, 77ff

La Mettrie, Julien Offroy de 153
Lampe, Jutta 2, 23
Lang, Alexander 117
Les Griots 18
Lessing, Gotthold Ephraim 7, 34, 115
Lévi-Strauss, Claude 181ff
Ludwig, Volker 7, 93ff

Mann, Thomas 165
Mathews, Anthony VIII
Matthus, Siegfried 112
Mecklenburgisches Staatstheater, Schwerin 113
Mihan, Jörg 122f
Minetti, Bernhard 3
Molière, Jean Baptiste Poquelin 115
Mozart, Wolfgang Amadeus 22, 26
Müller, Heiner VII, 5, 7f, 116f, 127, 135, 145ff

Nagel, Ivan 15–16
Neuenfels, Hans 13
Noren, Lars 16

O'Neill, Eugene 1, 27ff, 115
Ovid 50

Palitzsch, Peter 4, 10
Paryla, Katja 117
Peymann, Claus 4, 166f
Pinter, Harold 82
Piscator, Erwin 10
Piscator-Bühne 7

Plenzdorf, Ulrich 111, 122

Rehm, Walter 2
Reichskabarett 93ff, 100f, 178
Reinshagen, Gerlinde 6
Residenztheater, Munich 11
Roth, Friederike 6, 52ff
Roth, Joseph 164
Roth, Jürgen 80
Royal Shakespeare Company 119

Saeger, Uwe 120f
Sartre, Jean-Paul 1, 161f
Schall, Ekkehard 120
Schedler, Melchior 97
Schiller, Friedrich 7, 13, 115, 125, 127, 131, 136, 140f
Schloßtheater, Berlin 67
Schmitz, Marga VIII
Schnitzler, Arthur 164, 172
Schroth, Christoph 113, 115, 116
Seghers, Anna 154
Seidel, Georg 120
Semperoper, Dresden 112
Senghor, Leopold 22
Shakespeare, William 17, 40f, 113, 115, 125, 127, 136, 138, 142
Simonischek, Peter 23
Sperr, Martin 11, 78
Staatsschauspiel, Dresden 114
Stein, Peter VII, 2, 4, 5, 10, 12, 18ff, 35, 42
Strauss, Botho VII, 5, 31ff, 78, 79, 82, 85
Strindberg, August 67, 117
Strittmatter, Erwin 120
Szondi, Peter 70

Toller, Ernst 81

Verdi, Giuseppe 21
Vishnevski 19, 28
Vitrac, Roger 33
Voltaire, François Marie Aronet 180

Walser, Martin 2
Wedekind, Frank 131
Weigel, Helene 112
Weiss, Peter 2, 11, 12
Welsh Opera, Cardiff 5, 26
Wilder, Thornton 1
Williams, Tennessee 1
Wolf, Christa 148

Zadek, Peter 4, 10
Zweig, Stefan 164

197